SLAMMIN'

Wrestling's Greatest Heroes and Villains

David Hofstede

ECW PRESS

CANADIAN CATALOGUING IN PUBLICATION DATA
Hofstede, David
Slammin' : wrestling's greatest heroes and villains

ISBN 1-55022-370-4

1. Wrestling — History. 2. Wrestling. I. Title.

GV1195.H63 1999   796.812   C99-930843-2

Text design by Tania Craan
Typesetting by Mary Bowness
Front cover photograph credits, clockwise from center photo:
Marko Shark; James A. Steinfeldt/ Shooting Star; Marko Shark; Photofest;
Marko Shark; Ed Geller/ Globe Photos, Inc.; Dave Benett/ Alpha/ Globe Photos, Inc.
Spine photograph credit: Lisa Rose/ Globe Photos, Inc.
Back cover photograph credits, clockwise from top right: Marko Shark; Marko
Shark; Globe Photos, Inc.; Everett Collection; Albert Ferreira/ Globe
Photos, Inc.; Adam Scull/ Rangefinders/ Globe Photos, Inc.
Printed by Transcontinental, Beauceville, Québec
Distributed in Canada by General Distribution Services,
325 Humber College Blvd., Etobicoke, ON, M9W 7C3
Distributed in the United States by LPC Group,
1436 West Randolph Street, Chicago, Illinois, U.S.A. 60607
Distributed in the United Kingdom by Turnaround Publisher Services,
Unit 3 Olympia Trading Estate, Coburg Road, Wood Green, London N22 6TZ

Published by ECW PRESS
2120 Queen Street East, Suite 200
Toronto, Ontario M4E 1E2
www.ecw.ca/press

PRINTED AND BOUND IN CANADA

The publication of *Slammin'* has been generously supported by The Canada Council, the
Ontario Arts Council, and the Government of Canada through the Book Publishing Industry
Development Program.

SLAMMIN'

Table Of Contents

Introduction   ix

A Glossary of Wrestling Terms and Federations   xi

The First Five Thousand Years:

     From the Old Testament to the New World Order   3

PROFILES

Stone Cold Steve Austin   15

Chris Benoit   22

Ric Flair   26

Mick Foley   38

The Giant   43

Bill Goldberg   47

Scott Hall   51

Bret Hart   55

Owen Hart   63

Hunter Hearst Helmsley 67

Curt Hennig 71

Hulk Hogan 76

Chris Jericho 85

The Legion of Doom 89

Lex Luger 97

Dean Malenko 103

Shawn Michaels 106

Rey Misterio Jr. 114

Kevin Nash 118

The New Age Outlaws 123

Diamond Dallas Page 129

Rowdy Roddy Piper 134

The Rock 141

Randy Savage 144

Ken Shamrock 151

Sting 155

The Ultimate Warrior 162

The Undertaker 167

Vader 173

Sean Waltman 178

The 10 Best Wrestling Matches of All Time 183

The Top 10 Wrestling Events (By Attendance) 194

The Top 10 Wrestling Events in the United States

 (By Attendance) 198

The 10 Most Embarrassing Wrestling Matches/Gimmicks 200

The Women of Wrestling 204

Wrestling in Japan and Mexico 212

Title Histories 219

Two-Sport Stars 245

Bibliography 250

Acknowledgments

Special thanks to Dorran Jack Epstein for his comments, criticism, and expertise, particularly on the international wrestling scene. Thanks also to Mitch Brody, Brian Bukantis, Mike Chapman, Jack Condon, Jack David, the International Wrestling Institute and Museum, Jack Koenig, Kelly Kuhn, Howard Mandelbaum, and Michael Shulman.

Introduction

"Whether phony or real, fun or frightening, harmless or worrisome for society, professional wrestling's new forms are connecting with an audience in a way that television industry experts and social philosophers say demands that it finally be taken seriously, either for the money it makes or the message it sends."

— Kirk Johnson, *New York Times*, March 30, 1998

How do you begin to describe the wild, wacky, wonderful world of professional wrestling? It's a sport; it's entertainment; it's a goof; it's a guilty pleasure.

One thing's for certain — it is very, very popular. Both World Championship Wrestling's *Monday Nitro* and the World Wrestling Federation's *Monday Night Raw* consistently rank at, or near, the top of the ratings list for all cable programs. There are currently seven weekly wrestling programs, a total of 13 original action-packed hours. Taking all telecasts into account, according to *Time* magazine, about 34 million people watch wrestling every week.

If your question is whether or not the matches are fake, you're missing the point. Wrestling is not about athletic competition as much as it is about escapism, loud music, colorful costumes, cheering the good guys and booing the bad guys. Having said that, I should also note that professional wrestlers are genuinely skilled — even gifted — athletes. One incorrectly positioned piledriver or one wrong landing of a dive over the top rope can result in serious injury, so the sense of danger and drama is not entirely manufactured.

The charismatic stars who brought wrestling through its 1980s heyday and into its current, unprecedented prominence — Hulk Hogan, Ric Flair, Shawn Michaels, Stone Cold Steve Austin — are profiled in the pages that follow. For each, I have provided title histories. These histories are as complete as possible; records, especially among regional federations prior to 1980, are notoriously sketchy. Championship belts were exchanged for a variety of reasons, most of which had little to do with the comparative talent of the wrestlers. Deals between competitors allowing one to win in his hometown then lose when the show moved on went unrecorded.

As for later title changes, particularly as they apply to the WWF, we have to remember that some episodes of *Monday Night Raw* were taped a week or two before they were broadcast; for the sake of consistency, the date listed corresponds to the date the title match was aired on television.

A Glossary of Wrestling Terms and Federations

TERMS

BABYFACE: One of the good guys; a popular wrestler; usually just referred to as a "face."

BLADE: A wrestler cutting himself, usually on the forehead, with a palmed razor blade, to produce a torrent of blood and make a match appear more violent.

BUMP: A wrestler absorbing a severe-looking attack, usually in the form of a fall out of the ring or from a high place.

CHAIR SHOT: A blow with one of those folding chairs that always seem to be near ringside.

DQ: Disqualification.

GETTING OVER: A wrestler "gets over" when he receives an enthusiastic response from the fans for being either a "babyface" or a "heel."

HEEL: A bad guy; the opposite of a "babyface."

JOB: To lose a match on purpose. Wrestlers who make a career of this are called "jobbers."

MARK: A wrestling fan who believes that wrestling is real, and/or that the storylines are true.

POP: A loud audience reaction to a wrestler's introduction or to an impressive move during a match.

SCREWJOB: Losing a match through outside interference or any means other than a clean pinfall or submission.

SELL: Making a wrestling match look authentic or your opponent look good.

SHOOT: An actual, nonscripted fight. The term can also be applied to an interview in which a wrestler responds to questions out of character.

WORK: A preplanned event that is presented as spontaneous.

FEDERATIONS

AWA: American Wrestling Association

CWA: Catch Wrestling Association

ECW: Extreme Championship Wrestling, formerly Eastern Championship Wrestling

GWF: Global Wrestling Federation

ICW: International Championship Wrestling

IWGP: International Wrestling Grand Prix

NWA: National Wrestling Association (1929–48); National Wrestling Alliance (1948–88)

NWO: New World Order

PWA: Professional Wrestling Association

USWA: United States Wrestling Association

UWA: Universal Wrestling Association

UWF: Universal Wrestling Federation

WCW: World Championship Wrestling

WCWA: World Class Wrestling Association

WWA: World Wrestling Association

WWF: World Wrestling Federation, formerly World Wide Wrestling Federation

The First Five Thousand Years:

From the Old Testament to the New World Order

Wrestling is the oldest sport known to humanity. Though it developed in countless variations, almost every ancient culture on Earth has left evidence — through hieroglyphs, ancient writings, or other records — that wrestling was practiced as a sporting activity or as a way to settle disputes.

The Old Testament of the Bible tells us that Jacob wrestled with an angel for one night. There are copper statues of wrestlers in combat dating back to the year 3,000 BV (Before Vince), from the Babylonian Second Early Dynastic Period. The *Epic of Gilgamesh*, one of the great literary works of antiquity, tells the story of a wrestling match between Sumerian heroes Gilgamesh and Enkidu. There are historical accounts of wrestling in ancient Egypt, in Mesopotamia, in China, Japan, India, Africa, and South America.

But the popular perception of the origin of wrestling dates back to ancient Greece, where the sport was celebrated in history and myth. There are enough stories of matches between heroic legends to fill a pay-per-view card: Hercules vs. Antaeus, Theseus vs. Cercyon, and Odysseus vs. Ajax would be the main events. At the first Olympic Games, the combatants wrestled nude — a practice that, thankfully, was discontinued before the arrival of Dusty Rhodes and George "The Animal" Steele.

"Greco-Roman" is the term now used to describe a specific style of wrestling in which no holds are permitted below the waist and the use of the legs is forbidden. But the truth is there are no records detailing the actual manner in which the Greeks competed. As for the Romans, they never took to wrestling with the same zeal as the Greeks; in fact, there is no mention of competitions for several centuries after the Olympiad of the year AD 393.

By the Middle Ages, organized wrestling competitions were a part of everyday life throughout Europe and Asia. In Japan, sumo wrestling evolved between AD 710 and 1185 from a violent submission sport to a highly ritualized toppling match in which a wrestler attained victory by forcing his opponent out of a 15-foot circle. In England, a form of wrestling called "Cornwall and Devon" emerged in which wrestlers used their opponents' clothes as a means of achieving grips. Variations of this came to be known as "belt-and-jacket." After a military battle between England and France in 1502, King Henry VIII wrestled the French king, Francis I, following a series of bouts between the soldiers of their respective armies.

In the mid-1800s, a Frenchman from Lyon named Exbroyat organized various styles of wrestling into a professional sport resembling the one that's still practiced in the amateur competitions of today. The Paris Exhibitions became the mecca of pro wrestling. After events held in 1855 and 1867, the top wrestlers went on tour to promote the sport. Though the competition was strictly judged and adhered to the rules of Exbroyat, there was already a theatrical influence to the proceedings; in 1873, wrestling's first masked wrestler, billed as (what else?) The Masked Wrestler, made his debut in Paris.

Attempts to introduce the sport in England and North America sometime around 1870 met with only limited success. In the United States, a different type of wrestling had taken hold (so to speak). It was brought to America by Irish settlers, who referred to it as "catch-hold," or "collar-and-elbow," though most people just called is "scuffling."

Before he was elected president, Abraham Lincoln could scuffle with the best of 'em. According to George Gipe's *The Great American Sports Book*, Lincoln earned his reputation while working as a clerk in New Salem, Illinois, after he defeated a local streetfighter named Jack Armstrong. According to Gipe, people came from 50 miles away to see the fight, and the betting action was brisk, with Armstrong the clear favorite. "But once the fight started," claims Gipe, "it was no contest." "Lincoln lifted him by the throat," writes Lincoln biographer Carl Sandburg, "shook him like a rag, and then slammed him to a hard fall." Lincoln wrestled more than 300 matches as a young man. In fact, the legendary Abraham Lincoln-Stephen Douglas presidential debates were ultimately settled in a steel cage. . . . Well, okay, not really.

During the American Civil War, soldiers would participate in wrestling contests between military units. After the war, several veterans joined carnivals and other traveling shows, wrestling for money against anyone with the guts to step into the ring. Scuffling was still the predominant style, but in 1880 a new style emerged that was dubbed "catch-as-catch-can." In these matches, wrestlers faced each other from a standing position and were allowed to use any kind of hold. They differed from scuffling matches, in which the contestants would seize each other in a prescribed grip before the contest began.

Carnival promoters, to make certain they wouldn't lose money, hired only the best wrestlers, and they would resort to any tactic, illegal or not, to win. These men were known as "hookers" (no jokes, please). On those rare occasions when a hooker faced a serious challenge in the ring, it was usually from a "shooter," the name given to experienced wrestlers who came from the amateur ranks or from universities and who played by the rules. From the ranks of the hookers and shooters came the first group of men to wrestle professionally in the United States.

By the time of the 1889 and 1900 Paris Exhibitions, there were competitions pitting the French champions against those from Germany, Denmark, and Austria-Hungary, featuring such famous names as Karl Abs and the Greco-Roman specialist George Hackenschmidt. In 1900, Hackenschmidt, born in Estonia and dubbed "The Russian Lion," competed in a London catch tournament, and when he pinned Tom Jenkins, an American catch specialist, he was recognized as the world's best wrestler — in any style.

Wrestling was the most popular sport in the United States at the turn of the century and was actually considered more "dignified" than boxing. Its popularity received an additional boost when Hackenschmidt toured America in 1908 and wrestled former hooker Frank Gotch.

"Hackenschmidt put wrestling on the map," says wrestling historian Mike Chapman. "For about five years, he was maybe the strongest man on the planet." But he met his match in Frank Gotch, whom Chapman describes as "the greatest wrestler who ever lived, by any criteria."

Gotch, born in 1878 in Humboldt, Iowa, wrestled over 400 official matches in his career, plus thousands more in circus sideshows, according to Chapman's book, *From Gotch to Gable*. He lost only six times. "It was a war back then; wrestlers would throw a crossface, and try to tear your nose off," explains Chapman. "Gotch's first recognized match, when he was nineteen, was on a cinder track. Dan McCloud, who was already American champion, was 35 years old and had 15 years experience. He figured he could put this kid away in ten minutes, but they wrestled for an hour and a half. They had cinders embedded in their skin, they were bleeding, choking from cinders in their throat to the point where they couldn't swallow, but they refused to quit."

Gotch was trained by Martin Burns, who, as "Farmer Burns," may have been the first nationally known wrestling champion in America. Under Burns's tutelage, Gotch defeated all challengers. He forced Hackenschmidt to surrender after a grueling two-hour match on April 3, 1908. There were reports that Gotch had used fouls and "roughhouse tactics" (in the words of one sportswriter) to defeat The Russian Lion, and that he had doused his body in oil to make it more difficult for Hackenschmidt to maintain a hold.

The rematch, held in 1911, drew 33,000 people to Chicago's Comiskey Park. "The town almost closed down," remarks Chapman. Once again, Gotch won in two straight falls. The gate of more than $87,000 was the biggest ever for a wrestling match. Again, rumors swirled that Gotch was in on a scheme to injure Hackenschmidt's knee the night before the match. Such stories certainly connect wrestling in its golden age to the sports-entertainment phenomenon of today, but they have never been proven.

Considering Gotch's unquestioned skills, it's hard to believe he needed a handicap to defeat any opponent. "He was tremendously strong, amazingly fast and catlike in movement," declared the *Minneapolis Tribune*. "Frank was the master of all holds on offense and blocks for these moves on defense. He also mastered leverage to the nth degree and was the last word in courage."

Two years after his second victory over Hackenschmidt, Frank Gotch retired, but his fame never diminished. When he attended a Chicago Cubs game, the game stopped while he was introduced, and afterward all the Cubs went to get his autograph. He was invited to the White House twice by President Teddy Roosevelt. At the time of his death in 1917, Gotch was the best-known athlete in the country.

The first two decades of the twentieth century produced several legendary wrestlers who became the yardstick by which future generations would be judged. Tom Jenkins won the American Heavyweight championship in 1901 and could boast wins over both Frank Gotch and George Hackenschmidt. "One of the toughest men to ever step into the ring," says Chapman of Jenkins. "He would wrestle anybody, then fight them in the street afterwards."

Ed "Strangler" Lewis, who was a five-time Heavyweight champion between 1920 and 1932, is rated by Chapman as second only to Gotch in skill. But it was Lewis's decision to throw a match that makes him one of the sport's most pivotal figures. "In 1925, Wayne Munn beat Strangler Lewis in Kansas City to win the title. Munn was a University of Nebraska football player — his chance of beating Lewis should have been zero. But Lewis was given money to lose the title," Chapman reports.

Whether Ed "Strangler" Lewis was really the first wrestler to "job," or lose on purpose, is almost impossible to determine. But because he did so, Lewis is credited (or blamed, depending on your perspective) with initiating wrestling's shift away from pure sport and towards "sports entertainment."

Not that show business hadn't already become a part of the mix; at a wrestling tournament in 1915, a hooded wrestler calling himself The Masked Marvel emerged from the crowd and forced his way into the competition. He

A "Rassle Royal"

lost, but his gimmick caught on, and the following year he was wrestling Joe Stecher for the World title.

Lewis's actions, quickly adopted by other wrestlers and greedy promoters, have had this effect: no wrestling-match decision made after 1925 can be taken at face value. "There were shoots (real fights), but most of them happened backstage. The goal of promoters for the last 60 years has been to entertain," says Chapman. "But for decades," he adds, "wrestlers still cared about their pecking order." For this reason, champions took pride in wearing the belt; it represented a perception of superior skills and the proven ability to draw a crowd.

Wrestling from the 1920s through the 1940s was a curious mix of occasional fact and a lot of fiction. It was a time when the sport of Gotch was gradually being replaced by an exhibition of athletic feats performed by two men who were often working together. Ironically, it was Ed "Strangler" Lewis, the first man to lose on purpose, who was one of the most vocal critics of the change; he pronounced as "terrible and awful" the new type of "slam-bang grappling," with its "fixed matches and manufactured heroes and villains."

The predetermined outcomes also considerably shortened the length of matches. From 1900 to 1920, title matches would routinely last one hour, and they sometimes ran much longer. In 1916, Joe Stecher and Ed "Strangler" Lewis wrestled to a five-hour draw; imagine watching a single match for five hours and having it end in a tie! No wonder fans threw their seat cushions into the ring afterward.

New stars emerged to follow, and successfully compete against, the pioneers of the sport. Handsome Jim Londos, the son of a Greek amateur champion, was the Shawn Michaels of his day and is also credited with inventing the sleeper hold. "Simply a new hold I've perfected which shuts off the jugular vein," he told the *New York Sun*. He debuted the hold against

Ray Steele in a 1931 match before more than 20,000 fans at New York's Yankee Stadium.

In 1933, a wrestler named "Jumping" Joe Savoldi beat Londos for the World title. Londos, however, refused to acknowledge that he had lost and continued to bill himself as the World champion. Another competitor, Jim Browning, was also recognized in some states as the champ. A multitude of claims to the one World title would lead to the creation of different federations, each controlled by different promoters and represented by one of the claimants. Among the many "World champions" were ex-football-player Bronko Nagurski and Lou Thesz.

The first serious investigation into wrestling's authenticity was launched in January of 1934 by the New York State Athletic Commission. Accusations of "title juggling" and "secret agreements" resulted in a week of testimony from the top wrestlers of the day, including Londos, Ed White, and Dick Shikat. The commission outlawed syndicate agreements between promoters and also decided to ban the dropkick from competition. Nobody paid much attention to either edict.

Wrestling was still big business, even with a tainted reputation. On September 20, 1934, Jim Londos defeated Ed "Strangler" Lewis in a match at Chicago's Wrigley Field that was refereed by former Heavyweight boxing champ Jack Dempsey. The event drew of record gate of more than $96,000, an astonishing figure at the height of the Depression. Primo Carnera, former Heavyweight boxing champion of the world, switched to wrestling in 1941 at the age of 34. He compiled a winning streak of 321 straight matches (take that, Goldberg!) before losing to Antonino Rocca on April 20, 1949.

But the 1940s saw the fascination with wrestling begin to wane as football and basketball picked up fans and baseball solidified its status as the national pastime. Promoters responded by pushing the envelope further in the area of flash and spectacle. Wrestlers began wearing wild, colorful costumes and sporting names like The Purple Shadow, Man Mountain Dean, Whiskers Savage, Killer Kowalski, and Wild Red Berry.

Tag-team matches, which date back to 1901 in San Francisco, became more popular because the action was faster. Houston promoter Morris Sigel introduced the "Texas Tornado" tag-team match, in which all four wrestlers could enter the ring at the same time. In 1944, a joint benefit was held featuring wrestlers and the Houston Symphony Orchestra. Matches were set to music on a bizarre card in which Lou Thesz defeated Wild Bill Longson in the main event. After Ellis Bashara pinned opponent Dave Levin, he pushed the conductor aside and began leading the orchestra himself.

All of which was still not enough. Wrestling was headed for obsolescence by the late 1940s, only to be rescued by a new electronic marvel called television. America fell in love with TV right away, though there wasn't much programming to choose from in the early days of the medium. Families would leave their sets on just to look at the test pattern.

Wrestling made its television debut on July 30, 1948, on the Dumont network. The ABC, CBS, and NBC networks also broadcast matches; between 1949 and 1951, the first channel surfers could find wrestling shows six nights a week. Most originated from New York City-area venues such as the Jamaica Arena and Sunnyside Gardens, though Chicago had the longest-running wrestling show; announcer Jack Brickhouse called the action from the Windy City's Marigold Garden arena for six years.

Gorgeous George flexes for the cameras while his valet holds his velvet robe

(Photo Credit: Corbis/Bettman–UPI)

Television coverage transformed the wrestlers of the 1950s into household names. The wrestling shows also put emphasis on the interview, which soon became an integral part of the broadcast. Wrestlers who could "work the microphone" received more exposure and higher-profile matches, regardless of their skills in the ring. "It used to be about who could beat who, then it was about who could outdraw who, then both," said Lou Thesz, "and now nothing matters but box office."

Thesz, who held his first championship belt at the age of 21, was regarded by knowledgable wrestling fans as the competitor with the most skill. "The fourth best of all time, after Frank Gotch, Ed "Strangler" Lewis, and Joe Stecher," believes Mike Chapman, who grew up idolizing Thesz and Verne Gagne while his friends worshiped quarterback Johnny Unitas. Of all the professed champions in the 1950s, Thesz was the one who had the best chance to back it up in a shoot. He could only be beaten if he wanted to be.

In the course of an impossibly long and storied career, Lou Thesz took the National Wrestling Association (NWA; after 1948, the National Wrestling Alliance) Heavyweight title first in 1937 and won the same belt for the sixth time in 1963. He tried to merge as many of the disparate titles as possible, and his victory over Baron Michele Leone in 1952, which brought the California version of the title under the NWA Heavyweight belt, brought Thesz the closest any one man could get to being the undisputed champion. The match also drew the first gate of over $100,000 in wrestling history.

A list of wrestling milestones attained by Lou Thesz would require a separate book: he wrestled Rikidozan in 1957 in the first NWA World title match ever held in Japan; he pinned Jersey Joe Walcott in the fourth round of a boxer-wrestler match in 1963; he held the Universal Wrestling Association

(UWA) Heavyweight title in 1977, 40 years after he won his first belt; in 1990, at the age of 74, he wrestled a competitive match against 27-year-old Masa Chono in Japan. No wrestler has ever given more to the sport, or performed with more dignity when dignity was no longer required.

A roll call of wrestling's first television-era superstars has to begin with Gorgeous George (George Wagner), a flamboyant, effeminate heel whose pre-match routine laid the groundwork for the type of theatrics that have now become standard. A female valet would enter first, sprinkling rose petals in the aisle and spraying the ring with perfume. George would follow, tossing tiny mirrors or golden bobby pins into the crowd as he strutted to the ring in a frilly, flowing robe. "Sometimes he would pick out one woman in the crowd, it didn't matter what she looked like, and he'd stare at her for awhile and then say, 'My god, you're ugly!'" says Chapman. "By the time he got to the ring, the crowd was in an uproar."

In 1949, it was Gorgeous George who headlined the first wrestling card at New York's Madison Square Garden in 12 years. In 1962, he could still draw a full house — as he did when he was shaved bald after losing a hair match to The Destroyer in Los Angeles. George's skills as a wrestler were above average ("Surprisingly, Lou Thesz told me he really knew how to wrestle," comments Chapman), but he had no equal in self-promotion.

George's only competition in the area of outlandish behavior came from "Nature Boy" Buddy Rogers, who practically invented the rules for raucous, arrogant prematch interviews. In 1947, Rogers wrestled Billy Darnell in New York, and the match turned into such a wild brawl that one ringside fan died of a heart attack. After that, Rogers and Darnell were both barred from wrestling in New York for two years. Rogers won the Heavyweight title in 1961 and held it for almost two years before losing to Lou Thesz. His "Nature Boy" nickname, taken from a song by Nat King Cole, lives on through one of Rogers's biggest fans: Ric Flair.

Ethnic characters first became popular in the 1950s, though the stereotypes they promoted would hardly be considered politically correct today. Hans Schmidt played the role of a Nazi from Munich, Germany, who would bait the crowd with anti-American speeches. Less than 10 years after World War II, Schmidt became the sport's most hated villain. In reality, he was a French Canadian. Other "foreign menaces" were represented by Mr. Moto (Japan) and Nicolai Volkoff (Russia). Ethnic "babyfaces" included Argentinian Antonino Rocca, who brought an exotic style to the ring that incorporated elements from soccer and gymnastics, as well as Native Americans Chief Jay Strongbow and High Chief Peter Maivia (The Rock's grandfather).

The best wrestler to debut in the television era was Verne Gagne, a two-time collegiate champion who wrestled for the 1948 United States Olympic team. He turned pro in 1949 after turning down offers to play professional football from the Chicago Bears and Cleveland Browns. Gagne's 90-minute matches with Lou Thesz were incomparable exhibitions of wrestling acumen and a throwback to a bygone era.

By the 1960s, wrestling was no longer on prime-time television, though matches were still broadcast on local stations across the country. New York, Chicago, Memphis, Miami, Minneapolis, and Houston had thriving regional circuits, each with its own stable of stars. The NWA was the dominant organization, though the American Wrestling Association (AWA) boasted such stars as Verne Gagne, The Crusher, and Nick Bockwinkel.

Bruno Sammartino wrestles Ivan Koloff, January 18, 1971

In 1963, Lou Thesz defeated NWA champion Buddy Rogers in Toronto, Ontario, Canada. Promoters in the northeast territory of the NWA were unhappy with the decision and formed a new organization, the World Wide Wrestling Federation (WWWF). The federation (renamed the World Wrestling Federation [WWF] in 1979) continued to recognize Rogers as the champion.

"Bigger is better" became wrestling's new motto as promoters attempted to bolster the once-again dwindling crowd counts with larger-than-life players and ferocious man-beasts with little regard for civilized competition. There were prototypes in the 1950s, such as Haystacks Calhoun, a 650-pound farm boy who wrestled in overalls, and The Gorilla, who was wheeled to the ring in a cage. But the era of monsters and superheavyweights really began in the 1960s.

On the Midwest regional circuit, the most feared wrestler was former NFL star Dick Afflis, billed as "Dick the Bruiser." A hardcore wrestler even before the term was invented, Afflis never met an opponent he couldn't whack over the head with a steel chair. "He was never a wrestler, only a performer and a damn good brawler," said Lou Thesz, but The Bruiser's antics drew some of the sport's biggest crowds from the 1950s to the early 1970s. Most were in attendance to see him get pinned, if not killed. "The fans hate me and I sure have no love for them," he said in 1963. "They can hate me all they want as long as they buy tickets to watch me massacre their heroes."

In 1964, a Frenchman named Andre Rene Rusinoff made his professional wrestling debut as The Butcher. He toured North America under a variety of names, including Jean Ferre and "Monsieur Eiffel Tower," but when he joined the WWF in 1973, he called himself Andre the Giant. He became wrestling's biggest star, both literally and figuratively. Billed as the "Eighth Wonder of the World," he was 7' 4", 525 pounds, and simply too big to ignore. In 1981, he was profiled in *Sports Illustrated*, one of the very few instances before Hulk Hogan in which a wrestler received any recognition in the mainstream media. "From what I saw of him he couldn't wrestle at all," remarks Chapman. "But he was so huge that it didn't matter."

A few talented wrestlers were able to brave the land of the giants, and they managed impressive title reigns in the 1960s and early 1970s. The most prominent of these was Bruno Sammartino. A working-class hero of Italian descent, Sammartino debuted in 1959 and became the WWF's most bankable star before the arrival of Andre. On May 17, 1963, he pinned Buddy Rogers in just 55 seconds to win the WWF title, which he held until 1971. He came out of retirement in the 1980s, during the first wave of Hulkamania, and held his own against the likes of Roddy Piper, Paul Orndorff, and Cowboy Bob Orton.

In the 1980s, Hulk Hogan became wrestling's most charismatic and recognizable superstar since Gorgeous George and the man who would transform the sport into mainstream family entertainment. However, the pivotal figure in wrestling's recent evolution is WWF president Vince McMahon.

Not one of them ever laced up boots or held a title, but the McMahons can rightly claim status as the first family of wrestling. Vince's grandfather, Jess, promoted his first boxing card in 1925, then switched to wrestling promotion in New York and Philadelphia. His father, Vincent J. McMahon, controlled wrestling over much of the northeastern United States beginning in the 1950s and founded the WWWF in 1963. In 1982, Vince McMahon Jr. purchased the Capitol Wrestling Corporation from his father and began to acquire regional operators and their athletes. He paid local stations to carry WWF events and built a national network of syndicated stations for his organization.

"In the old days, there were wrestling fiefdoms all over the country, each with its own little lord in charge," McMahon told *Sports Illustrated* in 1991. "No takeovers or raids were allowed. There were maybe 30 of these tiny kingdoms in the U.S. and if I hadn't bought out my dad, there would still be 30 of them, fragmented and struggling. I, of course, had no allegiance to those little lords."

Brian Bukantis worked as a photographer and publicist for three of those "fiefdoms" from 1970 to the early 1980s. He started out with the NWA promotion in Detroit and later worked for the World Wrestling Association (WWA) in Detroit and Indianapolis, as well as Big Bear Sports, which covered southern Ontario, Canada. Matches at the time featured such mainstays as The Sheik, Bobo Brazil, Baron Von Raschke, Ernie Ladd, and The Valiant Brothers.

Bukantis disputes McMahon's claim that the regional circuits were always struggling. "Cobo Arena in Detroit sold out on a regular basis in the

'70s. Everybody came to see the Sheik lose, which he rarely did. In Indiana, the Indianapolis Expo Center was generally filled to capacity for the monthly cards. The independent scene in southern Ontario was likewise. They played to much smaller venues, but the fans filled the seats and were very rabid."

When the WWF broadcasts went national, the independents lost a lot of their support, though Bukantis acknowledged that McMahon wasn't the only problem. "The Sheik's promotion lost fan interest due to a myriad of factors, including continual 'no shows' by advertised stars, and the same finishes to matches with the Sheik always winning." The NWA Detroit promotion played to dwindling crowds in smaller arenas until finally closing up shop. The WWA and Big Bear Sports later followed suit.

The WWF's prominence was finally challenged when billionaire Ted Turner purchased the cornerstone of the NWA, Jim Crockett Promotions. Crockett, like McMahon, had devoted his life to wrestling. His father, Jim Crockett Sr., controlled the NWA from 1935 to 1973, a career that spanned title reigns from Jim Londos to Ric Flair. Jim Crockett Jr. took over in 1973 and then sold to Turner in 1988. Turner transformed the NWA into World Championship Wrestling (WCW) in 1991 and aired matches live on the TNT network, his national cable station.

The demise of the regional federations and the global domination of the wrestling market by the WWF and the WCW is a mixed blessing, according to Bukantis. "It was good for Vince and Ted and for selected wrestlers, but bad for everyone else. The problem was that I think they saw Vince as less of a threat than he turned out to be. The guys on top are making more money than ever, but I think the fact that there are no more territories is harmful to the growth of talent in the business," he said.

In the 1990s, the competition for wrestlers, fans, and television ratings between Vince McMahon and Ted Turner has been as nasty as any feud that has developed in the rings of their respective federations. "I dislike (Turner) very much," McMahon told *Newsweek* in 1998. "I think he's an asshole." Turner responded through WCW president Eric Bischoff, who railed against the WWF's more adult-oriented telecasts. Fielding a *Los Angeles Times* question about whether McMahon's PG-rated shows have succeeded, Bischoff snapped, "Every pimp on every street corner in every city knows you can sell sex."

The competition has forced both organizations to be more creative in their storylines, to work harder at creating new characters and at presenting their top stars from fresh angles. The fans have been the real beneficiaries of this rivalry — wrestling has never been more interesting, or more fun to watch, than it is right now.

Profiles

REAL NAME:
Steve Anderson

ALSO KNOWN AS:
Steve Williams, Stunning Steve Austin, The Stevester, The Ringmaster, The Rattlesnake

BORN:
December 18, 1964, Austin, Texas

HEIGHT:
6' 2"

WEIGHT:
262 pounds

PROFESSIONAL DEBUT:
December 1989

PROFESSIONAL AFFILIATIONS:
The Dangerous Alliance, The Hollywood Blonds

FINISHING MOVE:
the Stone Cold stunner

USWA **Southern Heavyweight title**
Won: January 25, 1991, over Jeff Jarrett
Decision reversed

WCW **Television title**
Won: June 3, 1991, over Bobby Eaton
Lost: April 27, 1992, to Barry Windham
Regained: May 23, 1992, over Barry Windham
Lost: September 2, 1992, to Ricky Steamboat

NWA/WCW **Tag-Team title**
(with Brian Pillman as The Hollywood Blonds)
Won: March 2, 1993, over Ricky Steamboat and Shane Douglas
Lost: August 18, 1993, to Arn Anderson and Paul Roma

WCW **United States Heavyweight title**
Won: December 27, 1993, over Dustin Rhodes
Lost: August 24, 1994, to Ricky Steamboat
Regained: September 18, 1994 (awarded title when Ricky Steamboat is unable to defend)
Lost: September 18, 1994, to Hacksaw Jim Duggan

WWF **King of the Ring 1996**

WWF **Tag-Team title**

(with Shawn Michaels)
Won: May 26, 1997, over Owen Hart and Davey Boy Smith
Titles vacated in June 1997, when Shawn Michaels is unable to defend

(with Dude Love)
Won: July 14, 1997, over Owen Hart and Davey Boy Smith
Titles vacated on September 7, 1997, when Steve Austin is unable to defend

(with The Undertaker)
Won: July 26, 1998, over Kane and Mankind
Lost: August 10, 1998, to Kane and

Mankind, The New Age Outlaws, and Owen Hart and The Rock (four-corners match)

wwf Intercontinental title
Won: August 3, 1997, over Owen Hart
Titles vacated on September 7, 1997, when Steve Austin is unable to defend
Regained: November 9, 1997, over Owen Hart

Title forfeited to Rocky Maivia on December 8, 1997

wwf World Heavyweight title
Won: April 28, 1998, over Shawn Michaels
Lost: June 28, 1998, to Kane
Regained: June 29, 1998, over Kane
Lost: October 18, 1998 (title stripped by Vince McMahon)
Regained: March 28, 1999, over The Rock

In the early 1990s, when the popularity of wrestling had slipped considerably from the dizzying heights of the 1980s, fans wondered when, or if, another wrestler would ever ascend to the status enjoyed by Hulk Hogan a decade earlier. When it finally happened, it certainly wasn't in a way they could have anticipated.

Stone Cold Steve Austin could hardly be called an overnight sensation. He had been around a long time, in both wcw and the wwf. He had won and lost several belts, wrestled in singles and tag matches, and had already created a character that was well known, if not exactly popular. But when "Stunning" Steve Austin became "Stone Cold" Steve Austin, he also became the first wrestler since Hogan to achieve name recognition among people who never watch wrestling.

Rolling Stone magazine called him the new American hero, but his character is not the kind that usually makes for a classic face. He dresses in basic black, he swears constantly, he breaks rules like a heel, and his favorite gesture is the raised middle finger, which he directs at both opponents and officials. "If it was 15 years ago, doing the stuff I do, people would hate my guts," he told *Newsweek*. If he is, indeed, the new American hero, Austin's success says as much about America as it does about wrestling.

He was born Steve Anderson in Austin, Texas, the second of three children, all of whom were abandoned by their biological father early on. He was raised by his mother and a stepfather whose last name — Williams — he still uses away from the ring. At Edna High School, Steve excelled in football, earning a scholarship to North Texas State University. He didn't wrestle, but he was already a fan; he'd watch the Von Erichs on television and attend live events at Houston's Sportatorium.

In college, Austin played defensive tackle and ended his senior season with fifty-five tackles, four sacks, and one interception. But he didn't go on to graduate after his scholarship ran out and he was not drafted by the NFL. Instead, he went to work on a freight dock, loading and unloading trucks. He still went to the Sportatorium on his days off, now convinced he could become a professional wrestler.

Steve spent five months learning the basics at Chris Adams's wrestling school; five months later, he made his debut at the Sportatorium, then signed up as a jobber for the uswa. When he was moved to the federation's Tennessee territory, he was told that he could no longer wrestle as Steve Williams: that name had already been taken by Dr. Death Steve Williams. The promoter suggested "Steve Austin," like the character played by Lee Majors on The Six Million Dollar Man TV series. Steve didn't like it, but he couldn't think of anything better.

While he was still learning the ropes, Austin was booked into tag matches with his trainer, Chris Adams. He then turned against Adams and tried to ignite a singles career. In 1990, he became "Stunning" Steve Austin and hired Jeannie Clark, Adams's ex-wife, as his valet. This prompted a series of mixed-tag matches pitting Austin and Jeannie (both of whom had long blond hair) against Adams and his current wife, Toni. Steve Austin and Jeannie Clark married in 1991.

The high point of Austin's uswa stint was a victory over Jeff Jarrett for the Southern Heavyweight title, which was later overturned because Austin's feet were on the rope during the pin. Eighteen months after signing with the uswa, Austin was offered a contract by wcw. He debuted in April of

"Steve Williams" as he appeared in his high school yearbook

1991, still as Stunning Steve Austin, and was accompanied to the ring by a brunette billed as "Vivacious Veronica." She quickly disappeared, to be replaced by Jeannie as "Lady Blossom."

Austin started in the midcard, then received a boost by winning the Television title from Bobby Eaton. He held the title for nine months, longer than any of his predecessors. Withstanding challenges from Tom Zenk, Dustin Runnels, and P.N. News, he became a contender for the United States title. At an August 1991 tournament to crown a new U.S. champion, Austin lost to Sting in the finals.

Jeannie decided she'd had enough of the spotlight, so Lady Blossom left, and Austin's contract was "sold" to Paul E. Dangerously, manager of the Dangerous Alliance. In 1992, Austin switched his Television title with Barry Windham before losing it in August to Ricky Steamboat. He teamed with Rick Rude for a few matches, but when Paul Dangerously left wcw, the Dangerous Alliance split up. At Halloween Havoc, Austin was a last-minute replacement for Terry Gordy as a partner for Dr. Death Steve Williams. They faced Dustin Rhodes and Barry Windham for the nwa World Tag titles but came up short in a 30-minute, time-limit draw.

Though Austin preferred to wrestle singles matches, wcw liked him in tag situations and teamed him with Brian Pillman to form The Hollywood Blonds. They won the tag titles in March of 1993, but are better remembered for their cocky personas and their habit of bringing a video camera to the ring to shoot defeated opponents. "It was two guys who were complete jackasses," Austin told *Wrestling World*: "That was basically our method of operation."

The Blonds dropped the titles after a five-month reign, but not without controversy. Steven Regal replaced an injured Brian Pillman for a title match against Arn Anderson and Paul Roma. Anderson pinned Austin for the win, but The Blonds probably would have regained their belts after Pillman's return had Austin not hired a new manager in his absence. Colonel Rob Parker added Austin to his stable but refused to take on Pillman, resulting in a feud between the two former partners.

Austin's career was unaffected by the split; he won the United States Heavyweight title from Dustin Rhodes in December of 1993 in a best-of-three-falls match at Starrcade. He successfully defended the title against the Great Muta and Johnny B. Badd, lost to Ricky Steamboat in August, but got the belt back in September when an injured Steamboat was unable to defend the title. Unfortunately, Austin was ordered to wrestle Hacksaw Jim Duggan and lost it again.

During a 1995 tour with New Japan, Austin suffered a detached tricep in his right arm, which required surgery. While recuperating, he was fired by wcw and hired by former manager Paul E. Dangerously, now the head honcho of Extreme Championship Wrestling (ecw). Before his arm had healed, Austin was taping spots in a Hogan-style outfit and calling himself "The Stevester." He lashed out at Hogan and Eric Bischoff, showing signs of the take-no-bull attitude that would later make Stone Cold Steve Austin famous.

Actually, Austin's brief stint with ecw was more memorable for his interviews than for his matches, though he did feud with two of the federation's top attractions, Mikey Whipwreck and The Sandman. But when the wwf called, Austin did not hesitate to sign up. He debuted in December of 1995 as The Ringmaster, managed by Ted DiBiase. As the self-proclaimed "Million-Dollar Champion," he wore green tights and DiBiase's own custom-made belt, which was emblazoned with a large dollar sign. "It sucked. There was no personality, or anything, and I wasn't allowed to be myself," said Austin of the character, who — thankfully — was not around long enough to damage his career.

The character of Stone Cold Steve Austin was born after Austin saw the movie *Pulp Fiction* and, inspired by the Bruce Willis character, decided to shave his head. Gone were the long blond locks of Stunning Steve; they were replaced by a smooth pate and a closely trimmed mustache and beard.

Later, Austin watched an HBO film about serial killer Richard Kuklinski, who was nicknamed The Ice Man. Though he didn't want to be thought of as a serial killer, Austin liked the idea of a ruthless, cold-blooded character who backed down from nothing. The wwf agreed to let him go with the new look and attitude, though they weren't confident that a no-frills tough guy in black trunks and a black vest would catch on. The federation tried to find a variation of the "Ice Man" name for the character, but it was Austin's wife, Jeannie, who came up with "Stone Cold." To complete the makeover, Austin abandoned his old "cobra clutch" finishing move for a new finisher dubbed "the Stone Cold stunner."

In February of 1996, Stone Cold Steve Austin made his first WWF appearance. Fans were intrigued, but they weren't impressed by his series of losses to Savio Vega. DiBiase had staked his WWF career on a match between Austin and Vega and was forced to leave when Austin lost. Austin later hinted that he had lost on purpose, thus eliminating the last link to his old Ringmaster character.

By the time of the King of the Ring tournament in June, Austin's star was on the rise. That night, he was to get a significant boost by winning the tournament, but it was Austin's acceptance speech that did more for his career than the victory.

Prior to Austin's final-round match with Jake "The Snake" Roberts, Roberts used his mike time to deliver a religious sermon. He was already preaching in his private life and was now incorporating it

(Photo Credit: Marko Shark)

into the repertoire of his professional character. Austin was at a hospital getting 18 stitches to close up a gash in his lip that had been opened by Marc Mero in an earlier match. When he returned to the Mecca Arena in Milwaukee, he was told of Roberts's speech.

After Austin pinned The Snake, he grabbed the microphone. "You sit there and you thump your Bible and say your prayers, and it didn't get you anywhere," he yelled. "You talk about your psalms, you talk about John 3:16. Well, Austin 3:16 says I just whipped your ass!" Austin insists the phrase was ad-libbed, but, whether impromptu or scripted, "Austin 3:16" became Stone Cold's signature. More than two million T-shirts bearing that message have been sold, and it's still a popular choice on the signs that fill WWF arenas.

After that, Austin would "break out a can of whoop-ass" (his other catchphrase) for every opponent. A bizarre minifeud outside the ring with former tag partner Brian Pillman ended with Austin breaking into Pillman's home and Pillman threatening Stone Cold with a gun. Inside the ring, his winning streak was ended by Bret Hart at the 1996 Survivor Series.

The match prompted an epic feud between Hart and Austin, which had a significant impact on both wrestlers' careers. In Steve Austin, Bret had found the perfect illustration of why he now hated American fans. He scolded them for cheering a foul-mouthed thug like Austin and brought his heel turn to fruition. Austin's stock went up considerably when he held his own against one of the best mat wrestlers in the business.

Their feud climaxed at WrestleMania XIII when Hart applied his sharpshooter finishing hold. Austin refused to tap out and appeared to lapse into unconsciousness before special referee Ken Shamrock finally called for the bell. Hart got the win, but Austin had enhanced his reputation as, in his own words, "the toughest SOB in wrestling." Announcer Jim Ross called him "The Rattlesnake," and another T-shirt was printed. "My friends told me, 'Steve, you're a babyface now.' I'd say bullshit, I'm a heel. I've always been a heel . . . then I realized they were right."

In the summer of 1997, Austin declared war on the entire Hart Foundation, which consisted of Bret and Owen Hart, British Bulldog Davey Boy Smith, and Brian Pillman. He was now the WWF's most popular superstar, but he never changed his heel-like demeanor. Though he prided himself on having no friends in the federation, he reluctantly teamed with Shawn Michaels to get the chance to beat up tag-team champions Owen Hart and The British Bulldog. They won the match and the titles, but could not get along with each other.

After Michaels was injured at the 1997 King of the Ring, Austin had to choose a new partner to defend the tag belts. He tried to get clearance to wrestle against two men himself, but then accepted Mankind as a partner after Mankind rescued him from a Hart Foundation attack. After a successful title defense, Stone Cold put the stunner on his own partner, advising him, "Don't trust anybody!" Such a betrayal would normally incite the fans' wrath, but at that time Austin could have stunned Mother Teresa and gotten a standing ovation.

On August 3, 1997, at the Meadowlands in New Jersey, Steve Austin faced Owen Hart for the Intercontinental title. The SummerSlam match ended in frightening fashion when Hart left too much of Austin's head exposed during a piledriver. "When I hit, the first thing that popped into my mind was Christopher Reeve," Austin told *Wrestling World*. "I never thought I would move again." While Austin lay motionless in the ring, Hart, knowing he was supposed to lose the match, wasn't sure what to do. He pretended to be hurt, too, until Austin regained enough feeling in his limbs to roll over and make the pin.

Doctors told him he had spinal-shock syndrome and that maybe he ought to consider a new career. Austin surrendered his tag title and Intercontinental title and appeared on WWF telecast remotes from his home in Victoria, Texas. Viewers saw him firing arrows at targets emblazoned with pictures of Owen Hart and Vince McMahon and vowing to make his way back. McMahon refused to reinstate him unless he signed a liability waiver. Austin signed it, then stunned McMahon.

At the 1997 Survivor Series, Stone Cold Steve Austin became the Intercontinental champion again by defeating Owen Hart. He was not subjected to another piledriver, and has not allowed any wrestler to attempt the move since. He then surrendered the title to Rocky Maivia, but not before throwing the belt into a river. There was only one belt he cared about, he announced, and that was the Heavyweight title.

Vince McMahon, who had now been stunned repeatedly by Stone Cold Steve Austin, cemented his heel status by using every tactic at his disposal to keep Austin away from the title. But, in 1998, Steve Austin won the Royal Rumble, which entitled him to a shot at Shawn Michaels's championship belt at WrestleMania XIV. McMahon introduced a special referee for their match: boxing champion Mike Tyson, who had been seated alongside McMahon at the Rumble.

During a memorable *Raw* telecast prior to WrestleMania, Austin confronted Tyson. Words were exchanged, and a shoving match evolved into a riot. One week before the match, Tyson joined Michaels and Degeneration X for a *Raw* appearance. But he proved to be a nonfactor in the title match, calling it down the middle and making the three-count after Austin nailed Michaels with the stunner.

Austin's win only infuriated McMahon further. He responded by throwing every rule and every wrestler in the WWF against Austin. The Rattlesnake's continual triumph over stacked decks and hidden contract clauses only further endeared him to the fans, who roared every time he gave McMahon the finger or stunned McMahon's two business-suit-garbed yes-men, Jerry Brisco and Pat Patterson.

The feud between Vince McMahon and Stone Cold Steve Austin has provided the storyline for almost every pay-per-view card in 1998. The WWF boss finally succeeded in stripping Austin of his title in October of 1998, but it hardly mattered; Austin is now an automatic main event whose popularity extends beyond belts and titles. McMahon told *Rolling Stone* he has plans outlined for Austin for the next five years. As long as Stone Cold can draw a sellout crowd, McMahon will gladly take a few more stunners and chair shots — and limp all the way to the bank.

CHRIS BENOIT

REAL NAME:
Chris Michael Benoit

ALSO KNOWN AS: Dynamite Chris Benoit, Wild Pegasus, White Pegasus, The Pegasus Kid, The Canadian Crippler, The Wolverine

BORN:
May 21, 1967, Edmonton, Alberta, Canada

HEIGHT:
5' 10"

WEIGHT:
218 pounds

PROFESSIONAL DEBUT:
December 1985

PROFESSIONAL AFFILIATIONS:
The Triple Threat, The Four Horsemen

FINISHING MOVE:
the crippler cross-face

TITLES HELD

**Stampede Tag-Team title
(with Ben Bassarab)**
Won: March 1, 1986, over Wayne Ferris and Ron Starr
Lost: March 24, 1986, to Wayne Ferris and The Cuban Assassin

(with Keith Hart)
Won: May 9, 1986, over Wayne Ferris and The Cuban Assassin
Lost: May 30, 1986, in title dispute

(with Lance Idol)
Won: October 7, 1988, over The Cuban Commandos
Lost: October 28, 1988, to The Cuban Commandos

(with Biff Wellington)
Won: April 8, 1989, over Makhan Singh and Vokkan Singh
Lost: June 9, 1989, to Bob and Kerry Brown

Stampede British Commonwealth Mid-Heavyweight title
Won: March 19, 1988, over Gama Singh

Lost: June 10, 1988, to Johnny Smith
Regained: June 17, 1988, over Johnny Smith
Lost: June 24, 1988, to Johnny Smith
Regained: January 13, 1989, over Johnny Smith
Lost: July 7, 1989, to Johnny Smith
Regained: July 8, 1989, over Johnny Smith
Lost: August 4, 1989, to Gama Singh

IWGP Junior Heavyweight title
Won: August 19, 1990, over Jushin "Thunder" Liger
Lost: November 2, 1990, to Jushin "Thunder" Liger

UWA Light Heavyweight title
Won: March 3, 1991, over Villano III
Lost: September 13, 1992, to Villano III

**CWA Tag-Team title
(with Dave Taylor)**
Won: December 21, 1991, over Miles Zrno and Frans Schuman
Title vacated in June 1992

ECW Tag-Team title
(with Dean Malenko)
Won: February 25, 1995, over Tasmaniac
and Sabu
Lost: April 8, 1995, to Public Enemy, Tasmaniac, and Rick Steiner (triangle match)

WCW Television title
Won: April 30, 1998, over Booker T
Lost: May 1, 1998, to Booker T

Regained: May 2, 1998, over Booker T
Lost: May 3, 1998, to Booker T

WCW Tag-Team title
(with Dean Malenko)
Won: March 14, 1999, over Barry
Windham and Curt Hennig
Lost: March 29, 1999, to Kidman and Rey
Misterio, Jr.

What Cal Ripken Jr. is to baseball, Chris Benoit is to wrestling — a throwback to a bygone era in sports when dedicated athletes demonstrated staunch professionalism without ego or selfishness.

Benoit's U.S. title reigns are few and far between, though his abilities in the ring transcend those of almost every other competitor he's faced. He hasn't received the recognition he deserves because he goes about his business without the gaudiness that usually comes with the territory. Despite this lack of self-promotion, which can be a recipe for career suicide in wrestling, Benoit always receives a pop from fans who know the difference between superior technique and cheap theatrics.

Anyone who's watched Chris Benoit at work will not be surprised to learn that he competed as an amateur wrestler and bodybuilder in Canada before learning the professional game at the legendary Dungeon training facility of Stu Hart. He enrolled in the Dungeon in late 1985 and made his pro debut in Hart's Stampede circuit that December, teaming up with Rich Patterson to defeat Karl Moffat and Mike Hammer.

Benoit won the Stampede Tag-Team belts twice in 1986, once with Ben Bassarab and once with Keith Hart, the brother of Bret and Owen. Both reigns were brief, but Benoit's intensity and textbook mat skills were already prompting comparisons to those of The Dynamite Kid. Even in his earliest matches, he had already mastered one of the Kid's best moves: the flying headbutt.

Just before the year's end, Benoit made his first of many trips to Japan, where his popularity now equals (and perhaps exceeds) what he's achieved in North America. He debuted with New Japan Pro Wrestling on January 2, 1987, against Yuki Funaki, and remained in Japan for most of 1987, competing as "Dynamite" Chris Benoit (an obvious tribute to his wrestling idol).

He returned to Stampede in 1988, reclaimed tag-team gold (with Lance Idol), and won his first singles belt in the Mid-Heavyweight division. But when the federation folded at the end of 1989, he went back to Japan and assumed a new identity — The Pegasus Kid. Working under a mask for the first time, he made his second debut with New Japan on February 10, 1990, teaming with Naoki Sano against Jushin "Thunder" Liger and Akira Nogami.

The story of his career from this point on could be *A Tale of Two*

Wrestlers. Outside the United States, Benoit has become one of the most successful and admired wrestlers wherever he's competed. In Japan, he won the IWGP Junior Heavyweight title against Jushin Liger in 1990, and he participated in the prestigious Best of the Super Junior tournaments from 1991 to 1996. He won in 1993, beating El Samurai in the final match, and again, in 1995, over Shinjiro Ohtani. On April 16, 1994, Benoit also won the Super J Cup, beating the Great Sasuke in a match for the ages that solidified his status in the sport (see The 10 Best Wrestling Matches of All Time, page 191).

He dropped the mask angle in 1991 and changed his name from The Pegasus Kid to White Pegasus before settling on Wild Pegasus. Benoit also competed as a masked wrestler in Mexico, in the UWA, at a time when the federation had a working relationship with New Japan. He lost his mask there in a south-of-the-border battle with Villano III on November 3, 1991. One month later, in Germany, he won the CWA Tag-Team title with Dave Taylor.

Meanwhile, back in America, Benoit signed a one-year contract with WCW in 1993 and was used mostly in tag teams with lesser talents such as Biff Wellington and Bobby Eaton. Because he was still splitting his schedule between the U.S. and Japan, it's possible that WCW was reluctant to give Benoit much of a push. After fulfilling his contract, he worked briefly as a jobber during a tryout with the WWF before returning to the independent circuits.

Benoit fared better in ECW, where he debuted in September of 1994. After a one-minute match with Sabu, in which he inflicted a fractured vertebrae and a bruised spinal cord on his opponent, Benoit picked up a new nickname: "The Crippler." He defeated 2 Cold Scorpio and then went after Sabu again; in February of 1995, he powerbombed the Samoan wrestler off the top turnbuckle onto a table where Public Enemy member Rocko Rock lay prone. The resulting impact put Rocko in a wheelchair for a time and advanced Benoit's reputation in ECW as a no-nonsense competitor.

Benoit formed The Triple Threat with Dean Malenko and Eddie Guerrero, his former rivals in New Japan. Together, they helped put the young Philadelphia federation on the map. The tag team of Benoit and Malenko, probably the most technically proficient ever to enter a wrestling ring, won the belts from Sabu and Tasmaniac in February of 1995. In September, they re-entered WCW as a team and, along with Guerrero, formed the cornerstone of the federation's new cruiserweight division. Early in his second Atlanta stint, Benoit lost to both Kensuke Sasaki and Jushin Liger in matches that were less competitive than their clashes in Japan. Some fans would say his career has been stalled ever since.

In December of 1995, Benoit joined Arn Anderson, Ric Flair, and Brian Pillman in The Four Horsemen. Despite the alliance, he wrestled several intense matches with Pillman before engaging in what is his most memorable feud to date, with Taskmaster Kevin Sullivan. The feud intensified when The Horsemen's valet, Woman (Nancy Sullivan), began accompanying Benoit to the ring for his matches and it was revealed that Woman had a prior relationship with Sullivan.

Their matches evolved into falls-count-anywhere donnybrooks; Benoit and Sullivan would start pummeling each other in the ring and then battle down the aisle into the backstage area — and sometimes into the crowd. One match in Chicago ended up in the men's restroom. There were plenty of exciting moments, but the wisdom of sending one of the sport's best technicians into brawl after brawl is questionable: it did not play to his strengths.

The feud climaxed at the 1997 Bash at the Beach, when Sullivan lost a retirement match to Benoit and ended his ring career. However, there was widespread speculation that Sullivan continued to make life miserable for Benoit from his position as a WCW talent booker. Kevin and Nancy Sullivan were married and divorced in real life, and rumor had it that the relationship between Benoit and Woman was not exclusively professional. Was Sullivan jealous enough to make sure The Crippler never held WCW gold? Or was that just a good story to entertain the marks?

Whatever the reason, Benoit's inability to win a title is baffling. He executes every move in the ring with maximum impact; he's the only wrestler who can draw a round of applause for a simple suplex, because he does it with such crisp, snapping precision. His German suplexes, performed in a series without ever releasing his opponent, are an amazing display of strength and balance. From his usual opening series of reverse knife edges to his submission finisher, the crippler cross-face, Benoit is a wrestling machine.

Has it mattered? Benoit's role as a Horseman carried some prestige, but in August of 1996 he lost to The Giant in seconds at a Clash of the Champions event when Woman accidentally tangled him in his vest at the start of the match. That's the type of shtick you'd expect from clowns like Lodi and Stevie Richards. He spent 1997 feuding with Raven's "flock," which helped put them over with the crowd but did little to advance Benoit's standing.

Fortunately, the future for Chris Benoit in WCW is looking brighter. He turned in a brilliant performance in a triple-threat match against Raven and Diamond Dallas Page, though, as usual, he came away without the U.S. title, which was up for grabs. He beat Booker T twice for the Television title, but both matches were at house shows and he was forced to lose it right back the following night. Only Benoit could win the Television belt twice without appearing on television.

Now that The Four Horsemen have been rejuvenated and Dean Malenko has joined the group, the revival of the Benoit-Malenko team should restore some much-needed class to the WCW's tag annals and bring Benoit the status in America that he has long deserved.

RIC FLAIR

REAL NAME:
Richard Morgan Fliehr

ALSO KNOWN AS:
The Nature Boy, The Black Scorpion, "the real World champion"

BORN:
February 25, 1949, Edina, Minnesota

HEIGHT:
6' 1"

WEIGHT:
240 pounds

PROFESSIONAL DEBUT:
December 10, 1972

PROFESSIONAL AFFILIATION:
The Four Horsemen

FINISHING MOVE:
the figure-four leglock

TITLES HELD

NWA **Mid-Atlantic Tag-Team title**
(with Rip Hawk)
Won: July 4, 1974, over Paul Jones and Bob Bruggers
Lost: 1975, to Paul Jones and Tiger Conway Jr.

(with Greg Valentine)
Won: December 25, 1976, over Gene and Ole Anderson
Lost: May 8, 1977, to Gene and Ole Anderson
Regained: June, 1977, over Dino Bravo and Tiger Conway Jr.
Lost: August 22, 1977, to Paul Jones and Ricky Steamboat

(with John Studd)
Won: October 30, 1978, over Paul Jones and Ricky Steamboat
Lost: November 5, 1978, to Paul Jones and Ricky Steamboat

(with Blackjack Mulligan)
Won: August 8, 1979, over Baron Von Raschke and Paul Jones
Lost: August 22, 1979, to Baron Von Raschke and Paul Jones

NWA **Mid-Atlantic Television title**
Won: June 3, 1975, over Paul Jones
Lost: June 10, 1975, to Paul Jones
Regained: May 1977, over Rufus Jones
Lost: June 25, 1977, to Ricky Steamboat

NWA **Mid-Atlantic Heavyweight title**
Won: May 24, 1976, over Wahoo McDaniel
Lost: September 11, 1976, to Wahoo McDaniel
Regained: October 16, 1976, over Wahoo McDaniel
Lost: November 30, 1976, to Wahoo McDaniel

NWA **Mid-Atlantic United States Heavyweight title**
Won: July 29, 1977, over Bobo Brazil
Lost: November 11, 1977, to Ricky Steamboat
Regained: March 1978, over Mr. Wrestling

Lost: December 18, 1978, to Ricky Steamboat
Regained: April 1, 1979, over Ricky Steamboat
Title vacated after Ric Flair wins the Tag title on August 12, 1979
Regained: April 19, 1980, over Jimmy Snuka
Lost: July 26, 1980, to Greg Valentine
Regained: November 24, 1980, over Greg Valentine
Lost: January 27, 1981, to Roddy Piper

NWA World Heavyweight title
Won: September 17, 1981, over Dusty Rhodes
Lost: June 10, 1983, to Harley Race
Regained: November 24, 1983, over Harley Race
Lost: March 21, 1984, to Harley Race
Regained: March 23, 1984, over Harley Race
Lost: May 6, 1984, to Kerry Von Erich
Regained: May 24, 1984, over Kerry Von Erich
Lost: July 25, 1986, to Dusty Rhodes
Regained: August 7, 1986, over Dusty Rhodes
Lost: September 25, 1987, to Ronnie Garvin
Regained: November 26, 1987, over Ronnie Garvin
Lost: February 20, 1989, to Ricky Steamboat
Regained: May 7, 1989, over Ricky Steamboat
Lost: July 7, 1990, to Sting
Regained: January 11, 1991, over Sting
Lost: March 21, 1991, to Tatsumi Fujinami
Regained: May 18, 1991, over Tatsumi Fujinami
Title vacated when Ric Flair joins the WWF on July 1, 1991
Regained: July 18, 1993, over Barry Windham
Title redesignated as WCW International

Heavyweight title in September 1993
Lost: September 19, 1993, to Rick Rude
Regained: June 23, 1994, over Sting
Title unified with WCW Heavyweight title

NWA Missouri Heavyweight title
Won: July 15, 1983, over David Von Erich (tournament final)
Lost: September 16, 1983, to David Von Erich

WCW World Heavyweight title
Won: March 1991
Title created
Title vacated when Ric Flair joins the WWF on July 1, 1991
Regained: March 17, 1993, over Vader
Title held up on April 23, 1994, after controversial match with Ricky Steamboat
Regained: April 24, 1994, over Ricky Steamboat
Lost: July 17, 1994, to Hulk Hogan
Regained: December 27, 1995, over Randy Savage
Lost: January 22, 1996, to Randy Savage
Regained: February 11, 1996, over Randy Savage
Lost: April 22, 1996, to The Giant
Regained: March 14, 1999, over Hulk Hogan
Lost: April 11, 1999, to Diamond Dallas Page, Hulk Hogan, and Sting (four-corners match)

WWF World Heavyweight title
Won: January 19, 1992 (tournament win)
Lost: April 5, 1992, to Randy Savage
Regained: September 1, 1992, over Randy Savage
Lost: October 12, 1992, to Bret Hart

WCW United States Heavyweight title
Won: July 7, 1996, over Konnan
Title vacated November 1996, when Ric Flair is unable to defend

If the *Encyclopedia Britannica* was to devote an entry to professional wrestling, the picture that would accompany it would be of Ric Flair. He is a living bridge between two eras in the history of the sport and the most prolific title holder of modern times. There is hardly a major figure in the past 20 years — from Buddy Rogers to Sean Waltman — with whom he has not had an alliance or a feud.

Flair personifies the mental image of what the general public envisions when they hear the term "wrestler": the platinum blond hair, the gaudy ring robe, the loud mouth, the all-too-obvious performance in the ring (begging for mercy one minute, pummeling an opponent the next), and the complete disregard for rules and officials. As the self-described "dirtiest player in the game," he has been a heel for most of his three decades in the squared circle but one for whom affection and respect never lurk too far beneath the derision. At the twilight of his career, Ric Flair is as beloved as any wrestler who has ever stepped through the ropes — it's almost impossible to imagine the sport without him.

Richard Morgan Fliehr was born and raised in Edina, Minnesota, a few blocks away from the Edina Country Club. He was the son of a doctor, who, according to most reliable sources, never yelled "Whoo!" before performing surgery. The family moved to Wisconsin where, in 1967, Fliehr won the state high-school wrestling championship in the Heavyweight division. Five years later, as Ric Flair, he turned professional. On December 10, 1972, in Rice Lake, Wisconsin, Flair debuted in the AWA against George "Scrap Iron" Gadaski. They wrestled to a ten-minute time-limit draw.

Flair was a jobber early on, like most rookies. In fact, there is no record of a Flair victory in the ring until mid-1973, when he pinned a long-forgotten grappler named John Heidmann. He was still attending Verne Gagne's training camp at the time, alongside such future stars as Ken Patera and The Iron Sheik.

His first real breakthrough came when he jumped from the AWA to the NWA Mid-Atlantic circuit. Wrestler Rip Hawk needed a tag-team partner because his usual partner, Swede Hanson, had suffered a heart attack. Flair was recruited at the last minute and was introduced to the fans as Hawk's nephew. They won the match, and Flair stayed with Hawk for nearly a year. On July 4, 1974, Flair and Hawk won the Mid-Atlantic tag belts from Paul Jones and Bob Bruggers. It was at about this time that Flair decided to move to Charlotte, North Carolina, where he lives to this day, and to dye his hair blond in order to look more like his "uncle," Rip Hawk, and his wrestling role model, Buddy Rogers.

In search of a gimmick, Flair began calling himself "The Nature Boy," a nickname first used by Buddy Rogers in the 1950s. The name was suggested by NWA boss Jim Crockett. And then, just as his career began to take off, it nearly crash-landed — literally. On October 4, 1975, Flair boarded a twin-engine Cessna 310 with a group of other wrestlers, including Johnny Valentine, Bob Bruggers, David Crockett, and Tim "Mr. Wrestling" Woods.

They were en route to a house show in Wilmington, North Carolina, when tragedy struck. Just minutes from its destination, the plane ran out of gas and went into a four-thousand-foot plunge. Before hitting the ground, the nosediving plane struck a tree and a power wire, which straightened the aircraft out just before impact. Had this not happened, there most likely would have been no survivors. As it was, the pilot was killed and Valentine and Bruggers suffered career-ending injuries.

During the flight, Flair had talked Valentine into changing seats with him. "I was in the back playing chess with Tim Woods," Valentine recalled years later; "Flair absolutely didn't want to sit up front with the pilot. Something must have told him." Still, Flair's back was broken in the crash. He spent 10 days in a North Carolina hospital and was then flown to Houston for surgery. Four months later, on February 1, 1976, he returned to the ring and scored a count-out win over Wahoo McDaniel. In a sport that specializes in manufactured heroes, Flair's recovery and return to the ring can only be described as an act of genuine heroism.

Flair's first long-standing feuds were with Wahoo McDaniel and Ricky Steamboat, both of whom he battled throughout the late 1970s. Flair's first singles title was a NWA Mid-Atlantic belt, which he won from McDaniel in May of 1976. The match pitted McDaniel's belt against Flair's hair. In tag-team matches, Flair often appeared alongside Greg Valentine. They won the tag belts from Gene Anderson and his brother Ole, who would one day join Flair's Four Horsemen.

The early success of Ric Flair is a testament to his work ethic: he wrestled constantly, anywhere and everywhere, winning and losing belts several times every year on several circuits. He fought Giant Baba in Japan, Jerry Lawler in Memphis, Dusty Rhodes in Florida, Roddy Piper in Canada, and hall-of-famer Bobo Brazil at his Carolina home base. He even wrestled Buddy Rogers for the use of the "Nature Boy" billing. Flair pinned Rogers using the figure-four leglock, his preferred finisher; earlier in his career, Flair had used the elbow drop and the vertical suplex as a finishing move.

Flair won the NWA World Heavyweight title on September 17, 1981, defeating Dusty Rhodes. It would be the first of 14 NWA/WCW title reigns for The Nature Boy, a record that may never be broken. He defended the belt throughout 1982 against such opponents as Harley Race, Barry Windham, Kerry Von Erich, Jumbo Tsurata, and Ricky Steamboat.

The first NWA Starrcade, held in Greensboro, North Carolina, on November 24, 1983, featured Flair in the main event. Having relinquished the title to Harley Race months earlier, he beat Race in a cage match refereed by the legendary wrestler Gene Kiniski. The event, which predated the first WrestleMania by 16 months, drew a crowd of 15,000 and reached more than 30,000 fans via closed-circuit locations throughout the Mid-Atlantic region, some as far away as the Caribbean.

Later that year, Flair apparently lost the title to a masked wrestler billed as "The Midnight Rider." The decision was reversed, however, when the Rider refused to remove his mask; he was later revealed to be Dusty Rhodes, who was still serving a suspension at the time of the victory. If you think it would be virtually impossible not to recognize the rotund Rhodes just because he wore a mask, you're right.

Flair and Race exchanged the title again in 1984 in matches held at Wellington, New Zealand, and Kallang, Singapore. The exchange was not acknowledged on television for nearly 10 years. Flair would also switch the title that year with Kerry Von Erich, losing a famous match in Texas Stadium but regaining the belt in Japan 18 days later.

At Starrcade 1984, Flair defended his title in a million-dollar-challenge match against Dusty Rhodes, with boxer Joe Frazier as a special referee. Frazier stopped the match after 12 minutes because of a cut that opened above Rhodes's eye. Flair then faced Magnum T.A. in a series of matches; Magnum would routinely interfere in Flair's matches with other opponents, ostensibly to make sure Flair kept the title until he, Magnum, earned another shot. Flair put a stop to the interference by allying himself with Arn and Ole Anderson, though at the time no one knew how important that alliance would become.

Gradually, Ric Flair had become a babyface, though one still likely to win matches by using a strategically hidden foreign object. He was the overwhelming crowd favorite when he faced Nikita Koloff in a cage match at the Great American Bash of 1985. That same year, NWA wrestling debuted on the cable station WTBS, bringing Flair's exploits to a national audience for the first time.

At the bash, Flair was attacked by Koloff and his brother, Ivan. He received some unlikely help from Dusty Rhodes, who chased off the Koloffs, but while he was checking on Flair the Anderson brothers appeared and locked the door of the cage. They unleashed a three-on-one assault against Rhodes; at one point, Flair hurled himself off the top rope onto Rhodes's ankle, breaking it.

This set the stage for Starrcade 1985 and a rematch between Flair and Rhodes. Incredibly, the ending of this contest was even more bizarre than that of their previous one. After the referee was knocked out, Arn and Ole Anderson came to Flair's aid, but Rhodes held them off with a "loaded" boot. Flair had the pin at one point, but there was no ref to make the count. When a second official finally got to the ring, Rhodes caught Flair in a cradle and scored the pin.

The fans went home believing the title had changed, but Flair protested that because of the Andersons's outside interference the match should have ended in an automatic DQ, which would have allowed him to keep the belt. Since Flair was a more popular champion anyway, the decision was reversed.

With Hulkamania in full flower in the WWF, Jim Crockett attempted to elevate the NWA to similar heights, and he knew that Ric Flair would have to play a major role in the federation. After 1985, Flair's frequent travels to the

AWA (where he faced Sgt. Slaughter), the Mid-South circuit, and Japan were curtailed so he could build up a stronger television following. This was viewed as a tremendous loss by Japanese fans, who had thrilled to Flair's exhibitions against Riki Choshu, Jumbo Tsurata, and AWA champion Rick Martel.

But The Nature Boy stayed close to home for most of 1986. There he revived his feud with Dusty Rhodes and schooled a new-comer named Lex Luger. His long-standing alliance with Arn and Ole Anderson became official in May of 1986, when they joined with Tully Blanchard and manager James J. Dillon to form The Four Horsemen. The group was named after the Four Horsemen of the Apocalypse, a Bible reference that was first adopted by sports people in the 1920s, when it was used to describe the backfield of the Notre Dame College football team. Arn Anderson is generally credited with naming wrestling's Horsemen.

Ric Flair at his senior prom

(Photo Credit: Seth Poppel Yearbook Archives)

Though the fame of the notorious Horsemen grew quickly and generated heat in the NWA, an argument could be made that their ultimate impact on Flair's career was detrimental. Flair continued to switch titles with anyone who needed a push and whenever his role as challenger could sell more tickets, but many of his matches ended in DQ as a result of Horsemen interference, which drew the spotlight away from his ability to finish.

When Flair did win, it was usually through cheating, which was always fun to watch but did not compare favorably with the clean victories achieved by his WWF counterpart, Hulk Hogan. The persona Flair had developed had started to affect his credibility and, by 1987, his drawing power.

His feuds with the Garvin brothers, Ronnie and Jimmy, were more silly than spectacular. At one point, Flair won a date with Jimmy's sexy manager, Precious. The date was presented as a taped skit in which Flair opened the door to his home and was attacked by Jimmy, who was in drag. Flair lost and regained his title against Ronnie Garvin (which further decreased his credibility), but he saved his best that year for his matches in Japan. During a March tour he faced Tiger Mask and Yoshiaki Yatsu in better showings than he could find at home.

In its early incarnations, the lineup of The Four Horsemen was, to be charitable, unstable. Ole Anderson retired, Lex Luger was in for awhile and then out, as was Barry Windham; and after Arn Anderson and Tully Blanchard bolted for the WWF, there wasn't much sense in keeping the organization intact. The Horsemen were disbanded for nearly two years.

Jim Crockett and the NWA continued to operate in the shadow of the wwf, but Crockett was not going to go quietly. On March 27, 1988, the day of WrestleMania IV, he staged the first Clash of the Champions show on TBS. Because the show was aired on basic cable, it cut deeply into the WWF's pay-per-view ratings. For one night, at least, more wrestling fans watched Ric Flair (who wrestled Sting to a 45-minute draw) than Hulk Hogan.

In the end, though, it wasn't enough. Crockett finally sold his company to Ted Turner. Flair was all set to jump to the WWF — by this time, the animosity between himself and Rhodes was no longer limited to the ring. Flair was frustrated with the storylines coming his way, and Rhodes, who was also a booker for NWA, blamed The Nature Boy for the dwindling crowd counts. At Starrcade 1988, Rhodes ordered Flair to job the title to Rick Steiner in a five-minute match. Flair walked out.

Having already lost Arn Anderson and Tully Blanchard to the competition, Turner threatened to pull his offer unless Ric Flair was part of the package. As a result, the main event was changed to Flair vs. Lex Luger, with Flair scoring a rare clean pin. Turner closed the deal, The Nature Boy stayed and was given creative control over his title, and Rhodes lost his booking privileges.

In 1989, Flair reignited his feud with Ricky Steamboat, who was introduced as Eddie Gilbert's mystery partner for a scheduled match against Flair and Barry Windham. Steamboat, just back from the WWF, pinned his old nemesis, which earned him several title shots. The three matches between Flair and Steamboat between February and May of 1989 are considered among the finest that Flair has ever wrestled. Steamboat won the title in the first contest and then barely held onto it in the rematch, scoring two out of three falls in 55 minutes. In the third match, Flair regained his title.

One of the celebrity judges for that final match was Terry Funk, who congratulated Flair and then piledrove him into a ringside table. The feud that followed nearly equaled Flair vs. Steamboat; the matches were exciting but grueling, and their sheer violence surpassed that of those Flair-Steamboat contests. At the July 1989 Great American Bash, Funk tried to suffocate The Nature Boy by jamming his head inside a plastic bag. At Halloween Havoc they were still going at it, this time with partners; Flair and Sting met Funk and The Great Muta in what was billed as a "Thunderdome" cage match. The feud was resolved when Flair won an "I Quit" match the following month.

The NWA was on a roll; cable viewership and house-show attendance was up, a response to some of the best shows the federation had booked in years. A Flair vs. Sting "Iron Man" match at the 1989 Starrcade kept the string of great main events intact. Sting won and then paid a surprising, emotional tribute to his opponent: "Ric Flair is the greatest World champion of all time," he said.

Flair had been wrestling Luger across the country for the title, but now Sting was over with the fans and was promoted to the number-one contender spot. The Horsemen were reinstated, and Sting was offered membership, though that was just a ruse to lure him into the open, where he was stomped by the group's founders. Sting suffered a real knee injury in the attack, so Luger regained his position on the depth chart. Sting returned at the 1990 Great American Bash and pinned Flair to win the title.

Flair was a last-minute addition to the popular Black Scorpion storyline created by Ole Anderson, in which The Scorpion, a masked wrestler, starts a feud with Sting. Originally, the role was to be played by Barry Windham, but when that didn't pan out several different wrestlers were used at various shows. When it came time for the identity of The Scorpion to be revealed, at the 1990 Starrcade, Flair agreed to play the man beneath the mask, though it was the first time he had actually worn it.

This awkward finale to the Scorpion storyline cost Ole Anderson his booking job, and the NWA, now in the midst of its evolution into WCW, inexplicably chose to reinstate Dusty Rhodes. Though Flair performed admirably against Sting, Bobby Eaton, and Tatsumi Fujinami (with whom he switched the title, though it was not acknowledged right away), Rhodes began making his life miserable again. As the 1991 Great American Bash approached, Rhodes, with the support of WCW executive vice-president Jim Herd, told Flair to job the title to Lex Luger. Herd, convinced that Flair was too old, also asked him to take a pay cut.

There was speculation as to whether The Nature Boy would agree or whether he would even show up for the pay-per-view, so the decision was made that he would lose two weeks before the event to Barry Windham. When Flair's appearance at this match also began to seem doubtful, Herd fired him. The ax fell on July 2, 1991. The Great American Bash turned into a fiasco, with fans chanting "We want Flair!" during every match. Meanwhile, The Nature Boy had already signed with the WWF. On September 8, he was stripped of his NWA title. Two days later, he wrestled his first WWF match, in Cornwall, Ontario, Canada. He forced Jim Powers to submit to the figure-four leglock.

Manager and WWF announcer Bobby Heenan made the announcement that "the real World champion" was on his way and that Hulk Hogan was in trouble. Most intriguing was the belt Heenan held up to the camera — supposedly Flair's NWA belt. It could have been, since Jim Crockett had actually granted Flair ownership of the belt instead of his salary when Crockett's federation was struggling financially. In 1992, WCW sued for its return, and Flair negotiated a price for WCW to buy it back. However, the belt displayed by Heenan and worn by Flair in his first WWF appearances was a phony, though the WWF made sure that the televised image of the belt was blurred to preserve the illusion.

It's conceivable that Flair was seen by more fans in his 18 months with the WWF than in the 17 years he had spent in the NWA and WCW. At the age of 42 he could still put on a terrific show, as evidenced by his performance in the 1992 Royal Rumble. He was the third man in the ring, and he outlasted the two who preceded him and the 27 who followed, winning the Rumble and the then-vacant WWF World Heavyweight title.

The match that intrigued most fans, however, was Ric Flair vs. Hulk

Hogan. The two first met on October 23, 1991, in Dayton, Ohio, and Flair won by count-out. Though the sport's two top superstars wrestled often at house shows, the feud between them never quite realized its potential. Though Flair (who was not called The Nature Boy during his WWF tenure since the name was considered part of his trademark WCW character) had been built into one of the promotion's most formidable stars, he could not beat Hogan in an important match, so much of the drama dissipated.

Flair's best WWF feuds were with Randy Savage and Bret Hart. His matches with Savage were accompanied by allegations that Flair had enjoyed a prior relationship with Savage's manager, Elizabeth, and that he had the photos to prove it. Savage beat Flair at WrestleMania VIII to win the title, though Flair won it back six months later.

Bret Hart beat Flair for the title in October of 1992. They met again in a 60-minute match on January 9, 1993, which Flair called his best WWF showing. Nine days later, he lost a "loser leaves the WWF" match to Curt Hennig, though his actual final WWF match was against Bret Hart in Dortmund, Germany, on February 10, 1993. Vince McMahon released him after Flair protested a drop to midcard status, claiming he could still contend for the World title.

To a hero's welcome, Flair returned to WCW at SuperBrawl III on February 21, 1993, in Asheville, North Carolina — "Horsemen country," as announcer Tony Schiavone would say. He didn't actually wrestle again until June 17, when he teamed with Arn Anderson against The Hollywood Blonds (Brian Pillman and Steve Austin). He still wasn't getting featured matches, though he continued to compete for his old NWA title, which he won in Japan over Barry Windham.

Instead, the promotion focused on its much-hyped battle of the super-heavyweights, Vader and Sid Vicious, for the WCW belt at the upcoming Starrcade. Those plans derailed on October 28, 1993, during a WCW tour of England. Vicious attacked Arn Anderson in his hotel room with a pair of scissors, stabbing Anderson more than 20 times. Suffering a punctured lung in the brawl, Vicious was fired, and WCW was left without a main event. Once again, the federation called on Ric Flair.

"He was in the process of being phased down and out," commented the *Charlotte Observer*, "with Starrcade, the event he built . . . taking place in his hometown, and he was scheduled third from the top in a tag match with long-time nemesis Ricky Steamboat against the Nasty Boys. [When] someone has been number one in the world for ten years and considered by many as the greatest ever, any fall from that vaunted greatest position and from the top of the card, when the big event is in his hometown is going to be noticeable to everyone."

Somehow, the *Observer* noted — as happened in 1988 when Flair was blamed by a booker for being unable to draw, as happened in 1989 when he was deemed too old, as happened in 1990 when he was finally removed from the top only to be reinstated in 1991 and then written off again — the wrestler who had allegedly outlived his usefulness was asked to save the company again. "With nowhere to go, as happened time after time when the ideas that were going to save the company failed and the saviors self-destructed, the only idea left was to go back to Ric Flair," concluded the *Observer*.

As if to prove the point, Flair wrestled an amazing match against Vader, a behemoth who outweighed him by almost 300 pounds. After 21 minutes, he pinned Vader and began yet another World title reign. He followed with more matches against old friends and foes, such as Sting, Ricky Steamboat, and Barry Windham, while wcw remained in a holding pattern, devoting its attention to negotiating Hulk Hogan's return from retirement.

Once the deal was signed, Flair faced Sting to unite the wcw World title with the wcw International title, the new designation for the old nwa title. The titles were unified on June 23, 1994; Flair got the pin, and Hogan appeared to support Sting after his loss. On July 17, Hogan pinned Flair amidst much fanfare, an obvious attempt to return Hogan to the level of fame he had enjoyed in the wwf.

The feud climaxed in a retirement match, held on October 23, 1994. Flair, who had been uncomfortably manipulated back to heel status to add luster to Hogan's halo, lost a match whose outcome was never in doubt. He had agreed to job since he wanted some time off anyway in exchange for a contract extension.

He sat out for awhile, then returned to lobby for his reinstatement. The entertaining storyline developed for this undertaking had Flair hosting an interview segment called "A Flair for the Gold" in which he urged wcw to overturn his retirement with the rallying cry, "Be fair to Flair!" Still allowed to wrestle outside the country, Flair agreed to face Antonio Inoki on a New Japan card in Korea that drew nearly 190,000 fans. It has been alleged that Hogan, Inoki's first choice, wanted more money and refused to job.

Back in wcw, Flair began attacking Hogan and Randy Savage. During one match, he emerged from the crowd in drag (see The 10 Most Embarrassing Wrestling Matches/Gimmicks, page 201). At the 1995 Great American Bash, The Nature Boy slapped his figure-four leglock on Savage's 80-year-old father, Angelo Poffo. Hogan and Savage campaigned for Flair's reinstatement so they could pound on him, and they got their wish.

Flair took his medicine, then got back on offense by reforming The Four Horsemen; the new lineup consisted of Flair, Arn Anderson, Chris Benoit, and Brian Pillman, who was later replaced by Steve McMichael. But in late 1995, while wrestling Hiroyoshi Tenzan in Japan, Flair injured his shoulder. On September 21, 1996, on another tour of Japan, he reinjured that shoulder while taking on Kensuke Sasaki. This time, his rotator cuff was completely torn.

To explain his absence, WCW staged a backstage attack by the outlaw New World Order (NWO) on an episode of *Monday Nitro*. Sharp-eyed fans guessed correctly that the wrestler found lying face down was not Flair; Flair's cries of pain were lifted from a 1980s match and played on the soundtrack.

After an eight-month absence, Flair returned to active competition in his hometown of Charlotte. At Slamboree, he teamed with Roddy Piper and football player Kevin Greene to defeat the NWO's Scott Hall, Kevin Nash, and Syxx.

The retirement of Arn Anderson put the future of The Horsemen in doubt until Curt Hennig was invited to take Anderson's place as the team's "enforcer." He graciously accepted, then betrayed the team at the WarGames of 1997. In a final act of defiance, Hennig revealed his NWO membership and slammed Flair's head in the door of a steel cage. On September 29, 1997, Ric Flair disbanded The Horsemen so he could concentrate on destroying Hennig and the NWO. It was a great idea, but one that received little attention after being introduced. Flair wrestled Hennig at Starrcade three months later but was injured in another NWO gang attack.

Flair's WCW contract expired in early 1998. He had been cast in a mild rivalry with Bret Hart, but given the presence of Hogan and Kevin Nash and the growing popularity of Goldberg, it seemed that there would be no grand plan to bring him back to the top. His appearances were primarily interview segments with Gene Okerlund in which he was introduced as "the 13-time Heavyweight champion of the world" to a standing ovation. With his mike skills, which if anything only improved with age, he could still work the crowd better than most other wrestlers had ever done.

In April of 1998, Tony Schiavone announced that Flair would appear on a WCW *Thunder* broadcast, but he never showed up. Eric Bischoff, who was playing the heel executive in charge of WCW and NWO, announced the no-show and then ripped into Flair, calling him at one point "a piece of garbage." Arn Anderson came to his old friend's defense and hinted there were good reasons for Flair's absence. In fact, Flair was attending a national-level amateur wrestling meet in which his son had qualified. He claimed to have informed WCW well in advance of his schedule change.

After that, angles got mixed with truth as Bischoff and Flair exchanged accusations both on and off camera. What was originally dismissed as a misunderstanding escalated into a lawsuit filed by WCW against Flair over missed appearances and violation of a letter of intent. Flair filed a counter-suit and was rumored to be weighing an offer from the WWF.

Cool heads ultimately prevailed, and Flair returned to WCW, on September 15, 1998, in an emotional ceremony. The Horsemen — including new member Dean Malenko — dressed in black tie for the event. Arn

Anderson made the introductions to a sold-out crowd. Flair, fighting back tears, emerged to one of the biggest pops ever received on a wcw broadcast. He thanked the fans for their support and then confronted Bischoff in what was rumored to be a shoot, although it had Bischoff's approval. Flair used language not often heard on family-friendly wcw shows, accusing Bischoff of abusing his power and calling him an "asshole."

At Starrcade 1998, Ric Flair wrestled Eric Bischoff. The match, Flair's first in 10 months, was thrown out after Curt Hennig saved Bischoff from a severe beating. But Flair won the rematch the following night on *Nitro*, staking his career against Bischoff's leadership of wcw and nwo. The victory gave him control over World Championship Wrestling for 90 days. Angles aside, those 90 days may turn out to have been a dress rehearsal for the role that Ric Flair will play in wcw when he finally hangs up his tights.

MICK FOLEY

REAL NAME:
Mick Foley

ALSO KNOWN AS:
Jack Manson, Cactus Jack Manson, Cactus Jack, Dude Love, Mankind

BORN:
May 14, 1965, Long Island, New York

HEIGHT:
6' 4"

WEIGHT:
277 pounds

PROFESSIONAL DEBUT:
June 24, 1983

PROFESSIONAL AFFILIATIONS:
the Union

FINISHING MOVE:
the mandible claw

TITLES HELD

CWA Tag-Team title
(with Gary Young)
Won: October 23, 1988, over Bill Dundee and Todd Morton
Lost: February 25, 1989, to Robert Fuller and Jimmy Golden

WCWA Tag-Team title
(with Super Zodiac II)
Won: May 19, 1989, over Jeff Jarrett and Kerry Von Erich
Lost: June 9, 1989, to Jeff Jarrett and Mil Mascaras

(with Scott Braddock)
Won: August 4, 1989, over Jeff Jarrett and Matt Borne
Lost: August 11, 1989, to Jeff Jarrett and Matt Borne

WCW Tag-Team title
(with Kevin Sullivan)
Won: May 22, 1994, over The Nasty Boys (Brian Knobbs and Jerry Saggs)
Lost: July 17, 1994, to Paul Roma and Paul Orndorff

ECW Tag-Team title
(with Mikey Whipwreck)
Won: August 27, 1994, over Public Enemy
Lost: November 5, 1994, to Public Enemy
Regained: December 29, 1995, over 2 Cold Scorpio and Sandman (titles awarded after Mikey Whipwreck defeats Scorpio in a singles match)
Lost: February 3, 1996, to The Eliminators

WWF Tag-Team title
(with Stone Cold Steve Austin)
Won: July 14, 1997, over Owen Hart and Davey Boy Smith
Titles vacated on September 7, 1997, when team disbands

(with Terry Funk)
Won: March 29, 1998, over The New Age Outlaws (The Road Dog Jesse James and Bad-Ass Billy Gunn)
Lost: March 30, 1998, to The New Age Outlaws

(with Kane)
Won: July 13, 1998, over The New Age
Outlaws
Lost: July 26, 1998, to Steve Austin and
The Undertaker
Regained: August 10, 1998, over The
New Age Outlaws, Steve Austin and The
Undertaker, and Owen Hart and The
Rock (four-corners match)

Lost: August 30, 1998, to The New Age
Outlaws

wwf **World Heavyweight title**
Won: January 4, 1999, over The Rock
Lost: January 24, 1999, to The Rock
Regained: January 31, 1999, over The
Rock
Lost: February 15, 1999, to The Rock

Fans will forever debate which wrestler is the most popular, which is the most technically skilled, and which has the best gimmick. But when the category is "most fearless wrestler," there can be only one candidate.

For more than 15 years, Mick Foley has sacrificed his body for his work. Whether he does it for love or money, or whether he's just plain crazy, Foley has subjected himself to the type of bumps that other wrestlers would run from. He has paid the price for his daring — a list of Foley's wrestling injuries reads like a month's log at a big-city emergency room: he swallowed his front teeth after they were knocked down his throat by Sting; he's suffered six concussions (between 1986 and 1998), a broken jaw (1986), a broken nose on two occasions (1993), and a broken cheekbone (1998); he's lost two-thirds of his ear (1993), sustained second-degree burns (1995), broken his wrist (1989) and six ribs (between 1991 and 1998); he's had over 300 stitches.

But every time you figure he can't possibly absorb any more abuse or stun another crowd with his ultraviolent battle tactics, Foley outdoes himself once again. His fall off a 16-foot steel cage at the wwf's 1998 King of the Ring is something those in attendance will never forget.

Billed in the mark sheets as a native of Truth or Consequences, New Mexico, Michael Foley was actually born and raised in Long Island, New York. Home movies once aired on a wwf broadcast show Foley as a teenager already obsessed with wrestling. Playing a character called Dude Love, he once dove off the roof of a friend's two-story house onto a pile of mattresses.

Video of this and other stunts found its way to Dominic DeNucci, a former wrestler turned trainer. Foley enrolled in DeNucci's school and became one of three students to graduate (the others were ecw star Shane Douglas and wwf referee Mark Curtis). He would routinely drive more than 200 miles to the school and often slept in his car.

Incredibly, the man who would rewrite the book on high-risk moves was in the audience at Madison Square Garden on June 28, 1982, when Jimmy Snuka performed his now-legendary "superfly" flying bodypress from the top of a steel cage. Three years later, Foley began wrestling in the independent circuits under his real name, then as Jack Manson, then as "Cactus" Jack Manson. He wrestled for any federation, anywhere, that would allow him on the card. In 1986, he incited a riot in Lagos, Nigeria, after beating

Power Uti, the local favorite. After the match, he was stitched up on a dirt floor with sewing thread and sent home.

Ending a stint in the CWA, during which Foley earned his first belt (a tag title with Gary Young), Cactus Jack Manson joined the Studd Stable, and in 1989 he was lured into the NWA. There, he began to push the limits of acceptable violence in professional wrestling in a series of matches with the notorious Abdullah the Butcher. Surprisingly, one of his gimmicks back then was to bring a novel to the ring, usually *The Road Less Traveled*.

Foley was jobbed through most of his NWA/WCW stint, but he did earn title shots against Sting and Ron Simmons, both of which were unsuccessful. Falls-count-anywhere matches became Foley's specialty; he beat Van Hammer, Paul Orndorff, and numerous others who were not as comfortable brawling in the stands.

In April of 1993, Cactus Jack began his most significant feud to date, with then-WCW champion Vader. He won their first match by DQ, though he required stitches afterward; he was nearly paralyzed in the rematch when he was subjected to a powerbomb on concrete. Cactus Jack then disappeared for weeks due to amnesia — according to the storyline. In reality, he left to spend time with his wife and newborn daughter, Noel. After being "discovered" — the storyline continued — by a WCW camera crew wandering aimlessly among the homeless in Cleveland, Cactus Jack returned to action, losing to Vader in a Texas death match in August and again in a strap match in October. He got another shot at Vader at Halloween Havoc, but he lost after being hit with a stun gun by Harley Race.

The ultimate Cactus-Vader match, however, took place in Germany on March 16, 1994. Cactus Jack got his head tied up between the top and middle ring ropes, and when he tried to slip out the tension was severe enough to badly tear his left ear and to tear his right ear almost completely off. Amazingly, he continued the match for another two minutes before losing to Vader by pinfall. Part of the right ear was iced and saved; the referee picked it up and gave it to a ring attendant. Foley's left ear required 12 stitches.

In the ambulance on the way to the hospital, Foley uttered the immortal words, "*Vergessen sie nicht bitte mein ohr in der plastik tascha zu ringen*" ("Don't forget to bring my ear in a plastic bag"). He suffered no hearing damage and refused to take time off for reconstructive surgery. Foley returned to the ring one month later.

The incident made international headlines, as did a much-anticipated rematch. But WCW wouldn't let it happen, perhaps fearing another bloody battle. Ted Turner had just signed Hulk Hogan to a longterm contract and wanted to make the federation more family oriented. Outraged, Cactus Jack left the federation in September and returned to the independent circuit. He wrestled in the Smokey Mountain promotion and began a near-legendary war with Terry Funk in ECW. In 1994, the pair caused a riot after inciting fans to throw their chairs into the ring. The feud reached its zenith at the King of the Death Match tournament in Kawasaki, Japan (see The 10 Best Wrestling Matches of All Time, page 189).

In ECW, Cactus Jack won the tag belts with Mikey Whipwreck, who got the push alongside Foley after Terry Funk missed his plane. He feuded with Sandman, the ECW Heavyweight champion, but got screwed in all his matches, a trend that would haunt him throughout his career. The popular Cactus Jack turned heel in 1995 by attacking Tommy Dreamer during a 10-man tag match.

In December of 1995, Mick Foley entered the WWF for the first time. He was reluctant to allow the federation to copyright the Cactus Jack name and gimmick for merchandising, so he created a new character: the deranged Mankind. Later, after he had signed a three-year contract extension, Foley felt more secure in the WWF, and so Cactus Jack made his return to action on September 22, 1997.

Lunatic behavior was nothing new to Foley — in ECW, he claimed his heel turn against Mikey Whipwreck was a result of an eating disorder triggered by Dorito's tortilla chips. Mankind's madness had equally bizarre origins; he was, the story went, a neglected child, forced to take piano lessons, who snapped one day and smashed his own fingers with a hammer. Leaving home, he became a hermit whose only companions were sewer rats.

The character debuted on April 1, 1996, on a *Monday Night Raw* that aired one day after WrestleMania XII. He beat Bob Holly with his finishing hold, the "mandible claw," which Foley had actually debuted in his last ECW match, against Mikey Whipwreck at the Big Ass Extreme Bash. After destroying Holly, Mankind returned and viciously attacked The Undertaker, sparking a feud that continued for more than two years.

In early 1997, the WWF aired a series of interviews with Mankind conducted by Jim Ross. Foley talked about his childhood, his lifelong love of wrestling, and his bitterness over his earlier treatment by the WWF. Drifting in and out of character, Foley was rediscovered by the WWF fans, who began cheering for him at that year's King of the Ring tournament. Responding to the reception, the WWF began to soften his image. The ultimate loner, Mankind decided in 1997 that he wanted to be Stone Cold Steve Austin's tag-team partner. He wore "Pick me, Steve" T-shirts to the ring but received a Stone Cold stunner for his efforts.

After Austin rejected Mankind, Foley tried a new approach — he campaigned for the job again, this time as a new character, a hippie named Dude Love. On July 14, 1997, Dude Love (which had also been Foley's teenage wrestling alias) joined Austin and won the tag belts over Owen Hart and the British Bulldog.

At present, Mick Foley continues to draw on all three of his wrestling characters for various matches, though for his most memorable battles he has adopted the guise of Mankind. These include a boiler-room brawl with The Undertaker in August of 1996, a buried-alive match — also against The

Undertaker — two months later, and a title shot against Shawn Michaels that December.

No match was more unbelievable, however, than Hell in the Cell II at the 1998 King of the Ring (see The 10 Best Wrestling Matches of All Time, page 192. The fall Foley took from the roof of a 16-foot cage was his idea. He had told a few people that he planned to do something special during his cage match against The Undertaker — an insane bump into the famous Spanish announcers' table — but the move itself was a surprise, which explains the genuinely horrified reactions of announcers Jim Ross and Jerry Lawler.

The Mankind outfit had some padding, but Foley could not possibly have emerged unscathed from such a fall. He blacked out briefly, broke several ribs, and dislocated his jaw. His trainer set the jaw, and Foley, after allowing himself to be carried off on a stretcher, suddenly bounded back to the ring. Once again, he climbed the cage, and The Undertaker greeted him with a choke-slam. Foley fell through the top of the cage and crashed back into the ring. The cage was not supposed to break, and Foley blacked out once again. This time, he broke his ankle in two places, but still he continued the match. He was pinned, after being choke-slammed into a ring full of thumbtacks, but walked out to a standing ovation.

In the summer of 1998, the WWF created a new title belt, the Hardcore, and Foley was its first champion. His love-hate relationship with Vince McMahon's corporation of heel wrestlers was finally severed in January of 1999, when Mankind applied a submission hold to McMahon's son, Shane, and demanded a Heavyweight title shot against The Rock. Vince McMahon consented before Shane's arm was broken, and Mick Foley defeated The Rock in a brutal no-DQ battle. The arena exploded into thunderous applause when Foley finally realized his dream of becoming World champion.

"Any physician in the world will tell you there's no way a human being should be able to take as many shots to the head as I have and still be able to carry on a conversation," Foley said in 1998. Why he wrestles the way he does — why anyone would — is a puzzle. But as long as Mick Foley can still climb between the ropes, wrestling will not have lost its capacity to thrill.

REAL NAME:
Paul Wight

ALSO KNOWN AS:
The Big Nasty, The Big Show

BORN
February 8, 1972, Tampa, Florida

HEIGHT:
7' 4"

WEIGHT:
430 pounds

PROFESSIONAL DEBUT:
July 16, 1995

PROFESSIONAL AFFILIATIONS:
The Dungeon of Doom, New World Order, The Corporation, The Union

FINISHING MOVE:
the choke-slam

TITLES HELD

wcw **World Heavyweight title**
Won: October 29, 1995, over Hulk Hogan
Title stripped on November 6, 1995
Regained: April 22, 1996, over Ric Flair
Lost: August 10, 1996, to Hulk Hogan

wcw **Tag-Team title**
(with Lex Luger)
Won: February 23, 1997, over The
Outsiders (Scott Hall and Kevin Nash)
Decision reversed on February 24, 1997

(with Sting)
Won: May 17, 1998, over The Outsiders
Lost: June 14, 1998 (in singles match vs.
Sting for ownership of title)

(with Scott Hall)
Won: July 20, 1998, over Sting and Kevin
Nash
Lost: October 26, 1998, to Rick Steiner
and Kenny Kaos

It didn't take long for The Giant to make an impression in wcw — a guy who's 7' 4" and almost 500 pounds is hard to miss. Less than six months after his first professional match, the man once known as Paul Wight had defeated Hulk Hogan for the wcw World Heavyweight title. Trust me, that was a lot more impressive before Goldberg showed up.

At first, Wight claimed to be the son of Andre the Giant. He still wears basic-black ring attire like wrestling's original Giant, with one shoulder exposed Tarzan-style. At the 1995 Bash at the Beach, he confronted Hulk

Hogan with a French-style shirt of the type that Andre used to wear and screamed, "Remember this?" The claim was false, but Wight did have a lot in common with Andre, specifically the unpleasant experience of being different from all the other kids.

"I have always been so much bigger than anyone else," he once said. "When you're 6' 9" in the eighth grade, have chest hair and shave, you are a freak." Wight played basketball in high school and attended Wichita State University on a basketball scholarship. He was considered a leading prospect for the NBA, and we can only imagine the collisions that might have occurred between wrestling's Giant and basketball's giant, Shaquille O'Neal.

But Wight was also a lifelong fan of wrestling — and especially of Ric Flair. Encouraged by his friends, he showed up at the WCW Power Plant for a tryout and was pegged for stardom early on. It wasn't just his size and his barrel-chested physique that impressed the trainers and federation officials — Wight also displayed a surprising agility in early workouts, even executing a few moves coming off the top rope!

After a few unheralded appearances on WCW *Saturday Night*, The Giant debuted at Bash at the Beach in July of 1995 and immediately got in the face of champion Hulk Hogan. He allied himself with Kevin Sullivan's Dungeon of Doom, and three months later he earned his first title shot. At Halloween Havoc, The Giant earned a DQ victory despite outside interference. The decision was reversed one week later.

A short-lived alliance with Flair against Hogan and Randy Savage ended in confrontation, and in April of 1996 The Giant defeated his wrestling idol to earn the Heavyweight title. He was still a heavy (literally and figuratively) when the New World Order storyline kicked in, and after Hogan turned heel it was The Giant who won over the fans by remaining in the WCW camp. In the first major skirmish between WCW and NWO, at the 1996 Hog Wild, The Giant lost the title to Hogan after interference from Scott Hall and Kevin Nash.

Just weeks later, The Giant switched sides for reasons that were never adequately explained. The dumbest argument, offered by Hogan, was that he had promised The Giant a chance to direct his next film. As if getting your name in the credits of *Mr. Nanny* II would prompt anyone to make a career change! Whatever the rationale, The Giant's acquisition by the NWO was considered important enough to shift the balance of power away from WCW. He won the World War III battle royal in 1996, a victory that traditionally led to a title shot. Hogan seemed to be ducking the challenge from his "ally," however, and criticized The Giant during his ubiquitous *Monday Nitro* ring commentaries.

At Starrcade, The Giant, already frustrated after losing to Lex Luger, was on the receiving end of another furious Hogan tirade as the champ tried to shift the blame for his main-event loss to Roddy Piper. With the fans urging him on, The Giant attacked Hogan and became the first NWO defector.

Another Hogan-Giant match was inevitable, but, at NWO Souled Out, they wrestled to a no decision (this was the era of spray-painting-gang attacks at WCW, and pins were a rarity). The Giant drifted through a forgettable angle as Lex Luger's tag-team partner until he found his most intriguing NWO opposite in Kevin Nash. Seven feet tall, Nash could look The Giant in the eye, and his acerbic microphone commentary was an effective contrast to The Giant's mild-mannered approach during interviews.

The Nash-Giant feud built in heat through the summer of 1997, but scheduled pay-per-view matches in September and October were postponed because Nash had sustained some injuries. These delays WCW attempted to incorporate into a storyline that had Nash afraid to fight. Finally, at the January 1998 Uncensored, fans got to witness the match that would decide who was the "real" giant of professional wrestling. Nash won in frightening fashion — his jackknife powerbomb slammed The Giant's neck into the ring at a dangerously awkward angle. Replays showed that the injury was no work — The Giant was lucky to walk out of the ring.

The powerbomb was outlawed in WCW as a result, though Nash kept using it anyway, supposedly paying a $50,000 fine with every infraction. The Giant returned in March, and requested that the powerbomb be reinstated for his revenge match against Nash. He got his wish, but inexplicably lost again after another NWO gang attack.

He earned some measure of revenge after teaming with Sting to take the tag belts from Nash and Scott Hall. But after the NWO split into two factions, The Giant joined up with Hogan's squad, a decision that made even less sense this time than it had the last. Had anyone else ever gone from heel-to-face-to-heel-to-face-to-heel in less than two years? The Giant battled Sting for the right to control the belts and choose a new partner; he lost, though it was the big guy's best showing in a year.

A disgusting angle that had him smoking on the way to the ring and dropping ashes on defeated opponents was quickly and mercifully scrapped. In July of 1998, he teamed up with Scott Hall to win the tag belts from Sting and Kevin Nash, and then he found himself next in line to job for Goldberg. Away from the ring, he made his film debut in *The Waterboy*, starring Adam Sandler.

There is every reason to believe that The Giant's best days are yet to come. After working from the ropes early in his career, he now seems content to rely on head butts, belly bounces, and leg drops before winning with the choke-slam. Pretty soon, probably after he turns face again, we should see a return to the type of aerial maneuvers that bring gasps when he executes them at the Power Plant. In October of 1998, he electrified the crowd with a missile dropkick on Diamond Dallas Page.

When will he debut "the Giantsault" in competition? "When everything else stops working," he said. "It's not the kind of thing I want to use for entertainment value. I will use it when I need it." Renamed 'The Big Show' in 1999, his arrival in the WWF is great news for fans, as well as for Kane and The Undertaker, who finally have someone else to fight besides each other.

REAL NAME:
William Scott Goldberg

BORN:
December 27, 1966, Tulsa, Oklahoma

HEIGHT:
6' 3"

WEIGHT:
285 pounds

PROFESSIONAL DEBUT:
September 22, 1997

PROFESSIONAL AFFILIATIONS:
none

FINISHING MOVE:
the jackhammer

TITLES HELD

wcw **United States Heavyweight title**
Won: April 20, 1998, over Raven
Title vacated on July 6, 1998, when
Goldberg wins the World Heavyweight
title

wcw **World Heavyweight title**
Won: July 6, 1998, over Hulk Hogan
Lost: December 27, 1998, to Kevin Nash

By the time you read these words, Bill Goldberg could be the wcw Heavyweight champion of the world and one of the talents that will carry the sport strongly into the next century. Or, he could be slapping himself in the head in a midcard match prior to battling another headliner of yesterday.

Like The Spice Girls, New Coke, and Swatches, today's craze often becomes tomorrow's trivia question. The meteoric ascent of Goldberg is unprecedented in wrestling; the closest comparison would be to the rise of The Ultimate Warrior, and even Jim Hellwig had to pay some dues before his dynamic character caught on. "Goldberg is a phenomenon you don't normally see. I haven't seen it for years," said Arn Anderson. But careers that take off like a rocket can plummet back to Earth at the same speed and on the same trajectory. And the positioning of Goldberg as an irresistible, unbeatable force does not bode well for his longterm success. What's going to happen now that he's lost?

Among the most ardent and knowledgeable wrestling fans, Goldberg has more detractors than admirers. He has been labeled a Steve Austin wannabe (though he looks more like Nikita Koloff) with berserker mannerisms borrowed from Ken Shamrock. His matches have fallen into a familiar pattern and are shorter than Randy Savage's Slim Jim commercials. Critics are convinced that he'll lose much of his appeal now that his winning streak has ended and that his inexperience will show once he's forced to wrestle for more than five minutes.

Goldberg faces more resentment in the locker room, where established stars like Curt Hennig have voiced their displeasure at jobbing for the new phenomenon. Within less than a year after his debut, he won both the U.S. Heavyweight title and the World Heavyweight title, while talented veterans like Chris Benoit and Dean Malenko continue to await their turn. "I might feel the same way if I were in their position," Goldberg admits. Of course, it's not Goldberg's fault that wcw is touting him as the next Hulk Hogan, but even Hogan lost a few along the way.

Very little was known about William Scott Goldberg as his rise to prominence began. Even after certain facts trickled out in wrestling articles and on the Internet, wcw chose to sustain the mystery for as long as possible. One year after his debut, Goldberg was still being introduced as hailing from "parts unknown."

Actually, Bill was born and raised in Tulsa, Oklahoma, the youngest of four children born to Jed Goldberg, an obstetrician, and his wife, Ethel, a concert violinist. He grew up a football fan, idolizing Oakland Raider great John Matuszak. Goldberg shattered disparaging stereotypes about Jewish athletes while playing nose tackle for the University of Georgia Bulldogs. He recorded 348 career tackles and twice earned All-Southeast Conference honors while earning a degree in psychology.

Goldberg was drafted by the Los Angeles Rams in the eleventh round and roomed for a time with future all-pro Kevin Greene before being cut in training camp. He played nose tackle for the Atlanta Falcons from 1992 to 1993, but in the 1994 preseason he tore the abdominal muscles off his pelvis, an injury that ended his NFL career. He spent one season with the arena football team Sacramento Surge before retiring to work as a bouncer. Goldberg's brother, Steve, also played in the NFL, with both the Oakland Raiders and the Minnesota Vikings.

"I never even considered wrestling to be an option, because I thought it was silly," Goldberg told a reporter in June of 1998. "There was no way I was going to go out in front of a million people wearing nothing but my underwear." The idea was first suggested to him by Diamond Dallas Page, who had met Goldberg in an "adult nightclub" back in 1991. Still determined to make it in the NFL, Goldberg passed on the offer, though Page assured him he'd never be as big in football as he would be in wrestling — "and I hadn't even known the guy for ten minutes," Page recalled.

In late 1996, while weight training at the Main Event Fitness Center in Atlanta, Goldberg was approached by owners Lex Luger and Sting. Once again, he was invited to visit the Power Plant. His former Rams roommate, Kevin Greene, also offered encouragement, having enjoyed his forays into the squared circle. This time Goldberg relented, and he spent six months training under veteran Jody Hamilton (The Assassin).

Goldberg "debuted" on WCW *Monday Nitro* on September 22, 1997, beating Hugh Morrus. Following the victory, he turned to the camera and said, "That's number one." The win was considered a mild upset, as Morrus was a veteran midcarder who may have been ripe for another push. Actually, Goldberg had first appeared on *Nitro* in March of 1997, during a skit in which Roddy Piper planned to recruit a team of WCW wrestlers and pit them against an NWO team for the Uncensored pay-per-view (John Tenta was also among the candidates). The idea of Piper with three unknowns did not go over with the fans and was

(Photo Credit: Erik S. Lesser/AP Photo)

Bill Goldberg puts Scott Hall to the mat during a WCW match

scrapped the following week, when an injured Ric Flair offered Piper The Four Horsemen to take into battle.

After beating Morrus, Goldberg feuded briefly with another ex-football player, Steve "Mongo" McMichael. Goldberg stole the former Chicago Bear's Super Bowl ring and defeated him at the 1997 Starrcade. During the feud, Goldberg failed to make it to the ring for a *Nitro* match; the camera captured him face down in the backstage area; he had apparently been hit with a lead pipe. Does this forfeit constitute an early loss on his long-unblemished record? No one has mentioned the incident since Goldberg's undefeated status became a hook. Rumors also abound that he lost dark matches to Hector Guerrero at house shows before anyone started counting.

In 1998, Bill Goldberg shortened his billing to just "Goldberg," though some fans wondered why he used his real name at all. "Let's be realistic, if I was going to pick a ring-name, I don't think it would be Bill Goldberg," he said, adding that it sounded like the name of "someone who sits behind a desk and does your taxes." He briefly considered calling himself "The Warlord" or "Mossad," after the Israeli spy agency.

Week after week on *Monday Nitro*, Goldberg would destroy another low-carder or midcarder. Disco Inferno, Ray Traylor, Lodi, Van Hammer, Stevie Ray, and The Barbarian all fell victim to his two-minute, two-move attack. The setup is a vicious spear to the midsection, followed by a combination suplex/body-slam called the jackhammer. "If I am getting over with two moves, why do more?" he said in an interview on Diamond Dallas Page's Web site.

Goldberg's limited repertoire was good enough to beat Raven for the

U.S. title in April of 1998. Three months later, in what was billed as the biggest *Nitro* ever, Goldberg brought his 106–0 record to Atlanta, the city where he had played college and professional football. On July 6, before nearly 40,000 fans in the Georgia Dome, he beat both Scott Hall and Hulk Hogan to win the Heavyweight belt. Fans expecting the usual NWO outside interference were shocked at the clean pin scored on the legendary Hulkster. Was this the passing of the same torch that Hogan had inherited from Andre the Giant at WrestleMania III?

Goldberg gave his first *Nitro* interview on July 28 — in retrospect, it's amazing he earned two belts without uttering a single word. Fans were curious as to why he had been kept off the microphone for so long. But he did the spot with the same raspy, shouting voice of a hundred other wrestlers. No better, no worse.

In August, Goldberg wrestled The Giant at house shows and won a battle royal at the Road Wild pay-per-view. His body-slam and jackhammer of the 500-pound Giant was undeniably impressive. Goldberg wrestled Meng, who in no way could be considered the number-one contender, on the August 10 *Nitro*. Diamond Dallas Page jobbed for him at October's Halloween Havoc, but it was getting difficult to find wrestlers to pad the champion's record.

At Starrcade on December 27, 1998, Goldberg faced Kevin Nash in a no-DQ match for the Heavyweight title. He fought off outside interference from both Disco Inferno and Bam Bam Bigelow but collapsed in a heap after being hit with a tazer by Scott Hall. Nash executed the landmark pin on Goldberg, ending his winning streak at 173 matches.

It was Nash who demanded a rematch, citing the controversial way in which he had won the title. But his magnanimous gesture turned out to be a charade, as 40,000 fans witnessed in the Georgia Dome on January 4, 1999. An elaborate plot was hatched that began when Goldberg was detained by the Atlanta police for stalking Miss Elizabeth, an ally of NWO. Hulk Hogan, who was apparently at the Georgia Dome simply to say farewell to his fans after announcing his retirement, applauded Goldberg's arrest. Nash challenged Hogan to take Goldberg's place and then rolled over for him, allowing Hogan to regain the title he had lost to Goldberg six months earlier.

Once Elizabeth dropped the stalking charge, Goldberg returned to the ring, only to be assaulted by the original, reunited New World Order, including new member Lex Luger. How this sudden run of vulnerability and bad luck will affect Goldberg's career will be one of wrestling's most intriguing stories throughout 1999 and beyond.

REAL NAME:
Scott Hall

ALSO KNOWN AS:
Starship Coyote, Texas Scott, The Diamond Studd, Razor Ramon, The Bad Guy, The Lone Wolf

BORN:
October 20, 1959, Miami, Florida

HEIGHT:
6' 8"

WEIGHT:
290 pounds

PROFESSIONAL DEBUT:
October 1984

PROFESSIONAL AFFILIATIONS:
American Starship, The Outsiders, New World Order, NWO Hollywood

FINISHING MOVE:
the outsider edge

AWA **Tag-Team title (with Curt Hennig)**
Won: January 18, 1986, over Jim Garvin and Steve Regal
Lost: May 17, 1986, to Buddy Rose and Doug Somers

USWA **Heavyweight title**
Won: April 3, 1995, over Bill Dundee
Lost: May 1, 1995, to Jerry Lawler

WCW **United States Heavyweight title**
Won: February 21, 1999, over Rowdy Roddy Piper
Title stripped March 18, 1999, due to injury

WWF **Intercontinental title**
Won: September 27, 1993, over Rick Martel (tournament win)
Lost: April 13, 1994, to Diesel (Kevin Nash)
Regained: August 29, 1994, over Diesel
Lost: January 22, 1995, to Jeff Jarrett
Regained: May 19, 1995, over Jeff Jarrett
Lost: May 21, 1995, to Jeff Jarrett
Regained: October 22, 1995, over Dean Douglas

Lost: January 21, 1996, to Goldust

WCW **Tag-Team title (with Kevin Nash as The Outsiders)**
Won: October 27, 1996, over Harlem Heat (Booker T and Stevie Ray)
Lost: January 26, 1997, to The Steiner Brothers
Regained: January 27, 1997 (decision of January 26 reversed)
Lost: February 23, 1997, to Lex Luger and The Giant
Regained: February 24, 1997 (decision of February 23 reversed)
Lost: October 13, 1997, to The Steiner Brothers (Sean Waltman substitutes for Kevin Nash)
Regained: January 12, 1998, over The Steiner Brothers
Lost: February 9, 1998, to The Steiner Brothers
Regained: February 22, 1998, over The Steiner Brothers
Lost: May 17, 1998, to Sting and The Giant

Scott Hall is wrestling's most troubled superstar. After a long and difficult climb through several promotions, he has reached the top of his profession only to risk losing everything in a battle with personal problems that are not as easily dispatched as his opponents in the ring. His characters have been loved and hated, but those who care about wrestling can only support Hall as he struggles to overcome his demons; we want him to continue to entertain us for years to come.

After graduating from the College of William and Mary with a premed degree, the Miami-born, Charlotte, North Carolina-raised Hall passed on becoming a doctor to follow his friend Barry Windham into a wrestling career. He paid his dues around the world in small promotions, including some in Germany, Japan, and Puerto Rico.

He was "Texas Scott" in the early days, but found his first lasting identity in Florida Championship Wrestling as Coyote, a member of the tag team American Starship. His partner was Dan Spivey, who later teamed with Mark Calloway (The Undertaker) in The Skyscrapers. The team dissolved in 1984; Hall took the Starship Coyote character to the AWA the following year, but he soon reverted to wrestling as "Big" Scott Hall. He teamed with Curt Hennig for a five-month title reign as AWA tag champs, but Hennig was considered the strength of the team, and Hall was unable to silence his critics after losing to Rick Martel in a match for the federation's Heavyweight title.

When Diamond Dallas Page joined AWA as a manager, Hall became one of his first clients. He followed Page to the NWA in 1991, changing his character to The Diamond Studd. There, he introduced a new finishing move, a crucifix powerbomb he called "the diamond death drop" (later renamed "the razor's edge," or "the outsider edge").

The Diamond Studd was to be the federation's macho ladykiller, and he received a big buildup through film clips similar to those later used to introduce Goldust and Val Venis to the WWF. He had the looks, the microphone skills, and the wrestling ability, but for some reason The Studd never took off, even after gaining wider exposure when the NWA became WCW. He beat lesser talents and played minor roles in pay-per-views, most notably in an eight-man Chamber of Horrors match at the 1991 Halloween Havoc.

In 1992, Scott Hall joined the WWF, and with the help of Vince McMahon he found a character that finally put him over. With a few quarts of grease in his long, curly, black hair, a day's growth of beard, gold chains from Mr. T's garage sale, a toothpick sticking out of his mouth, and a Rico Suave accent, Scott Hall became Razor Ramon. He didn't look the least bit Hispanic, but when he got onto the mike and growled, "Hey, chico, you don' wan' no part o' the bad guy," the crowd loved it.

At first he was a popular heel. Ric Flair introduced him at the 1992 Survivor Series as protection against The Nature Boy's federation rivals, Randy Savage and Curt Hennig. Rising quickly through the ranks, Razor Ramon earned a shot at Bret Hart's Heavyweight title at the 1993 Royal Rumble, but he lost after a competitive match. Hart would beat him again at that year's King of the Ring, though after this Razor would win his next seven pay-per-view appearances.

Ironically, Hall's career got its greatest boost when he was pinned in a routine *Monday Night Raw* match by newcomer Sean "The Kid" Waltman. His "Latin" pride wounded by the embarrassing defeat, Razor demanded a rematch — and lost again. The shocking turn of events created more heat around Razor Ramon than any 10 victories would have. Ted DiBiase, "The Million Dollar Man," took on The Kid next, vowing to show Razor how he should have handled the match. Razor distracted DiBiase and helped The Kid get the pin.

Waltman and Hall became friends inside and outside of the ring, and Razor Ramon, now a portrait of arrogance humbled, brought the crowd around to his side. He went on to beat DiBiase in the final match of his career in America and then feuded with the Million Dollar Man's former tag partner, Irwin R. Schyster.

On September 23, 1993, Razor Ramon won a 20-man battle royal to earn the vacated Intercontinental title. He would hold the belt four times in all — a WWF record. Among Hall's many memorable title matches, two "ladder matches" against Shawn Michaels stand out (see The 10 Best Wrestling Matches of All Time, page 187).

Razor Ramon's "oozing machismo" act was one of the WWF's top draws in 1994 and 1995. During this time, the WWF had a talent-exchange agreement with Jerry Lawler's USWA, which allowed Hall to win the USWA Heavyweight belt from Bill Dundee. He held it for about a month before dropping it (as everyone else did, sooner or later) to Lawler. He returned to the WWF for terrific matches with Diesel, Jeff Jarrett, Owen Hart, and The 1–2–3 Kid, who had turned heel since beating The Bad Guy three years earlier.

The year 1996 began with promise. Hall found himself in the most bizarre feud of his career. The flamboyant Goldust developed a crush on the supermacho Razor Ramon, who was forced to fend off kisses in addition to wrestling moves during a series of hilarious confrontations. But on February 19, Hall was suspended from the WWF for six weeks due to "unprofessional conduct." His match with Goldust at Wrestlemania XII had to be canceled. The suspension would be the first of many for Hall, whose struggle with substance abuse shortened his stay in the WWF. He made his final pay-per-view appearance at an April 28, 1996, In Your House, losing to Vader in a lackluster match.

Less than one month later, Hall walked unannounced into the first-ever two-hour *Monday Nitro*, and fired the opening salvo in what was to become a war between WCW and NWO. "You know who I am," he said to the shocked announcers, "and we are taking over." As part of The Outsiders tag team with Kevin Nash, Hall won the WCW Tag-Team belts, but he became more famous for his "survey," which he conducted on every *Nitro* and at every WCW house show. "Hey yo! It's real simple: we want to know if you're with us or against us," he would say. "So is anybody here to see . . . WCW? Or is everybody here to see the N . . . W . . . O!!!" A few weeks into the bit, the crowd would pick up the "NWO" chant, at which point Hall would boast, "One more for the good guys."

In the ring, he still flips his toothpick at opponents, and he still struts around with Razor Ramon's arrogance (his accent, however, has disappeared). But though he was center stage for all of NWO's group antics he wasn't given many memorable singles matches along the way. His disappearances — which lasted for days or even weeks at a time — were probably a factor in WCW's decision to not make any longterm plans for his character.

Still, there have been moments. Hall goaded WCW announcer (and former AWA foe) Larry Zbyszko out of retirement and pinned him with outside help from Dusty Rhodes. Rumors of actual fights between Hall and Zbyszko in various bars and hotels near wrestling arenas were commonplace. At the 1997 World War III, Hall won the 60-man battle royal, entitling him to a shot at Hulk Hogan's Heavyweight title. The match did not materialize until after Hogan lost the belt to Sting. Hall suffered the same fate as his NWO ally, then disappeared again to enter a drug rehab program and to deal with marital problems.

After a lengthy absence, Hall was allowed to appear at WCW house shows in May of 1998, but after appearing drunk on a March 16 Nitro, he was still considered too volatile and unpredictable for television. When the suspension was lifted for the July 6, 1998 Nitro, Hall's assignment was to job for Goldberg. It was hard to watch the match and not conclude that Hall was still being punished for past infractions.

The Outsiders team was dissolved that same month, paving the way for a Scott Hall vs. Kevin Nash match. Since Hall's personal problems were by now known to most fans, they were incorporated into a storyline of very questionable taste. On a September 1998 Nitro, Hall feigned drunkenness during a scheduled match and vomited on Eric Bischoff when it was suggested he leave the ring.

Then, just as WCW went public with Hall's alcoholism, the company also turned his recovery into an angle. A more subdued, repentant Scott Hall, now calling himself The Lone Wolf, appeared on telecasts to campaign for a revival of The Outsiders. He got his wish when the original NWO reunited on Nitro in January of 1999.

REAL NAME:
Bret Hart

ALSO KNOWN AS:
The Hit Man, The Excellence of Execution

BORN:
July 2, 1957, Calgary, Alberta, Canada

HEIGHT:
5' 11"

WEIGHT:
235 pounds

PROFESSIONAL DEBUT:
1973

PROFESSIONAL AFFILIATION:
The Hart Foundation

FINISHING MOVE:
the sharpshooter

WWC Caribbean Tag-Team title (with Smith Hart)
Won: 1978, over The Castillo Brothers
Lost: September 29, 1979, to Kengo Arakawa and Kendo Kimura

Stampede British Commonwealth Mid-Heavyweight title
Won: September 1978, over Norman Frederich Charles III
Lost: November 1978, to The Dynamite Kid
Regained: April 1979, over The Dynamite Kid
Lost: July 1979, to The Dynamite Kid

Stampede North American Heavyweight title
Won: early 1980, over Leo Burke
Lost: early 1980, to Leo Burke
Regained: May 1980, over Leo Burke
Lost: June 1980, to Leo Burke
Regained: July 1980, over Duke Meyers
Lost: mid-1981, to David Shults
Regained: June 26, 1982, over Leo Burke
Lost: August 3, 1982, to Bad News Allen
Regained: October 17, 1982, over Bad News Allen
Lost: January 14, 1983, to Leo Burke
Regained: May 3, 1983, over Leo Burke
Lost: June 1983, to Bad News Allen

WWF World Tag-Team title (with Jim Neidhart)
Won: January 26, 1987, over The British Bulldogs (Davey Boy Smith and Dynamite Kid)
Lost: September 26, 1987, to The Fabulous Rougeau Brothers
Regained: September 27, 1987, over The Fabulous Rougeau Brothers (reversing decision of September 26)
Lost: October 27, 1987, to Strike Force (Rick Martel and Tito Santana)
Regained: August 27, 1990, over Demolition (Axe and Smash)
Lost: October 30, 1990, to The Rockers (Shawn Michaels and Marty Jannetty)
Regained: November 4, 1991 (decision of October 30, 1990, reversed)
Lost: March 24, 1992, to The Nasty Boys (Brian Knobs and Jerry Sags)

WWF Intercontinental title
Won: August 26, 1991, over Curt Hennig
Lost: January 17, 1992, to The Mountie (Jacques Rougeau)
Regained: April 5, 1992, over Roddy Piper
Lost: August 29, 1992, to Davey Boy Smith

WWF World Heavyweight title
Won: October 12, 1992, over Ric Flair
Lost: April 4, 1993, to Yokozuna
Regained: March 20, 1994, over Yokozuna
Lost: November 23, 1994, to Bob Backlund
Regained: November 19, 1995, over Diesel (Kevin Nash)
Lost: March 31, 1996, to Shawn Michaels
Regained: February 16, 1997, over Steve Austin, Vader, and The Undertaker (four-corners match)

Lost: February 17, 1997, to Shawn Michaels
Regained: August 3, 1997, over The Undertaker
Lost: November 9, 1997, to Shawn Michaels

WWF King of the Ring 1993

WCW United States Heavyweight title
Won: July 20, 1998, over Diamond Dallas Page (tournament win)
Lost: August 10, 1998, to Lex Luger
Regained: August 13, 1998, over Lex Luger
Lost: October 26, 1998, to Diamond Dallas Page
Regained: November 30, 1998, over Diamond Dallas Page
Lost: February 8, 1999, to Roddy Piper

What is there left to say about Bret "Hit Man" Hart that he hasn't already said about himself? "I am The Excellence of Execution," he boasts; "The best there is, the best there was, and the best there ever will be." Bold words, but, as the saying goes, "It ain't bragging if you can do it." The Hit Man's accomplishments in the ring over the course of a 20-year career make for a convincing argument that he's right; Bret Hart has held every major title in the WWF more than once. His knowledge of scientific wrestling and textbook use of mat technique allowed him to offer a refreshing and no-less-entertaining alternative to the brawling styles of Hulk Hogan and The Ultimate Warrior during the WWF's glory days. And though he's yet to latch on to anything interesting in WCW, Bret Hart must still be considered the favorite in any match against any opponent.

Growing up the son of Stu Hart, the man who established the Calgary Stampede wrestling circuit, Bret's career choice may have seemed preordained. All the Hart boys — Keith, Bruce, Smith, and Owen — spent time in the squared circle; Bret was a successful amateur at East Manning High School in Calgary, but he decided at the age of 15 that he was not going to turn pro. "I saw it as a last-ditch profession," he admitted. "If everything else failed, there would be wrestling. I guess everything else failed."

Bret hoped to become a film director, and he studied the works of Eisenstein and Hitchcock as a broadcasting major at Mount Royal College. He also became the school's top wrestler and was scouted for the British Commonwealth Games. Low on funds, he took a semester off to earn some extra cash as a referee for Stampede. One semester turned into one year, and by then Bret was training in the Hart Dungeon, preparing to enter the family business.

Although Bret didn't join the Stampede circuit until 1976, he actually made his professional debut in the summer of 1973, in Amarillo, Texas, as a last-minute substitute for a wrestler who didn't show up. He was 16 years old. He lost. Despite this inauspicious debut, Bret still holds the record for selling the most wrestling programs in a single day — more than 1,000 — at the Calgary Stampede Fairgrounds.

Bret Hart's debut of record was in 1976 — in a Stampede match against Dennis Stamp. He earned his first title with his brother Smith when they took the WWC Caribbean tag belts from The Castillo Brothers in 1978. Bret won the British Common-wealth Mid-Heavyweight title that September but dropped it two months later to The

The Hart Foundation

Dynamite Kid. That match would be the first of countless memorable battles between The Hit Man and The Kid in both singles and tag competition. "Dynamite Kid was like Wayne Gretzky," says Bret. "He was that good — one of a kind . . . [and he] had a tremendous mind for wrestling." Their feud, which reached its peak in the British Bulldogs-Hart Foundation clashes of the mid-1980s, lasted almost 10 years.

From 1980 to 1983, Bret held the Stampede North American title six times. In 1984, he joined the WWF. Just prior to the first WrestleMania in 1985, Bret was almost talked into an identity makeover by WWF executive George Scott, who suggested the character of "Cowboy Bret Hart," a rhinestone cowboy who would ride to the ring on a different horse every night and use a lasso to hog-tie opponents. Bret rejected the idea — a risky thing for a wrestler to do if he wanted to continue working. He told Scott he couldn't ride a horse and didn't like country music. He had also known real cowboys in Calgary, men he respected and didn't want to emulate in a foolish way. Scott was convinced that Bret had thrown his future away and that he was destined to stay a midcarder for life.

Knowing he would need another gimmick, Bret asked if he could be teamed with Jim Neidhart and managed by Jimmy Hart since they all had similar last names. Instead, the WWF tried to put Bret over as a face. The fans weren't buying, though Bret would occasionally provoke a squeal from a female fan. Just as he was on the verge of quitting, Bret was contacted by Scott while he was backstage at a house show in Poughkeepsie, New York — the WWF had agreed to try his idea of a Bret Hart-Jim Niedhart-Jimmy Hart alliance.

In 1984, The Hart Foundation was born. Former football player Jim "The

Anvil" Neidhart provided the raw power and Bret "The Hit Man" Hart complemented The Anvil's brawn with superior speed and ring savvy. The "Hit Man" nickname dated back to childhood — "mostly from hitting my sisters," Bret once joked. By now, he was also wearing his trademark sunglasses, a habit he acquired because he was still shy around the television cameras.

The team began picking up heat after its participation in the 20-man battle royal at WrestleMania II. Both Bret and Neidhart were among the last entrants to be eliminated by the eventual winner, Andre the Giant. They quickly worked their way past the federation's lesser teams and, in the fall of 1986, were given a title shot against the most talented and popular team in the sport, The British Bulldogs. They lost, and kept losing for the next three months, to Davey Boy Smith and The Dynamite Kid.

When The Hart Foundation finally beat its British rivals in January of 1987, it did so in true heel fashion, by double-teaming Davey Boy and getting an assist from corrupt referee Danny Davis. The Hart Foundation reigned for seven months before losing to Strike Force (Rick Martel and Tito Santana). The team continued to take on all comers, including The Islanders (Taka and Haku), Jacques and Raymond Rougeau, The Killer Bees (B. Brian Blair and Jim Brunzell), The Dream Team (Greg Valentine and Dino Bravo), and The Young Stallions (Paul Roma and Jim Powers). In between, Bret managed a respectable solo showing at the first Royal Rumble (1988), foreshadowing his successful singles career.

Bret's first singles feud was with Bad News Brown, an opponent from his Calgary days. He began winning cheers for the first time in the WWF, and that popularity soon carried over into The Hart Foundation, especially after the team fired the weasel-like "Mouth of the South," Jimmy Hart. Jimmy responded by managing both The Rougeau Brothers and Demolition (Axe and Smash) against The Hart Foundation.

Injuries sustained by The Dynamite Kid forced The British Bulldogs to break up, which left a shortage of talented teams to contend with Bret and The Anvil. Only The Brainbusters (Arn Anderson and Tully Blanchard) managed to best them on the road to a brief title reign.

At WrestleMania VI in 1990, The Hart Foundation beat The Bolsheviks (Nikoli Volkoff and Boris Zukhov) in 19 seconds. The Rockers (Shawn Michaels and Marty Jannetty) were the hot new tag team in the federation, but matches between two fan favorites didn't happen often back then, so The Rockers and The Hart Foundation tangled only occasionally.

One particularly memorable contest occurred in Madison Square Garden; The Rockers defeated Bret and The Anvil, but the decision was reversed by WWF president Jack Tunney because one of the ropes broke, causing the ring to become unbalanced. The real reason, however, was that Neidhart planned to leave the federation in a contract dispute. When the two sides came to terms, the Foundation's belts were returned. The incident was not acknowledged on television.

The Hart Foundation lost the titles, for the final time, to The Nasty

Boys (Brian Knobs and Jerry Sags, managed by Jimmy Hart) at WrestleMania VII. In 1991, Bret resumed his singles career and earned a shot at Curt Hennig's Intercontinental title at SummerSlam in August. Bret won the match, acclaimed at the time as one of the best in WWF history, and debuted his new finishing hold, an adaptation of the Boston crab that he dubbed "the sharpshooter."

It was during Bret's second Intercontinental title reign, in 1992, that he started wrestling Shawn Michaels. Even in their earliest confrontations, there seemed to be a heat between them that went beyond the storyline.

Bret's match against his brother-in-law Davey Boy Smith (Neidhart is also a brother-in-law of Bret's), at SummerSlam 1992 ranks among the very best of The Hit Man's main events. Before more than 80,000 fans in

(Photo Credit: Steve Taylor/Photofest)

London's Wembley Stadium, The British Bulldog thrilled his countrymen by scoring a pin after 25 grueling minutes. Bret remained gracious in defeat, knowing, perhaps, that better days were soon to come.

Less than two months after losing the Intercontinental belt, Bret Hart won the WWF World Heavyweight title, defeating Ric Flair in Saskatoon, Saskatchewan, Canada. The decision was considered a phenomenal upset, as most fans expected the title to switch back to The Ultimate Warrior or Randy Savage.

In the course of Hart's celebrated title run, he forced almost everyone on the WWF's A list to submit to the sharpshooter, including then-Intercontinental champion Shawn Michaels. Bret lost his title, indirectly, through a work at WrestleMania IX, in which he stepped aside to let Hulk Hogan defeat Yokozuna and claim the belt. It was an unsatisfying resolution, but even The Hit Man's popularity could not rival the immortal Hulkster's.

So, Hogan had the title and Hart, logically, should have been the number-one contender; instead, a Hogan-Yokozuna rematch was scheduled for the 1993 King of the Ring. A Hulk Hogan-Bret Hart match would have meant that one of the WWF's two top stars would have had to job, and that wouldn't do. Strangely enough, Hogan wound up jobbing the title to Yokozuna anyway before leaving the WWF for good. One can only assume that The Hulkster (who called the shots for his own career) chose losing to a 600-pound behemoth over losing to a better wrestler. Bret earned the King of the Ring title that night, presumably as a consolation prize.

Given the drama and excitement that surrounded The Hit Man's "family feud" match with Davey Boy Smith, it was inevitable that he would one day clash with brother Owen, a talented mat technician in his own right, who had yet to really click with WWF fans. A misunderstanding between the two at the 1993 Survivor Series (see Owen Hart, page 65) quickly escalated into a war of words as Owen repeatedly challenged his brother to a singles match. At WrestleMania X, Owen scored a clean pin over The Hit Man after an outstanding exhibition of scientific wrestling (with a few cheap shots mixed in for fun). Later on that same card, Bret pinned Yokozuna to regain the Heavyweight title.

The feud continued as Bret's former tag partner Jim Neidhart sided with Owen, causing The Hit Man to lose a match with Diesel (Kevin Nash). Meanwhile, Owen had joined forces with former WWF champion Bob Backlund, who had foolishly been transformed from a veteran babyface into a psychopath. Backlund, who now resembled a Chucky doll from the *Child's Play* movies, started slapping his cross-face-chicken-wing submission hold on everybody, and it was up to Bret to stop the insanity.

A submission match — sharpshooter vs. chicken wing — was scheduled for the 1994 Survivor Series. The match would end when one of the wrestlers' seconds threw in the towel. Bret chose The British Bulldog while Owen Hart accompanied Backlund. Owen interfered during the match, causing Bret to break the sharpshooter he had on Backlund. Later, Backlund applied his submission hold on Bret and, as The Bulldog had been incapacitated, no one was available to throw in the towel. Feigning concern for his brother, Owen begged his mother, seated at ringside, to save her son. She did, and Bret lost, though he never submitted.

Backlund's title reign was short — he lost to Diesel three days later. The match between Bret and Diesel at the 1995 Royal Rumble was marred by interference from Owen, Shawn Michaels, Jeff Jarrett, and anyone else who had some free time backstage. Bret lost his temper, and retaliated with attacks on Owen and Bob Backlund as they approached the ring for the rumble. The Hit Man's heel turn was about to begin.

Following forgettable clashes with Jerry Lawler, Hakushi, and Dr. Isaac Yankum (Glenn Jacobs, now known as Kane), Bret renewed his feud with Diesel and scrapped with both Davey Boy Smith and The Undertaker. Though he would regain the Heavyweight title, pins were hard to come by as nearly every match was subjected to outside interference. Bret was growing frustrated with the unresolved angles and the involvement of Shawn Michaels in several of his matches. During the buildup to WrestleMania XII, in which Michaels and Bret would square off in a 60-minute Iron-Man match, The Hit Man engaged in the type of trash talking that came more from his heart than from the script.

What took place was a classic battle (see The 10 Best Wrestling Matches of All Time, page 188) that proved Michaels was more than a pretty face who knew how to fall. After one hour of clean wrestling, neither man could claim a pin. Bret reclaimed his belt and left the ring, but he was called back by WWF president Gorilla Monsoon, who ordered him to continue the match. Michaels won in an overtime session that Bret didn't expect, another controversial loss that cost Hart the title.

"Screwed" became Bret Hart's favorite word. After the towel incident in the match against Backlund and the WrestleMania XII decision, The Hit Man's complaints became louder. Fans weren't buying it — hey, it's wrestling; everybody gets screwed — plus, Bret went on to win the title back again anyway, in a tournament victory over The Undertaker.

While Bret's protests prompted a response of "Stop whining and start wrestling!" more screwjobs followed. He lost the title to Sycho Sid after taking a chair shot from Stone Cold Steve Austin. The rematch was marred by interference from Austin and The Undertaker, and Bret lost again. Afterward, when Vince McMahon suggested he was "frustrated," Bret grabbed the microphone and yelled, "Frustrated isn't the goddamn word for it! This is bullshit!"

At WrestleMania XIII, Bret Hart achieved his last great WWF victory, in a donnybrook brawl with Austin that was fought in the ring and in the stands and with any foreign object that was in reach. After the match, Bret unleashed a verbal tirade against Sid, The Undertaker, and Shawn Michaels, causing Sid to shout, "Hey! Take your whining ass out of here!" The feud was a defining moment in Austin's WWF career and turned The Rattlesnake into a main eventer.

The following night, on *Monday Night Raw*, Bret apologized to everyone "except those in the United States." Before long, there was a new Hart Foundation in the WWF, consisting of Bret, Owen, Jim Neidhart, Davey Boy Smith, and the late Brian Pillman. They hoisted the Canadian flag and delighted in calling all American fans "scum." It remains one of the most ill-advised angles ever devised by the WWF. Jingoism was nothing new, of course; without it, there would have been no Iron Sheik or Nikolai Volkoff. But could any American really work up a good hatred for Canada? Especially after it had given us Shania Twain? But the marks went along with it, chanting "Canada sucks!" as if the Great White North was the Evil Empire.

Bret lost to The Patriot, a talented wrestler and All-Japan veteran who was a virtual unknown in North America. He bounced back to win the Heavyweight title for the fifth time after a bizarre match with The Undertaker. He squared off against Hunter Hearst Helmsley, Steve Austin, and Ken Shamrock before once again facing his oldest nemesis, Shawn Michaels.

Survivor Series, November 9, 1997. The Hit Man and The Heartbreak Kid tangled one last time, and the result ranks among the most controversial matches in the history of wrestling. A plan was in place for Bret to drop the title; it was common knowledge by then that he was leaving the WWF. However, it was supposed to happen the following night, after Bret pinned Michaels on pay-per-view. Bret's WWF contract ran through December, and he had planned to drop the belt before the holidays.

But Vince McMahon had other ideas. He knew Bret was about to join

WCW and had actually told Bret that the move would be in his best interest. That night, however, McMahon became afraid that Bret might change the storyline without telling anyone, so he did it first. The moment Michaels locked Bret in Hart's own sharpshooter hold, McMahon ordered the referee to end the match and award the decision to Michaels. It was obvious to everyone that Bret never tapped out of the hold, but McMahon claimed otherwise.

An outraged Hart spit in McMahon's face. He destroyed ringside monitors and left the arena in disgust. Michaels also stormed out of the ring, after yelling profanities at McMahon and the referee. He left holding the belt, but he was genuinely upset over the incident. Backstage, Bret punched McMahon in the face, giving him a black eye, then confronted Michaels, who reiterated his own objection to what had happened. The following night, several wrestlers boycotted the *Raw* telecast to protest McMahon's action. Ever since this incident, McMahon has ruled the WWF in the character of "Vince McMahon, corporate dictator."

Bret made his WCW debut as "special referee" for a Starrcade match between Larry Zbyszko and Eric Bischoff. Later, during the much-anticipated main event between Sting and Hollywood Hogan, Bret used his status as an official to throw Hogan's pin of Sting out, claiming the count was fast. The match was restarted and Sting won; the decision was the popular and pre-ordained one, but there had actually been nothing wrong with the count that gave the decision to Hogan.

Following that inauspicious beginning, Bret battled Ric Flair and Curt Hennig as speculation intensified as to whether he would ally himself with the outlaw New World Order. Any drama that might have resulted from this, however, rapidly disappeared — Bret was shuffled from one botched angle to another. He rarely performs on *Monday Nitro* now, and he fails to generate much heat as hero or villain.

In December of 1998, the Arts and Entertainment Network aired *Hitman Hart: Wrestling with Shadows*, a documentary on Hart's life and career that serves as an excellent reminder of how much Bret Hart means to wrestling. Let's hope the WCW bookers were watching.

REAL NAME:
Owen James Hart

ALSO KNOWN AS: The Avenger, Owen James, The Blue Blazer, The Rocket, The King of Harts, The Black Hart

BORN:
May 7, 1966, Calgary, Alberta, Canada

HEIGHT:
5' 11"

WEIGHT:
227 pounds

PROFESSIONAL DEBUT:
1986

PROFESSIONAL AFFILIATIONS: High Energy, The Hart Foundation, The Nation of Domination, Canadian Country

FINISHING MOVE:
the sharpshooter

TITLES HELD

Stampede British Commonwealth Mid-Heavyweight title
Won: October 25, 1986, over Les Thornton
Lost: August 7, 1987, to Gama Singh

Stampede North American Heavyweight title
Won: January 19, 1987, over Makhan Singh
Lost: January 30, 1987, to Makhan Singh
Regained: April 10, 1987, over Makhan Singh
Lost: May 6, 1988, to Makhan Singh

IWGP Junior Heavyweight title
Won: May 27, 1988, over Hiroshi Hase
Lost: June 24, 1988, to Shiro Koshinaka

USWA Heavyweight title
Won: June 21, 1993, over Papa Shango
Lost: July 5, 1993, to Jerry Lawler

WWF King of the Ring 1994

WWF Tag-Team title
(with Yokozuna)
Won: April 2, 1995, over The Smoking Gunns (Billy and Bart Gunn)
Lost: September 24, 1995, to Shawn Michaels and Diesel

Regained: September 25, 1995 (decision of September 24 reversed)
Lost: September 25, 1995, to The Smoking Gunns

(with Davey Boy Smith)
Won: September 22, 1996, over The Smoking Gunns
Lost: May 26, 1997, to Shawn Michaels and Stone Cold Steve Austin

(with Jeff Jarrett)
Won: January 25, 1999, over The Big Boss Man and Ken Shamrock
Lost: March 30, 1999, to Kane and X-Pac

WWF Intercontinental title
Won: April 28, 1997, over Rocky Maivia
Lost: August 3, 1997, to Stone Cold Steve Austin
Regained: October 5, 1997 (tournament win)
Lost: November 9, 1997, to Stone Cold Steve Austin

WWF European title
Won: January 20, 1998, over Goldust
Lost: March 17, 1998, to Hunter Hearst Helmsley

Owen Hart was the Frank Stallone of wrestling. For more than a decade he worked steadily, constantly reinventing himself to play whatever role was available, and paying his dues by dutifully jobbing to lesser talents. He won numerous titles, and earned a reputation among his fellow wrestlers as a skilled technician and a fierce competitor who was equally adept in both individual and tag team competition.

And yet, for all his success, Owen still labored in the shadow of his famous brother, Bret "Hit Man" Hart. Even a clean victory over Bret in the high-profile setting of WrestleMania x didn't alter his second-class status. Said Owen in a 1996 interview, "That's the discrimination and aversion that I have dealt with my whole life." But after he was killed in a freak accident during a 1999 WWF pay-per-view, Owen was praised by his fellow wrestlers for his old-school work ethic, his unselfish performances, and his ready smile and nonstop pranks in the locker room.

The youngest son of Stu and Helen Hart (see Bret Hart), Owen learned the family trade the way his brother did, in Stu Hart's Calgary-based Stampede circuit. As an amateur, his win/loss record was better than Bret's. In 1986, he won the International Tag Team Championship with partner Ben Bassarab, and held the North American Heavyweight Title for more than a year.

In 1988, Owen toured with New Japan, and defeated Hiroshi Hase to become the first westerner to win the Junior Heavyweight Title, though he lost to Shiro Koshinaka a month later. He worked small promotions in Mexico, Japan, and Germany, before joining the WWF as the masked "Blue Blazer." The idea for the character, according to Owen, came from his brother, Bret. The Blazer's daring aerial maneuvers and suicide dives through the ropes always received a big pop from the crowd, but with that name people didn't know if he was a wrestler or a sport coat.

Shortly after WrestleMania v, Owen left the WWF to again work in promotions throughout Europe and Canada. He spent a few uneventful months in WCW, before agreeing to give the WWF another chance. For a time he replaced Bret Hart in "The New Foundation" tag team opposite brother-in-law Jim Neidhart, but he was lost in the legacy of his brother and the original Hart Foundation, one of the most popular and successful teams in history.

When Neidhart left WWF, Owen began a short-lived stint as a member of the tag team "High Energy" (with "Bird Man" Koko B. Ware). The alliance seemed on its way up, but in 1992 Owen was sidelined with a knee injury, and by the time he recovered the Bird Man had flown the coop. "In the early days as the Blue Blazer and when I was with Koko B. Ware, I don't think I was given a fair chance," he recalled.

Once more he left the federation, and joined the USWA, with whom the WWF had a talent exchange program. As "The Rocket" Owen Hart, he reigned for two weeks as the United World Heavyweight champ (beating Papa Shango), and then lost to Jerry Lawler. So it was back to the WWF, where he was reduced to jobbing for the company's top stars.

"It was only when I got a chance to fight Bret . . . that I got a fair chance to show my ability," Owen said. The angle grew out of a 1993 Survivor Series match, in which Bret inadvertently caused Owen's elimination from a "family feud" pitting Bret, Owen, and their brothers Bruce and Keith against Shawn Michaels and three masked jobbers. "The Rocket" exploded after being the only Hart to be eliminated, and began using his interview time to complain about his inadequate treatment. Though Bret vowed never to fight his brother (yeah, right), tension between the two continued to build throughout 1993.

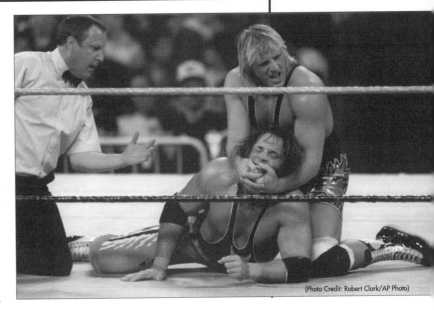

(Photo Credit: Robert Clark/AP Photo)

Owen Hart applies a choke hold to brother Bret at WrestleMania X

Their feud culminated at Wrestle-Mania X. After the usual back-and-forth swings, Owen reversed a pin attempt with a victory roll and won the match. Bret, however, ended the evening by beating Yokozuna for the WWF Heavy-weight title, making Owen's earlier victory seem unimportant. There was still enough heat between them, however, to keep the feud building toward a rematch.

The 1994 King of the Ring tournament was Owen Hart's finest hour. To earn the shot at Bret and the title, he pinned in succession Adam Bomb, Tatanka, the 1-2-3 Kid and Razor Ramon. That night, he declared himself "King of Harts." At SummerSlam later that year, it was brother vs. brother once again, this time inside a steel cage. Outside interference from relatives the British Bulldog and Jim Neidhart tarnished a superb battle, won by Bret, and set the stage for a series of family feud tag matches pitting Bret and the Bulldog against Owen and Neidhart.

Since Owen's "I don't get no respect" routine didn't score much sympathy from the fans, he turned heel and aligned himself with motormouth manager Jim Cornette. At WrestleMania XI, tag team champs the Smoking Gunns accepted a challenge from Cornette and Owen, that allowed Cornette to keep the identity of Owen's partner a secret. It was an effective gimmick that built interest in the match and, when the big night came, out waddled the big fat sumo wrestler Yokozuna, who sat on the Gunns and helped Owen win his first WWF tag title. They held the tag belts for more than a year, before losing to the Smoking Gunns in a rematch.

Reduced to jobbing again, Owen claimed a Slammy Award (which he never actually won) by sending Shawn Michaels to the hospital with a concussion, though no feud resulted from the incident. He reteamed with the British Bulldog and regained the tag team title from the Smoking Gunns, but the alliance was doomed from the start; fans cheered the Bulldog, but wouldn't throw Owen a bone.

By this time, Bret Hart had already embarked on the celebrated heel turn that ultimately led to his departure from the WWF. After whining about several controversial decisions, and his newfound unpopularity among fans, Bret convinced Owen and the Bulldog to band together as the new Hart Foundation. Thus began a series of Canadian flag-waving, America-bashing exhibitions. It was a deplorable choice of angles that prompted numerous ugly displays within the ring (Bret calling all American fans "scum") and in the arenas, now suddenly filled with signs reading "Canada Sucks."

Still, Owen excelled in the new partnership, winning the Intercontinental title from Rocky Maivia in 1997. He lost the belt to the red-hot Stone Cold Steve Austin, but not before nearly ending Austin's career with a piledriver, that resulted in Austin suffering spinal shock syndrome (see Steve Austin). A major feud resulted, during which Owen finally became a hated heel on his own, without help from Bret. He wore an "Owen 3:16—I just broke your neck" t-shirt, to further enrage the fans.

For awhile, after Bret, the British Bulldog, and Jim Neidhart all bolted to wcw, Owen heard cheers again from wwf fans for his company loyalty. The "I hate Americans" routine had thankfully been forgotten, but Owen, billed as "The Black Hart," couldn't find another satisfying angle. A gimmick of biting the ear of his opponents (like Mike Tyson) didn't last long, and smacked of desperation, as did his newfound allegiance to the Nation of Domination, and a revival of his Blue Blazer character.

Owen began taking a page from his brother's former "crybaby" persona, walking to the ring to the strains of his own voice screaming, "Enough is enough, and it's time for a change! I tried to be a nice guy!" Rather than make him a respectable heel, however, the rant opened him up to ridicule. Owen heard chants from the crowd calling him a "nugget," a reference that dated back to a Shawn Michaels insult from a year earlier.

In 1999, Owen teamed up with Jeff Jarrett and manager Debra McMichael to form "Canadian Country." The team enjoyed one title reign, and served as a launching pad for Owen's revival of his Blue Blazer character. This time, the gimmick had potential — Owen played the Blazer as a vintage superhero, and his grandiose speeches about defending truth and justice were drawing the anticipated bemusement from fans.

On May 23, 1999, at a pay-per-view dubbed "Over the Edge," the new Blue Blazer was scheduled to compete against the reigning Intercontinental champion, the Godfather. But any concerns about the title or the storyline were forgotten when the fantasy world of wrestling was invaded by a tragic reality. Owen was to repel from the roof of the Kemper Arena in St. Louis, Missouri, but instead plunged 50 feet to his death before a stunned, sold-out crowd of more than 16,000. Inexplicably, the show continued for another 90 minutes, though neither the wrestlers nor the fans could muster any enthusiasm.

The following night, on an emotional Raw telecast, Owen Hart was mourned in a series of emotional tributes, as wwf wrestlers, executives and referees broke character to remember a friend. The impact of this tragedy on future events has yet to be determined, but one thing is certain: professional wrestling has lost one of its good guys.

REAL NAME:	Paul Michael Levesque
ALSO KNOWN AS:	Jean-Paul LeVeque, Terra Rizing, Triple H
BORN:	July 27, 1969, Greenwich, Connecticut
HEIGHT:	6' 5"
WEIGHT:	280 pounds
PROFESSIONAL DEBUT:	March, 1992
PROFESSIONAL AFFILIATIONS:	Degeneration X, the Corporate Ministry, the Corporation
FINISHING MOVE:	the pedigree

TITLES HELD

WWF **Intercontinental title**
Won: October 21, 1996, over Marc Mero
Lost: February 13, 1997, to Rocky Maivia
Regained: August 30, 1998, over Rocky Maivia
Lost: October 9, 1998 (unable to defend due to injury)

WWF **European title**
Won: December 11, 1997, over Shawn Michaels
Lost: January 20, 1998, to Owen Hart
Regained: March 17, 1998, over Owen Hart
Lost: July 14, 1998, to D-Lo Brown

WWF **King of the Ring 1997**

He's not an aristocrat, but he plays one on television. Or at least he used to. From his WCW debut through his early days in the WWF, Hunter Hearst Helmsley was the second coming of Lord Steven Regal — an impeccably dressed, perfectly coiffed blue blood who, with a patronizing sneer, would bow to his opponent before pummeling him into submission.

The attitude came naturally to Helmsley, a.k.a. Paul Levesque. Like his character, he really was born and raised in Greenwich, Connecticut — one of the old-money capitals of the United States. Emerging from such highbrow origins, Levesque pursued the lowbrow career of wrestling by training with the great Killer Kowalski. As Terra Rizing (Terrorizing), he debuted on Kowalski's New England circuit, and just two years later he moved up to WCW.

Still using the Terra Rizing name, Levesque defeated Brian Armstrong in his first televised match. But WCW was not happy with his persona and suggested a variation on his surname. Levesque was repackaged as Jean-Paul

LeVeque, a wealthy, cultivated French Canadian, but he remained relegated to jobber status. He appeared in only one WCW pay-per-view match in 1994, a loss to Alex Wright at that year's Starrcade.

The Atlanta brass promised bigger and better things to come — Steve Regal had actually requested Levesque as his tag-team partner — but the impatient "aristocrat" instead bolted for the WWF where he became Hunter Hearst Helmsley. The name was appropriate: "Hearst" came from William Randolph Hearst, the arrogant billionaire newspaper baron; "Helmsley" was borrowed from Leona Helmsley, the infamous wife of a luxury-hotel magnate who went to jail for tax evasion. Garbed in a black riding outfit, Hunter was to embody all the worst attributes of the idle rich. Even his finishing move, a piledriver out of a front face-lock, was called "the pedigree."

Helmsley debuted in July of 1995, feuding first with his polar opposite in the WWF, hog farmer Henry Godwin. He continued his war against the federation's blue-collar types by attacking Fatu and Duke "The Dumpster" Droese. He sprayed perfume on Fatu before consenting to wrestle him, a gimmick that dates back to Gorgeous George.

Though his persona was that of the quintessential heel, Helmsley started getting over with fans for several reasons. First, the guys he was beating weren't any more popular than he was. Second, his long blond hair and penetrating eyes had caught the attention of female fans. Male fans looked forward to his appearances as well, as he was usually accompanied to the ring by one of several beautiful female valets. The most famous of these glamour girls was a buxom blond known as Sable, whom Helmsley would verbally abuse every time he lost a match. Soon after Helmsley was defeated in less than two minutes by The Ultimate Warrior at WrestleMania XII he also lost Sable to Marc Mero. In reality, as fans later became aware, Sable is Mero's wife, Rena. The feud between Helmsley and Mero lasted the rest of 1996.

Just before Scott Hall and Kevin Nash left the WWF for WCW, Helmsley and some other wrestlers broke character to wish the pair well at the end of a Madison Square Garden house show. Helmsley later explained that the incident was not premeditated: "There was a strong bond between us and it being Kevin and Scott's last stand, it was a very emotional night for all of us." However, the WWF frowned upon their actions, and since the federation couldn't punish Shawn Michaels (who was one of the wrestlers who broke character) because he was too popular, it was Helmsley who incurred its wrath. The King of the Ring title he was supposed to win that year was instead given to Steve Austin. "Do I regret the incident? Emotionally, no . . . from a business standpoint maybe just a tiny bit," Helmsley later admitted.

Helmsley hired Curt Hennig as his manager, and together they pulled a con job on Intercontinental champion Marc Mero in October of 1996. It seemed as though their partnership would be shortlived when Hennig began escorting Helmsley's female valets from ringside. Helmsley challenged Hennig to a match, which turned out to be the setup; Hennig faked an injury, Marc Mero offered to step in, but Helmsley would only agree to the substitution if Mero put up the belt. When Mero consented, Hennig revealed his true loyalty by helping Helmsley defeat Mero and win the title.

During a subsequent feud with Goldust, Helmsley began showing interest in Goldust's manager, Marlena, but behind the scenes he was trying to convince Vince McMahon to hire a friend of his, someone he'd met at Killer Kowalski's gym. Helmsley thought Joanie Laurer, a female bodybuilder, would make quite a splash in the WWF as his bodyguard. McMahon finally relented and, as "Chyna," Joanie joined Hunter and immediately made her presence known by viciously attacking Marlena.

Meanwhile, Helmsley's rise to prominence continued, despite his loss of the Intercontinental title to The Rock at a February 1997 In Your House pay-per-view. He won the King of the Ring that year and had his best feud yet with Mick Foley, man of many faces. Helmsley showed a surprising resilience in hardcore-style matches, a quality that reinforced the skills he'd already proven to have in the ring.

Shawn Michaels was forced to team with Helmsley to face a tag challenge against then-champions Mankind and Stone Cold Steve Austin. The pairing proved to be inspired; Helmsley gradually evolved away from his blue-blood persona and became Michaels's prankish partner in mischief. Together with Chyna and Rick Rude, they formed Degeneration X (DX), an uproarious gang of rule breakers specializing in outside interference, getting bleeped on national television, and mooning arena crowds.

Rude departed for WCW, but Degeneration X thrived, though it was Michaels who fought most of the group's major battles. Helmsley feuded with Owen Hart, losing and regaining the European title to him during 1998. After Michaels lost the Heavyweight belt to Stone Cold Steve Austin, he took several months off to recuperate from a severe back injury, placing the future of DX in jeopardy.

There was significant doubt as to whether Helmsley, now referred to as Triple H, could step in as DX leader. But with the additions of Sean Waltman and The New Age Outlaws, the Helmsley-led DX achieved unprecedented popularity. Comedy skits presented on WWF weekly shows, in which DX marches on arenas hosting WCW events, revealed an undiscovered humorous side to the former aristocrat's personality. His send-up of Michael Buffer's ring introductions — culminating in the line, "Let's get ready to . . . suck it!" — became a crowd favorite.

Image aside, the members of DX, particularly Helmsley, have also proven themselves in the ring. Skirmishes between DX and The Nation of Domination comprised one of the WWF's best feuds of the late 1990s. The groups' respective leaders, Helmsley and The Rock, had several outstanding matches in 1998, including a ladder match at SummerSlam that snared Triple H the Intercontinental title.

The return of Shawn Michaels in November of 1998 has opened up a world of possibilities, the most interesting of which is a feud between the two former DX leaders. The condition of Michaels's chronically injured back will most likely determine whether Triple H takes on The Heartbreak Kid or awaits his shot at The Rock's Heavyweight title.

REAL NAME:
Curt Hennig

ALSO KNOWN AS:
Mr. Perfect

BORN:
March 28, 1958, Minneapolis, Minnesota

HEIGHT:
6' 3"

WEIGHT:
235 pounds

PROFESSIONAL DEBUT:
1979

PROFESSIONAL AFFILIATIONS:
The Four Horsemen, New World Order, NWO Hollywood

FINISHING MOVE:
the perfect plex

TITLES HELD

AWA **World Tag-Team title (with Scott Hall)**
Won: January 18, 1986, over Jim Garvin and Steve Regal
Lost: May 7, 1986, to Buddy Rose and Doug Somers

AWA **World Heavyweight title**
Won: May 2, 1987, over Nick Bockwinkel
Lost: May 9, 1988, to Jerry Lawler

WWF **Intercontinental title**
Won: April 23, 1990, over Tito Santana
Lost: August 27, 1990, to Kerry Von Erich
Regained: November 19, 1990, over Kerry Von Erich
Lost: August 26, 1991, to Bret Hart

WCW **World Tag-Team title (with Barry Windham)**
Won: February 21, 1999, over Chris Benoit and Dean Malenko
Lost: March 14, 1999, to Chris Benoit and Dean Malenko

WCW **United States Heavyweight title**
Won: September 15, 1997, over Steve McMichael
Lost: December 28, 1997, to Diamond Dallas Page

The injuries he has sustained throughout his career have prevented Curt Hennig from taking his place among wrestling's elite competitors, though the frequent interruptions they've caused have not prevented him from racking up an impressive collection of titles in three different federations.

Before he'd turned 35, Hennig had undergone surgery four times on his left knee and once on his right, and he had been treated for degenerating disks in his neck and lower back. He's walked away from the spotlight more than once because, in his own words, "I didn't want to grow old with so many medical problems that I couldn't enjoy life." But he keeps coming back as the megaheel who makes life miserable for the fans' favorite superstars.

Among his other distinctions in the sport, Hennig holds the title of wrestler most likely to have his name misspelled. Even otherwise reliable sources refer to him as Curt "Hennig." They did it to his father, too: Larry "The Axe" Hennig was a four-time AWA tag-team champion who taught his son the business back home in Minneapolis, Minnesota. There must be something in the water there, as Hennig's closest childhood friend, Rick Rood, also became a wrestler, under the name of Ravishing Rick Rude.

Curt graduated from Verne Gagne's training camp, and his lessons continued after he broke into the sport as a jobber for the WWF. Matched against Bob Backlund at house shows, Hennig surely picked up a few moves while losing to one of the sport's best amateur competitors.

When the WWF opted not to pick up his contract, Hennig joined the AWA, his father's federation. He teamed with another newcomer, Scott Hall, and together they won the tag titles in 1986 from Jim Garvin and Steve Regal. Hennig was recognized as the more skillful wrestler of the team. Though his shoulders and chest resembled a weightlifter's, he was surprisingly flexible and agile in the ring — a mat technician in a muscleman's body. Hall tired of being the team underdog and moved on to WCW; Hennig realized a dream by joining his father in a tag match against the mighty Legion of Doom. The dream turned into a nightmare when Curt became entangled in the ropes and Hawk played the drums on his head with a steel chair.

The Hennig name meant instant babyface status for young Curt, but his true talent lay in playing the villain. He attacked Greg Gagne to begin his heel turn, then went after one of his father's rivals, Nick Bockwinkel. In a controversial 1987 match, Hennig kayoed Bockwinkel with a palmed roll of nickels to win the World Heavyweight title. He held onto the belt for one year, softening up most of his opponents with a lethal dropkick before scoring a pin with a cradle suplex.

Hennig lost his title to Jerry Lawler in 1988, then took some time off to recoup from various injuries before accepting the WWF's offer to return. He played "Mr. Perfect," a wrestler who did everything perfectly. To drive the point home, the WWF aired film clips during its broadcasts showing Hennig hitting baseballs over the home-run fence, nailing the bullseye with darts, and driving a golf ball to a hole in one.

Entering the arena to the dramatic strains of the theme from *Exodus*, Hennig began to make a name for himself at the 1988 Survivor Series, where he eliminated Jake "The Snake" Roberts from a team-vs.-team match. He embarked on an undefeated streak, surviving challenges from The Blue Blazer (Owen Hart) at WrestleMania V and The Red Rooster (Terry Taylor) at the 1989 SummerSlam. He also debuted a new finishing move, a fisherman suplex he redubbed "the perfect plex." During his five years with the WWF, only four wrestlers ever kicked out of the move: Bret Hart, Hulk Hogan, Roddy Piper, and The Ultimate Warrior.

The first time Hennig proved less than perfect in the WWF was during the 1990 Royal Rumble; though he was the last competitor eliminated in the 30-man, 60-minute battle royal, even Mr. Perfect could not best Hulk Hogan. Just before WrestleMania VI, Hennig's undefeated singles streak also ended when he was pinned by The Ultimate Warrior at a house show. He scored a DQ victory over Hogan in the high-profile setting of Madison Square Garden, but at WrestleMania he lost again, this time to Brutus Beefcake.

On the same card, The Ultimate Warrior defeated Hulk Hogan to win the World Heavyweight title, and The Warrior's Intercontinental title was declared open. Hennig, with the luster of his Mr. Perfect identity fading by the minute, entered the eight-man tournament for the belt. With an assist from new manager Bobby Heenan, Hennig pinned Tito Santana to win his first WWF title.

He dropped the belt at SummerSlam to "Texas Tornado" Kerry Von Erich, a surprising development given Von Erich's newcomer status outside of the southern circuits. The victory, achieved in just five minutes, put Von Erich over with the fans but left Hennig thirsting for revenge. He won a rematch 86 days later, and this time he kept the belt for nine months. "Perfect" was now just a name and not a description — he'd lost plenty during the interim, most notably to The Big Boss Man at WrestleMania VII, but always by disqualification.

A nagging back problem ended his reign and caused Hennig to lose to Bret Hart at the 1991 SummerSlam. He had to seek treatment. The back injury was written into his storyline, which alleged that it had resulted from Hart's application of the sharpshooter. Warned not to wrestle by his doctors, Hennig returned in a managerial capacity, though he preferred the title "executive consultant." He joined forces with Bobby Heenan and Ric Flair, whose World title victory at the 1992 Royal Rumble kept Hennig on the front burner of federation storylines.

Hennig returned to the ring after accepting a surprise invitation to be Randy Savage's tag-team partner against Ric Flair and Razor Ramon. Heenan was outraged at the betrayal, and in a rare moment of courage he slapped Hennig, who retaliated by pouring a pitcher of water over The Weasel's head. Mr. Perfect and Savage won the tag match by DQ, and Hennig further antagonized Flair by eliminating him at the 1993 Royal Rumble. The Nature Boy's stay in the WWF was nearing its conclusion, and Hennig earned the honor of beating Flair in the loser-leaves match that explained his departure. The match was taped before the Royal Rumble and aired on television one week later.

Now a babyface for the first time since his early AWA days, Hennig battled Lex Luger (in his "Narcissist" persona) at WrestleMania IX, losing a screwjob decision. In the locker room, he was also attacked by Shawn Michaels. At the first King of the Ring tournament in 1993, Hennig lost in the second round to the eventual winner, Bret Hart, after an epic 18-minute match.

Mr. Perfect's last WWF pay-per-view appearance came at SummerSlam, in an Intercontinental title match against Shawn Michaels that compared favorably to the Don Muraco-Pedro Morales matches of two decades earlier. Hennig lost by DQ due to outside interference from Diesel. A rematch would have followed had Hennig's back problems not returned. He spent the rest of 1993 on the sidelines but returned in 1994 as the special referee for a WrestleMania X match between Lex Luger and Yokozuna. Luger was now a face, but Hennig remembered their feud of the previous year and refused to count Yokozuna out. When Luger protested, Hennig disqualified him and left the arena to the heel heat so dear to his heart.

Curt Hennig would not wrestle again until 1997. He worked as a commentator for the WWF and was an occasional guest referee. In 1995, he took part in an angle involving Hunter Hearst Helmsley. Hennig started to leave his microphone position to escort Helmsley's female valets away from ringside. Helmsley, understandably ticked off by this, challenged the one-time Mr. Perfect to a match.

Fans looked forward to Hennig's return to the ring, but on October 21, 1996, Helmsley injured Hennig's knee during a sneak attack. Hennig authorized Intercontinental champion Marc Mero to wrestle in his place, and Helmsley consented on the condition that the title be placed on the line. During the match, Mr. Perfect laid out Mero with a chair shot (while the referee was incapacitated, of course!), allowing Helmsley to win the match and the title. Their earlier feud was revealed as a work, and Mr. Perfect introduced himself as Helmsley's new manager. The storyline would have continued but Hennig left the WWF one week later citing health problems.

Nothing was heard from Curt Hennig until July 13, 1997, when he debuted in WCW as the mystery partner for Diamond Dallas Page at a Bash at the Beach tag match with Scott Hall and Randy Savage. It was Hennig's first match in nearly four years, and after executing a few basic moves he walked out on his partner. The resulting feud with Page worked the ring rust off the former Mr. Perfect, whose back had recovered sufficiently for him to once again snap off a flawless bridge suplex.

Despite Hennig's reputation for treachery, Arn Anderson, in August of 1997 on the eve of his retirement, approached Hennig. He offered Hennig his old position as the "enforcer" of The Four Horsemen; Anderson wanted to help the team that stood for WCW tradition combat the NWO. An emotional Hennig accepted the offer. But on September 14, at Fall Brawl, Hennig turned against The Horsemen and revealed his allegiance to the New World Order in dramatic fashion.

Near the end of the WarGames cage match, Hennig handcuffed Horsemen Chris Benoit and Steve McMichael to the cage then dragged a wounded Ric Flair towards the steel door. He slammed Flair's head in the door with authority, a dangerous move that was brilliantly sold. A bloodied Flair was carried from the ring and sidelined for two months. In one night, Hennig put The Horsemen out of business. Flair made it official on September 29, 1997, when he disbanded the group so he could focus on his revenge against Hennig and his manager/co-conspirator, Rick Rude.

Meanwhile, Hennig continued his one-man war by pinning McMichael for his United States title.

Flair wrestled Hennig at the next two wcw pay-per-views and lost both times. It's hard to explain why The Nature Boy was not allowed his revenge; Hennig was hardly unbeatable at the time — he had lost his United States title to Diamond Dallas Page at the 1997 Starrcade and jobbed for Goldberg more than once on *Monday Nitro*. After another injury leave, Hennig made a surprise return appearance at the 1998 Starrcade, saving Eric Bischoff from being thrashed by Ric Flair.

HULK HOGAN

REAL NAME:
Terry Gene Bollea

ALSO KNOWN AS: The Super Destroyer, Terry Boulder, Sterling Golden, Terry Hogan, The Hulkster, Hollywood Hogan

BORN:
August 11, 1953, Augusta, Georgia

HEIGHT:
6' 8"

WEIGHT:
275 pounds

PROFESSIONAL DEBUT:
1978

PROFESSIONAL AFFILIATIONS:
The Megapowers, New World Order, NWO Hollywood

FINISHING MOVE:
the leg drop

TITLES HELD

IWGP **Heavyweight title**
Won: June 2, 1983, over Antonio Inoki (tournament final)
Lost: June 14, 1984, to Antonio Inoki

WWF **World Heavyweight title**
Won: January 23, 1984, over the Iron Shiek
Lost: February 5, 1988, to Andre the Giant
Regained: April 2, 1989, over Randy Savage
Lost: April 1, 1990, to The Ultimate Warrior
Regained: March 24, 1991, over Sgt. Slaughter
Lost: November 27, 1991, to The Undertaker
Regained: December 3, 1991, over The Undertaker

Title held up on December 4, 1991, and awarded to Ric Flair after his victory in the Royal Rumble
Regained: April 4, 1993, over Yokozuna
Lost: June 13, 1993, to Yokozuna

WCW **World Heavyweight title**
Won: July 17, 1994, over Ric Flair
Lost: October 29, 1995, to The Giant
Regained: August 10, 1996, over The Giant
Lost: August 4, 1997, to Lex Luger
Regained: August 9, 1997, over Lex Luger
Lost: December 28, 1997, to Sting
Regained: April 20, 1998, over Randy Savage
Lost: July 6, 1998, to Goldberg
Regained: January 4, 1999, over Kevin Nash
Lost: March 14, 1999, to Ric Flair

No one, with the possible exception of Frank Gotch in the 1920s, has exerted a more profound influence on the history of professional wrestling than Hulk Hogan. A comparison of wrestling prior to his arrival on the national scene and what it became after his ascension to superstardom reveals an upsurge in popularity unparalleled in any other sport.

Hogan's impact on wrestling most resembles Michael Jordan's impact on basketball; but while Jordan revolutionized his game through sheer talent, Hogan's influence on wrestling has stemmed almost entirely from his personality and his ability to fire up a crowd. He is an imposing figure in the ring at 6' 8", 275 pounds, and those 24-inch pythons (biceps) he brags about are there for more than just show. But anyone who knows wrestling would argue that Hogan's technical skills and mat technique are practically nonexistent.

It doesn't actually matter, though, because wrestling did not make Hulk Hogan — Hulk Hogan made wrestling. Vince McMahon may have taken his federation national, but his bid for global domination would not have succeeded without a star who could sell tickets, headline pay-per-views, and bring a sport still perceived as corrupt and seedy into the mainstream. Had there never been a Hulk Hogan, there is a very real question as to whether wrestling would have achieved the heights of popularity that it enjoys today.

To children, he has been a living, breathing superhero — a role model whose message of "training, prayers, and vitamins" is also popular with parents. When he was a good guy, he was the biggest good guy in the sport; when he shocked the wrestling world in 1996 by turning heel, he instantly became the biggest heel in the sport. Everything he's done, it seems, has been larger than life. "He became," said Dusty Rhodes, "a part of Americana."

Born Terry Bollea in Augusta, Georgia, the future Hulkster attended his first wrestling matches with his father, Pete, at the Tampa Armory soon after his family moved to Florida. His mother, Ruth, was a dance teacher. "I guess Terry gets lots of his showmanship from me," she told *People* magazine in 1991.

At the age of 12, Terry weighed 195 pounds; he wrestled in high school and got into even more fights outside of school. When he was 14, he was sentenced to a stretch in reform school for streetfighting and emerged from the experience determined to turn his life around. He graduated from high school and went on to study business at the University of South Florida, but his dream was to become a professional wrestler.

In 1976, Bollea worked as a stevedore and played bass for a South Florida rock band, but he had been unable to break into wrestling in any regional circuit. His first tryout, in fact, left him with a broken leg. While attending a wrestling event in Miami, he was spotted at ringside by WWF wrestlers Jack and Jerry Brisco. They thought the blond, muscular Bollea had an interesting look and asked him if he had ever wanted to become a wrestler. "I've wanted to be one all my life," he replied.

Bollea trained for months with the Briscos, then made his debut in Florida as The Super Destroyer. He toured the South in regional circuits billed as Sterling Golden and, later, Terry Boulder. Though he was still an unknown jobber, there was something about Bollea that always drew a response from the crowd. "By the time he got into the ring, he was getting a standing ovation," said Jerry Brisco. "Nobody had a clue who this was, but they were cheering him like he was already a superstar."

It was in 1979, while Bollea was making $125 a week in Verne Gagne's AWA federation, that he was recruited to the WWF by Vince McMahon Sr. McMahon cast him as an Irish villain named Terry Hogan, later redubbed "Hulk," because of the popularity of the television series *The Incredible Hulk*, starring Lou Ferrigno. Hogan was managed by Freddie Blassie and was beaten regularly by the sport's top stars of the day, including Superstar Billy Graham and Bob Backlund.

Soon Hogan began to generate heat, as he had on the smaller circuits, and he received a significant career boost in 1982 when he was cast as a wrestler named "Thunderlips" in the film *Rocky III*. The same year, Vince McMahon Jr. bought the Capitol Wrestling Corporation from his father and assumed control of the WWF. When it came time to choose a standard-bearer for the new national federation, McMahon selected Hulk Hogan.

Surprisingly, Hogan's first title run happened not in the WWF but in Japan, where he defeated Antonio Inoki in a June 1983 tournament final to become the first-ever IWGP Heavyweight champion. Many years later, Hogan revealed that the IWGP belt was the one that "meant the most" to him, perhaps because it was the last belt he won without the aid of his image.

The beginning of "Hulkamania" can be traced back to January 23, 1984, when Hulk Hogan pinned The Iron Sheik to win the WWF World Heavyweight title. With increased television exposure, he soon became wrestling's most recognized face. His popularity was further boosted by a feud with Rowdy Roddy Piper, who deserves a lot of the credit for Hogan's breakthrough. Every hero needs a worthy adversary and, in 1984 and 1985, Piper was the villain that fans loved to hate.

Suddenly, wrestling was becoming hip — guest appearances by recording star Cyndi Lauper and Hogan's *Rocky III* costar Mr. T generated national media attention. On February 18, 1985, MTV aired *The War to Settle the Score* live from Madison Square Garden. Hogan won the main event over Roddy Piper when Lauper and Mr. T interfered.

On March 31, 1985, the WWF presented its first WrestleMania. Guest referee Muhammad Ali had his hands full with the tag-team main event, which pitted Hogan and Mr. T against Roddy Piper and Paul Orndorff. The card, made accessible to viewers across the country at closed-circuit locations, drew an audience of more than 400,000. Three days before the event, Hogan appeared with Mr. T on comedian Richard Belzer's cable-TV show *Hot Properties*. While demonstrating a front facelock, Hogan purposely dropped the acerbic host onto a cement floor. Belzer needed nine stitches in his head, and he sued Hogan and the WWF for five million dollars in damages. The case was settled out of court for an undisclosed sum of money.

His reputation untarnished by the Belzer incident, Hogan appeared on the cover of the April 29 issue of *Sports Illustrated*; next to the swimsuit issue, it was the magazine's biggest seller in 1985. Two weeks later, wrestling returned to network television after a 30-year absence when WWF *Saturday Night's Main Event* premiered on NBC. The main event featured — who else? — Hulk Hogan, who pinned Cowboy Bob Orton. Ratings for the telecast were higher than those for *Saturday Night Live*, the show it replaced. Suddenly, Hogan had become a bona-fide national superstar.

For the rest of the decade opponents came and went, but Hogan reigned supreme. His feud with Roddy Piper carried on through 1985; the Hulkster also dealt with Bob Orton and Paul Orndorff (who was seemingly an ally one week and an enemy the next). Hogan defeated King Kong Bundy in a cage match at WrestleMania II, then became embroiled in a feud with Andre the Giant that culminated in the most publicized wrestling match of the century (see The 10 Best Wrestling Matches of All Time, page 185).

Terry Bollea poses for a mens' clothing ad during his senior year of high school

(Photo Credit: Seth Poppel Yearbook Archives)

One of Hogan's more bizarre matches in the early days of Hulkamania was a cage match against Paul Orndorff in January of 1987. Both men appeared to touch the floor at the same time, and two officials were unable to decide who had won. It didn't seem like a work, but Hogan retained his title, so it probably was.

Contrary to popular belief, Andre the Giant did not retire after his WrestleMania III defeat; he continued to battle Hogan throughout 1987 and into 1988, by which time Hogan had allied himself with Randy "Macho Man" Savage and Miss Elizabeth to form The Megapowers.

Wrestling returned to prime-time (after 33 years!) at 9 P.M. on February 5, 1988, when NBC aired its monthly *Main Event* show. Vince McMahon wanted to make the show special, and did so by having Andre defeat Hogan for the Heavyweight title (the decision was a result of shenanigans involving official Earl Hebner). A tournament for the title at WrestleMania IV saw Hulk and Andre fight to a no contest, while Randy Savage came away with the belt. Hogan was the first in the ring to congratulate him.

The Megapowers squared off against Andre the Giant and Ted DiBiase at the 1988 SummerSlam; when Hogan and Savage seemed defeated, Elizabeth climbed onto the ring apron and dropped her skirt, freezing Andre and DiBiase in their tracks. Savage pinned DiBiase for the win, though most of the male fans were looking elsewhere.

The search for new opponents who could sell a competitive match against Hogan was a challenge for WWF bookers. In 1988, they introduced The Big Boss Man (Ray Traylor), a Southern good ol' boy who dressed like a prison guard and carried a nightstick. During a cage match on *Saturday Night's Main Event*, Hogan executed a ring-shaking superplex on The Boss Man from the top of the 10-foot cage. It was the biggest bump ever taken by Hogan, who usually did his flying in Lear jets.

Jealousy prompted the Hulkster's next feud. Randy Savage was growing resentful of the time Hogan spent with Elizabeth. When The Megapowers disbanded, Elizabeth remained with Hogan while Savage found a new manager in "Sensational" Sherri Martel. "The Megapowers Explode!" was the headline for WrestleMania v, in which Hogan pinned Savage to regain the World title.

Hogan's performance rarely deviated from one pattern: to the strains of Rick Derringer's "Real American," he would burst through the curtain wearing his familiar yellow trunks and tear-away T-shirt, his receding blond hair tucked into a red bandanna; he would walk purposefully towards the ring, cheeks inflated, mouth blowing hot air beneath a Fu Manchu mustache; he'd puff out his chest like a rooster and point derisively to his opponent, while the arena erupted with applause.

Hogan's matches also followed a familiar pattern: usually, he got the worst of it most of the way, and then, when all seemed lost, his arms would start to shake; the rest of him, feeding off the cheers of the crowd, would "Hulk up" until he was back on his feet and ready to take whatever his opponent could dish out. "He's impervious to pain!" was the familiar exclamation of Gorilla Monsoon, who called most of Hogan's matches. At this point, the Hulkster would begin to land blows on his opponent, following them up with a couple of clotheslines and then a whip into the ropes, a pickup, and a body slam. Hogan would then hurl himself into the ropes, building speed for a leg-drop finisher.

Still, the inevitable pin was not the end of the drama. The triumphant Hogan would bask in the cheers of the crowd, cupping his ear to the north, south, east, and west, acknowledging each outburst. Fans who had watched the routine a hundred times marked out once more. Anyone who didn't join in the adulation had probably rooted for the witch in *The Wizard of Oz*.

Hogan, no fool he, parlayed his popularity into an empire. He endorsed everything from vitamins to antiperspirant; more than 300 different Hulkster products were produced including dolls, lunchboxes, and pillowcases. Combining his WWF salary and his cut of the merchandising, Hogan's annual income totaled between five and ten million dollars a year.

To his credit, Hogan also used his celebrity status to raise money for charities, particularly those benefiting children. He made hospital visits at every WWF tour stop, often meeting with as many as 20 sick and dying children a week. Most of these visits were not publicized — Hogan did it because he wanted to, not to get his name in the paper. "I don't know anything that could compare with Hulk at the moment," said McMahon in 1991. "I think he's gone beyond Babe Ruth."

Other attempts to capitalize on his fame were not as successful. Hogan tried to launch a movie career in 1989 by playing a wrestler named Rip in the action film *No Holds Barred*. Actor Tiny Lister, who played Rip's opponent, Zeus, turned up at several WWF events to challenge Hogan, further blurring the line between fiction and reality (or reality in wrestling, at least). *No Holds Barred* was not a hit, however, and subsequent Hogan films have performed even worse at the box office.

"I'd like to be the John Wayne of the 1990s," said Hogan on the eve of his 1993 release, *Mr. Nanny*. That didn't happen, but he did find a wider audience for his acting pursuits in the medium that had made him famous: television. His TV movies *Thunder in Paradise* (1997) and *Assault on Devil's Island* (1998), both heavily promoted on WCW *Monday Nitro* and airing on the same cable network (TNT), drew respectable ratings.

The Ultimate Warrior scored a rare clean pin over Hogan at WrestleMania VI in 1990 (see The 10 Best Wrestling Matches of All Time, page 186), and Hogan was brutally attacked soon after by the monstrous Earthquake. The storyline had Hogan suffering injuries that threatened his career, and many WWF wrestlers wore armbands in tribute to the fallen champion. Hogan, of course, bounced right back to defeat Earthquake at SummerSlam.

After Sgt. Slaughter turned against America and defeated The Warrior to become WWF champion, it was American hero Hulk Hogan who busted Sarge back to private at WrestleMania VII. During his third title reign, he switched the belt with The Undertaker, thus granting the newcomer instant status. The Undertaker's victory was aided by outside interference from Ric Flair, recently arrived from WCW. Revenge was imminent, and fans looked forward to the clash between wrestling's two most prominent superstars. On October 23, 1991, in Dayton, Ohio, Hogan faced Ric Flair for the first time. Flair won the match by count-out.

The first genuine threat to Hulk Hogan's supremacy, however, did not occur in the ring — it happened within a court of law. Rumors of steroid abuse circulated around the WWF in 1991, tainting, in particular, Vince McMahon, who was accused of everything from turning the other way to handing out the drugs himself. But was Hulk Hogan, the idol of millions, really a product of something other than training, prayers, and vitamins? Hogan appeared on *The Arsenio Hall Show* in 1991 to dispute the charges (making statements he would later contradict during McMahon's 1994 trial). But the stories persisted. In 1992, a *People* magazine article was published featuring interviews with former wrestlers who accused Hogan of abusing marijuana, cocaine, and quaaludes as well.

The negative publicity pushed Hogan to the brink of retirement. Back inside the fantasy world of the WWF, the Heavyweight title was suspended as a result of rulebreaking in Hogan's match with The Undertaker; Hogan's attempt to regain the belt at the 1992 Royal Rumble was foiled by his former ally, Sid Justice. At WrestleMania VIII, Hogan faced Justice in what many thought could be his last match. McMahon would only acknowledge that Hogan would be taking a hiatus, that could last "six months or six years or forever, I don't know."

The World Heavyweight title match that night at Hoosier Dome in Indianapolis featured Randy Savage vs. Ric Flair; but the main event, the last match of the night, was Hulk Hogan vs. Sid Justice. The Hulkster's participation still automatically made any match the most important on the card, whether a belt was involved or not. Hogan won via disqualification, and he received a thunderous ovation from a sold out crowd.

Hogan returned to the WWF eight months later, but there was tension between him and McMahon over the handling of the steroid controversy. McMahon was already looking past Hogan and building the future of his federation around younger stars such as Bret Hart and Shawn Michaels. Hogan was reduced to teaming with Brutus Beefcake in tag matches against Money, Inc. (Ted DiBiase and Irwin R. Schyster).

At WrestleMania IX, Yokozuna defeated Bret Hart for the Heavyweight title then issued a challenge to Hogan, who had wrestled earlier in the evening. Hogan accepted and pinned the mighty Yokozuna. It seemed like a return to the good old days, but that was not to be. Two months later, at the King of the Ring, Hogan was pinned by Yokozuna after a fireball was shot from a photographer's flashbulb at ringside. That match, held on June 13, 1993, would be Hulk Hogan's last in the World Wrestling Federation. Later that year, he traveled to Japan to defeat the Great Muta in a nontitle IWGP match in New Japan.

On June 11, 1994, almost one year to the day after his WWF swan song, Hogan signed with WCW. An outraged McMahon began ridiculing Hogan on WWF broadcasts, a sad ending to an alliance that had made both men millionaires. In WCW, Hogan defeated Ric Flair for the World title in his debut match, feuded with his "close friend" Brutus (now "The Butcher") Beefcake, and renewed his on-again, off-again alliance with Randy Savage.

The following year — 1995 — saw Hogan pitted against two other superheavyweights; Vader (whom Hogan had defeated at the July Bash at the Beach), and newcomer The Giant, who claimed to be the son of Andre. The Hogan ritual before, during, and after a match had changed little since the previous decade, but his presence had not elevated WCW to the level of the WWF, which still dominated its competition in television ratings and pay-per-view buy rates.

That changed in 1996 with the introduction of the New World Order storyline. Hogan was away making a movie during the initial invasion of "Outsiders" Scott Hall and Kevin Nash but returned at the July Bash at the Beach as the mystery partner of Hall and Nash. Together, they defeated wcw's top good guys: Randy Savage, Sting, and Lex Luger. The unthinkable had happened — Hulk Hogan, henceforth known as "Hollywood" Hogan, had turned heel.

The hottest storyline in wrestling was now the exploits of the NWO, and it catapulted WCW to victory in its weekly TV ratings wars with the WWF. Hogan, seemingly reenergized by his new identity, now dressed in black and broke every rule in the book. At the October 1996 Halloween Havoc, he pinned Randy Savage but was then confronted in the ring by Rowdy Roddy Piper. One of wrestling's greatest feuds was rekindled, culminating at Starrcade on December 29. It was Hogan vs. Piper, as it had been at the first WrestleMania 11 years earlier. This time, the allegiance of the fans was firmly behind Piper; he handed Hogan his first clean defeat since Hogan's loss to The Ultimate Warrior in 1990.

Though brilliant in its inception, the NWO story fell into a repetitious rut in 1997; every *Nitro* broadcast ended with the outlaw band charging the ring and attacking some hapless face. Hogan lost to Piper on two more pay-per-views, though he some-

(Photo Credit: Fitzroy Barrett/Globe Photos, Inc.)

how managed to retain the title both times. He teamed with basketball star Dennis Rodman against Lex Luger and The Giant at Bash at the Beach, then switched the belt with Lex Luger in August.

The match fans were waiting for, however, was Hogan vs. Sting, who had been in self-imposed exile for more than a year after being falsely accused of joining the NWO. The battle was slated for December 28, 1997, at Starrcade. One of Hogan's better showings since his heel turn, the match ended sloppily after his victory was overruled by Bret Hart, who had been granted special referee privileges that night for another match. He claimed that Hogan had won due to a quick count by ref Nick Patrick, and he restarted the match. Sting put Hogan in a scorpion deathlock, scoring the submission victory and the Heavyweight title.

Matches with Sting and Randy Savage played like déjà vu in early 1998, and the splintering of NWO into two factions had wrestlers switching allegiances almost every week. Losing viewers to a resurgent WWF, WCW once again resorted to stunt casting. Hogan was reteamed with Dennis Rodman in a June pay-per-view against Diamond Dallas Page and Rodman's NBA nemesis Karl Malone. The match was a disaster. In August, Page teamed with *Tonight Show* host Jay Leno to take on Hogan and NWO boss Eric Bischoff (see The 10 Most Embarrassing Wrestling Matches/Gimmicks, page 203). Watching Hogan writhe in pain from a Leno arm bar was humiliating enough, but even sadder was the realization that Hulk Hogan was no longer the biggest draw at his own matches.

In between the Malone and Leno fiascos, Hogan lost his Heavyweight title to the phenomenon of Goldberg before a crowd of 40,000 at the Georgia Dome. Rumor had it that Hogan, who was certainly in control of his own career, agreed to job to Goldberg with the stipulation that he would later be the man to end Goldberg's much-publicized winning streak, presumably at the next Starrcade.

Before that, Hogan was confronted by another face from the past when The Ultimate Warrior made his WCW debut on August 17, 1998. But Hogan-Warrior II, a featured match at the 1998 Halloween Havoc, did not measure up to its predecessor eight years earlier. The buy rate was disappointing, and the event did little to reignite either man's career.

Hulk Hogan announced his retirement from wrestling on Thanksgiving Day, 1998, on *The Tonight Show* with Jay Leno. He reasserted his plan to run for president of the United States, a *Nitro* angle inspired by the Minnesota gubernatorial victory of former wrestler Jesse "The Body" Ventura. He sounded serious, but just two months later he was back on *Nitro* among the culprits in a plot to destroy Goldberg; during this undertaking, Hogan regained the belt in a farce of a match against his NWO crony Kevin Nash.

Fans may have felt cheated, but the Leno announcement really wasn't the way that wrestling's most prominent figure should have walked away. Most devotees, especially the Hulkamaniacs of old, would prefer to see Hogan make a face turn and defeat an unstoppable foe (perhaps Goldberg, recast as a heel) before stepping down to an ovation appropriate for someone who has meant so much to the sport. Wrestling being what it is, it could still happen.

REAL NAME:
Chris Irvine

ALSO KNOWN AS:
Lionheart, Corazon de Leon

BORN:
November 9, 1970, Vancouver, British Columbia, Canada

HEIGHT:
5' 10"

WEIGHT:
225 pounds

PROFESSIONAL DEBUT:
October 2, 1990

PROFESSIONAL AFFILIATION:
The Thrillseekers

FINISHING MOVE:
the liontamer

TITLES HELD

Canadian Middleweight title
Won: January 9, 1992, over Stevie Richards
Lost: date unknown

**WWA Tag-Team title
(with El Dandy)**
Won: July 21, 1993, over Texano and Silver King
Lost: September 1, 1993, to Texano and Silver King

NWA World Middleweight title
Won: December 4, 1993, over Mano Negra
Lost: November 8, 1994, to The Ultimo Dragon

Canadian Heavyweight title
Won: January 29, 1993, over Biff Wellington
Lost: date unknown

WAR International Junior Heavyweight title
Won: June 4, 1995, over Gedo
Lost: July 28, 1995, to The Ultimo Dragon

**WAR International Junior Heavyweight Tag-Team title
(with Gedo)**
Won: February 23, 1996, over Lance Storm and Yuji Yasuraoko (tournament win)
Lost: March 27, 1996, to Lance Storm and Yuji Yasuraoko

ECW World Television title
Won: June 22, 1996, over Pitbull #2
Lost: July 13, 1996, to Shane Douglas

WCW Cruiserweight title
Won: June 28, 1997, over Syxx (Sean Waltman)
Lost: July 28, 1997, to Alex Wright
Regained: August 12, 1997, over Alex Wright
Lost: September 14, 1997, to Eddy Guerrero
Regained: January 24, 1998, over Rey Misterio Jr.
Lost: May 17, 1998, to Dean Malenko
Regained: June 14, 1998, over Dean Malenko

Lost: July 12, 1998, to Rey Misterio Jr.
Regained: July 13, 1998, over Rey
Misterio Jr.
Lost: August 8, 1998, to Juventud
Guerrera

wcw **Television title**
Won: August 10, 1998, over Stevie Ray
Lost: November 30, 1998, to Konnan

Wrestling and comedy usually don't mix because wrestling strays dangerously close to self-parody even when it's played straight. Still, the sport has produced its share of genuine comic talents, among them Rowdy Roddy Piper ("Ole Anderson is strong as an ox . . . and almost as smart") and announcer Bobby Heenan, who once said of Kerry Von Erich, "He's the only man I know who can hide his own Easter eggs."

Wrestling's current clown prince is Chris Jericho, a fact that would shock anyone who had only followed his career up until 1998. He was always a talented, good-looking wrestler with a chiseled physique and the requisite curly blond mane, but after debuting in wcw to much pomp and circumstance he couldn't get arrested. For tv viewers, only Jeff Jarrett signaled "bathroom break" more than the man they call "Lionheart."

All that changed when perennial good guy Jericho began throwing temper tantrums following losses to lesser opponents. What began as a typical heel turn developed into a showcase for Jericho as a comedic loose cannon who alternated between egomania and paranoia. He still doesn't generate cheers when he strides to the ring, but the boos have stopped and his interviews and backstage antics have become a highlight of wcw broadcasts.

Jericho was born Chris Irvine, the son of National Hockey League player Ted Irvine. He grew up in Winnipeg, Manitoba, Canada, watching AWA wrestling shows and those presented by Stu Hart's Stampede circuit. Irvine was a standout athlete in high school, excelling at hockey and water polo, but after he graduated from college with a degree in journalism he set his sights on a wrestling career. In Canada, that road always led through the Hart Brothers Pro Wrestling Camp, a.k.a. the Dungeon. From June to September of 1990, he trained there with Chris Benoit, the late Brian Pillman, and Stu's son Bruce Hart. On October 2, Jericho made his professional debut.

As Chris Jericho, he worked Canadian independent shows during 1991, often teaming with Lance Storm. He won the Canadian Middleweight belt in January of 1992 and then became one of wrestling's most well-traveled journeymen; he joined Bay Area Wrestling in San Francisco in August 1992; in November, he began working in Monterrey, Mexico, as Corazon de Leon (Spanish for "Lionheart"). In January 1993, he returned to Canada and won the Canadian Heavyweight title over Biff Wellington. Three months later, Jericho debuted for EMLL in Mexico City, and in July he won the WWA Tag-Team title alongside the *luchadore* El Dandy.

In September he began a two-month stint in Hamburg, Germany, for CWA then returned to Mexico to claim the NWA Middleweight title from Mano

Negra. Still stockpiling the frequent-flyer miles, he debuted for WAR in Japan on February 24, 1994, then wrestled for Smoky Mountain Wrestling in Tennessee from March 1994 to March 1995. There, he reteamed with Canadian cohort Lance Storm to form the Thrillseekers tag team.

And so it went for Chris Jericho; though he never lacked for work, most of his early career highlights happened outside the United States. He won the WAR International Junior Heavyweight belt in 1994, and the following year he successfully defended the title against The Ultimo Dragon. He also made an impressive showing at the prestigious Super J Cup tournament that year, losing to Wild Pegasus (Chris Benoit) in the second round. But when he debuted in Philadelphia's fledgling ECW circuit, he was considered a newcomer.

In 1996, Jericho divided his schedule between Philadelphia and the Far East, competing for titles wherever he went. In between, in June, he wrestled Bam Bam Bigelow and Konnan at the Antonio Inoki World Peace Festival in Los Angeles. He won the ECW Television title over Pitbull #2, and made his WCW debut in August. Less than one month later, he was wrestling Chris Benoit on pay-per-view, and in January he was presented with the Newcomer of the Year award from the readers of WCW *Magazine*.

Jericho was primed to step up to the next level. His success in Japan was a testament to his mat skills, speed, and athleticism, and he was pitted against heels such as Syxx and The Ultimo Dragon to further put him over with the fans. The result was lukewarm good-guy applause. His frequent victories and defeats in Cruiserweight title matches had little effect on that response. The reasons are debatable, but the most obvious may be that with the arrival of the NWO and the influx of several former WWF stars, Jericho may simply have been lost in the shuffle.

What got him noticed was a hissy fit he threw after an unexpected loss. He cursed, pounded his fists, threw chairs, and stormed off the *Nitro* set. The following week, he apologized for his behavior, promising that it would "never, ever" happen again. But after another loss he snapped again. Turning into a petulant brat doesn't sound like a recipe for success, except that Jericho's indignation was really funny.

The year 1998 saw Jericho's breakthrough. In January, he pinned Rey Misterio Jr. to regain the Cruiserweight belt, and then he beat Juventud Guerrera in a title-vs.-mask match at the February Superbrawl. Jericho took to wearing Guerrera's mask around his waist, solidifying his heel turn. In March, he defeated Dean Malenko at Uncensored, and suddenly the impressive moves he had always displayed were being noticed and appreciated.

After Malenko beat Jericho for the belt in May, the new Jericho persona came into focus. Jericho railed at Malenko, Malenko's deceased father, WCW, and anyone who would listen. During a film clip shot in Washington, DC, he stood outside the White House holding a sign that read "conspiracy victim." He rechristened *Monday Nitro* "Monday Night Jericho" and dubbed his rabid (mostly imaginary) followers "Jerichoholics."

Jericho won the Cruiserweight belt for an unprecedented fifth time in July, lost it within weeks, and two days later won the Television title from Stevie Ray. By this time, however, fans were looking forward to his backstage antics as much as his athleticism in the ring.

His best routine to date was played out that September; wcw had taken to filming Goldberg from the moment he left his dressing room until he arrived in the ring, and Jericho did an uproarious send-up of the practice. With feigned self-importance he emerged from his own dressing room flanked by men wearing cardboard signs around their necks that read "security." Instead of walking towards the ring, however, Jericho kept making dramatic entrances through the wrong doors. While his opponent waited in the ring, Jericho pushed open a door with a grandiose flourish and found himself locked out of the arena.

NAME:
Road Warrior Hawk, Road Warrior Animal

ALSO KNOWN AS:
The Road Warriors, LOD 2000

PROFESSIONAL DEBUT:
1983

FINISHING MOVE:
the doomsday device

NWA National Tag-Team title
Won: June 11, 1983 (tournament win)
Lost: November 27, 1983, to Brett and Buzz Sawyer
Regained: November 30, 1983, over Brett and Buzz Sawyer
Lost: December 27, 1983, to Brett and Buzz Sawyer
Regained: January 28, 1984 (awarded titles when Buzz Sawyer leaves NWA)
Lost: May 6, 1984, to Masked Superstar and King Kong Bundy

AWA World Tag-Team title
Won: August 25, 1984, over Crusher Lisowski and Baron Von Raschke
Lost: September 29, 1985, to Jim Garvin and Steve Regal

NWA World Six-Man Tag title (with Dusty Rhodes)
Won: May 17, 1986, over Ivan Koloff, Nikita Koloff, and Baron Von Raschke
Lost: February 12, 1988, to Ivan Koloff and The Powers of Pain (Warlord and Barbarian)
Regained: July 9, 1988, over Ric Flair, Arn Anderson, and Tully Blanchard (tournament win)
Title abandoned in 1989

All-Japan Unified Tag title
Won: March 1987, over Jumbo Tsuruta and Genichiro Tenryu
Lost: June 10, 1988, to Jumbo Tsuruta and Yoshiaki Yatsu

NWA World Tag title
Won: October 29, 1988, over The Midnight Express (Bobby Eaton and Stan Lane)
Lost: April 2, 1989, to The Varsity Club (Mike Rotunda and Steve Williams)

WWF Tag-Team title
Won: August 26, 1991, over The Nasty Boys (Brian Knobbs and Jerry Saggs)
Lost: February 7, 1992, to Money, Inc. (Ted DiBiase and Irwin R. Schyster)
Regained: October 7, 1997, over Henry and Phineas Godwinn
Lost: November 24, 1997, to The New Age Outlaws (Jesse James and Billy Gunn)

HAWK

REAL NAME:
Mike Hegstrand

ALSO KNOWN AS:
Crusher Von Haig

BORN:
September 12, 1957, Chicago, Illinois

HEIGHT:
6' 3"

WEIGHT:
277 pounds

PROFESSIONAL DEBUT:
June 1983

PROFESSIONAL AFFILIATION:
The Hell Raisers

OTHER TITLES HELD

IWGP **Tag-Team title (with Power Warrior, as The Hell Raisers)**
Won: January 4, 1994, over The Jurassic Powers (Scott Norton and Hercules Hernandez)

Lost: November 25, 1994, to Hiroshi Hase and Keiji Muto (The Great Muta)
Regained: December 14, 1992, over Scott Norton and Tony Halme
Lost: August 5, 1993, to The Jurassic Powers

Road Warrior Hawk

(Photo Credit: Marko Shark)

REAL NAME:
Joe Laurintas

ALSO KNOWN AS:
Joe Lauren

BORN:
January 26, 1960, Chicago, Illinois

HEIGHT:
6' 1"

WEIGHT:
285 pounds

PROFESSIONAL DEBUT:
November, 1982

Other titles held:
none

On the very short list of indisputable truths in wrestling, The Legion of Doom must be acknowledged as the most successful tag team of all time. While they never exhibited the quickness of The Rockers, the technical proficiency of The British Bulldogs, or the flawless teamwork of Arn and Ole Anderson, The LOD has outlasted all the best teams of the last 15 years and still competes for the titles while its former competition languishes in retirement or obscurity.

Hawk and Animal have survived all these years on sheer toughness, which has often crossed the line into brutality. But, unlike the brawling teams of past generations such as The Crusher and Dick the Bruiser, The LOD combined their take-no-prisoners style with a strong foundation in mat wrestling and a team chemistry that only comes with years of experience. Of all their accomplishments, the most impressive and the most significant are their unprecedented title reigns in each of the top three promotions (AWA, NWA/WCW, and WWF).

Both Hawk (Mike Hegstrand) and Animal (Joe Laurintas) grew up in Chicago. As teenagers, they shared an interest in bodybuilding and wrestling. "We were in the gym every day pushing weights while the others were out shooting pool," said Animal. "We knew what we wanted and worked for it."

They received their early wrestling training from former pro Eddie Sharkey, but they began their careers in singles competition. In 1982, Hawk debuted in Canada as Crusher Von Haig and achieved some notoriety in Germany for his ring garb, which resembled a punk Nazi uniform.

The same year, Animal appeared on small Southern circuits, billed first as Joe Lauren and later as The Road Warrior. At this stage, however, he looked more like a Hell's Angel than a refugee from a *Mad Max* movie — this "warrior" dressed in denim cutoffs, a leather jacket with matching cap, and motorcycle boots with which he would stomp opponents into submission.

When Hawk returned from Germany, he sought out his friend from the Windy City, and the two were reunited on the Georgia Championship Wrestling circuit. "Precious" Paul Ellering, a manager with a stable billed as The Legion of Doom, teamed Hawk and Animal in June of 1983. They were introduced as The Road Warriors, and their gimmick was to charge the ring at full speed to the strains of Black Sabbath's "Iron Man" and jump their opponents before the bell could sound.

Wearing spiked red shoulder pads and sporting buzzcuts and face paint, Hawk and Animal were unlike anything the tag-team world had ever experienced. They demolished the Georgia competition, usually in matches that lasted less than five minutes. Three weeks after their debut, they won the tag belts but were nearly banned from the circuit for their ring tactics.

Seeking greater glory and a national spotlight, Ellering and The Warriors joined the AWA in 1984, and once again they dominated the division like no other team in history. The Crusher and Baron Von Raschke held the titles at that point, but both were past their prime and no match for Hawk and Animal, who defeated the two veterans that summer in a woefully one-sided contest.

Of all The Warriors' title reigns, their AWA supremacy ranks as the most impressive, given the quality of the competition. Their reputation was such that the federation could not sell a storyline in which they lost. They not only sent all the AWA teams into defeat, but they also vanquished imported NWA teams such as The Fabulous Freebirds and The Von Erichs. When the supply ran out, new teams were created out of singles wrestlers, all of whom suffered the same fate. Among the most infamous of The Road Warriors' AWA matches was a battle with Curt Hennig and his father, Larry "The Axe" Hennig. At one point, Curt became tangled in the ropes, and Hawk clobbered him with three lethal chair shots, drawing torrents of blood.

Their title reign ended in its second year, after a screwjob loss to "Gorgeous" Jimmy Garvin and Steve Regal that conveniently coincided with The Warriors' desire to return to the NWA. There, they renewed the closest thing they had to a competitive rivalry — with Ivan and Nikita Koloff.

Late in 1985, Hawk and Animal joined forces with Dusty Rhodes for a series of three-on-three matches against Ric Flair and Arn and Ole Anderson. In April of 1986, they won the World Six Man title from the Koloffs and their old enemy Baron Von Raschke. They also picked up the Jim Crockett Senior Memorial Cup in New Orleans for beating Magnum TA and Ron Garvin. The title supposedly came with one million dollars in prize money.

Jim Cornette's Midnight Express (Dennis Condrey and Bobby Eaton) defeated The Rock and Roll Express for the NWA tag titles, but a match against The Warriors was not forthcoming. The storyline had Cornette ducking The Warriors, which gave Hawk and Animal the opportunity to work singles matches.

Out of their earlier defeat of Flair and the Andersons grew an epic feud between The Road Warriors and The Four Horsemen. Though they are not remembered now for their win-loss record as singles, both Hawk and Animal turned in respectable efforts against Ric Flair. Various combinations among the respective teams wrestled throughout 1986 and 1987; often they were subjected to interference from those left on the sidelines. The Warriors held their own in what frequently became four-on-two confrontations, but for the first time in their career they were sometimes left face down in the ring.

Hawk and Animal finally got their shot at Cornette's Midnight Express at Starrcade 1986. Having already fought in cage and double-chain matches, The Warriors were ready to push the envelope again: they did so at Starrcade with an anything-goes scaffold match. The two teams, perched on a narrow metal scaffold 25 feet above the ring, fought until someone fell. Midnight Express members lost the contest, actually falling after hanging beneath the scaffold (not as impressive!), and the match remains one of the most unique of the 1980s.

During their second NWA title reign, The Warriors continued to battle The Four Horseman, then composed of Ric Flair, Arn and Ole Anderson, and Tully Blanchard. Dusty Rhodes remained their ally, and they would later receive help from old foe Nikita Koloff, whose wrestling style and ferocity prompted some fans to call him "The Russian Road Warrior."

The feud continued after Lex Luger replaced Ole Anderson in The Horsemen during the spring of 1987, and culminated in the first-ever NWA WarGames. Inside two rings covered by a steel cage, The Horsemen and their manager, J. J. Dillon, met Hawk, Animal, Dusty Rhodes, Nikita Koloff, and Paul Ellering. By the time the dust had settled, Dillon had suffered a separated shoulder, Koloff had sustained a career-threatening neck injury, and The Warriors had gotten the pin.

After a successful tour of Japan that made them international sensations, The Road Warriors fought The Horsemen for the rest of 1987, until fans finally began to grow tired of the conflict. Just in time, a new team appeared on the horizon to challenge The Warriors' supremacy. Managed by Ivan Koloff and Paul Jones, The Powers of Pain (Warlord and The Barbarian) first met The Warriors not in a wrestling match but at a weightlifting contest. As Animal attempted to bench-press 600 pounds, Ivan Koloff threw powder in his eyes and The Powers drove his face into the barbell, causing injury to his orbital socket.

After this incident, which almost cost Animal his sight in one eye, the two teams fought anywhere and everywhere — Chicago streetfights, barbed-wire matches, and six-man battles with Dusty Rhodes and Ivan Koloff. No longer the indestructible force they once were, The Warriors lost as often as they won, and no clear victor came out of the feud. The Powers of Pain left the NWA in June of 1988 with the issue still unsettled.

In an attempt to recoup some of their lost heat, The Road Warriors turned heel by attacking their partner, Sting, during a six-man match in October of 1988. The plan worked: less than a month later, The Warriors defeated The Midnight Express to regain the NWA tag belts.

The heel turn prompted a series of matches against former ally Dusty Rhodes, who was unable to best The Warriors even with Sting by his side. Hawk and Animal lost the belts to Mike Rotunda and Steve "Dr. Death" Williams on April 2, 1989, after an uneventful six-month feud. The decision was controversial, as was the rematch at WrestleWar 1989, which was marred by interference from Kevin Sullivan and Danny Spivey. Though The Warriors lost, Rotunda and Williams were stripped of the titles, and a tournament was established to fill the vacancy. Surprisingly, The Road Warriors were eliminated in the first round by Michael Hayes and Terry Gordy, the original Freebirds.

Hawk and Animal ended the 1980s by feuding with The Samoan Swat Team (Haku and Fatu) and The Skyscrapers (Dan Spivey and "Sycho" Sid Vicious). When Sid suffered a punctured lung in November of 1989, he was replaced by "Mean" Mark Callous before his rebirth as The Undertaker.

The now-forgotten team of Butch Reed and Ron Simmons, billed as Doom, tried to get a push by challenging The Warriors to a series of matches. That the NWA would have Hawk and Animal job to these masked midcarders was a sign that it was time to move on. The Warriors fought their last NWA match in June of 1990, defeating Arn Anderson and Barry Windham by DQ.

With the exception of Sting, The Road Warriors were the athletes that fans most hoped would make the jump to the red-hot WWF, then indisputably wrestling's senior circuit. They got their wish in 1990, when The Warriors debuted as The Legion of Doom, minus Paul Ellering. The name change was made to avoid confusion with The Ultimate Warrior. Though they'd sometimes lose by count-out or disqualification, The LOD was not pinned in a WWF match for almost two years.

Hawk and Animal seemed revitalized in their new surroundings as they battled The Hart Foundation, The Nasty Boys, and The Orient Express (Kato and Pat Tanaka). But the match that drew the most heat pitted The LOD against Demolition (Ax and Smash), who were labeled Warrior-wannabes when they were introduced by the WWF in 1987. Their names, ring style, face paint, and metallic outfits were obvious rip-offs, but they eventually caught on anyway and became three-time champions between 1988 and 1990.

Inexplicably, however, what could have been a classic feud fizzled out over the course of a handful of mundane matches, easily won by The LOD. Demolition tried adding a third member, Crush, and The LOD responded by teaming with The Ultimate Warrior and emerging victorious in the six-man matchup. With members of Demolition finally dismissed as the clones they were, The LOD moved on to beat The Nasty Boys for the WWF tag titles at

THE LEGION OF DOOM

SummerSlam 1991. It was a no-disqualification match, at that time a rarity in the WWF. Rematches with The Nasty Boys, notorious rulebreakers, forced The LOD to revert to the bruising style of their early NWA days.

Their next challenge came from two tons of fun called Earthquake and Typhoon — The Natural Disasters. The LOD met this pair of 400-pounders and lost by count-out, which allowed the team to keep the titles. But in February of 1992, despite the return of Paul Ellering, Hawk and Animal lost to the unheralded team of Money, Inc., composed of Ted DiBiase and Irwin R. Schyster. The loss compelled the team to go back to its Chicago roots. Hawk and Animal returned to battle The Beverly Brothers, who tried to make a name for themselves by taunting the LOD, calling them "The Legion of Sissies." At SummerSlam 1992, The LOD won a nontitle rematch with Money, Inc. It would be their last match in the WWF until 1997.

Ten years of body slams had taken their toll on Animal's back, and he announced his retirement. Hawk teamed with Kensuki Sasaki in Japan to form The Hell Raisers, and they won the IWGP tag belts over Scott Norton and Tony Halme. Later, he wrestled briefly for ECW and then rejoined WCW as Dustin Rhodes's mystery partner in a tag match against The Equalizer and Rick Rude.

At a 1995 singles match in Japan, The Road Warriors finally reemerged. There, Hawk defeated Scott Norton with some illegal help from Animal. Their first match as tag-team partners came in January of 1996. Reverting to their Road Warrior monikers, the team took on all comers in WCW, including Public Enemy, The Steiner Brothers, and Harlem Heat.

The Warriors left WCW in May of 1996, supposedly after a falling out with WCW boss Eric Bischoff over the rich contracts offered to Scott Hall and Kevin Nash. They worked briefly in the AWA before returning to the WWF in February of 1997. Though Hawk and Animal had a promising early run at the tag titles, then held by Owen Hart and Davey Boy Smith, recent times have not been the best for The Legion of Doom; the duo has been used primarily to help novice teams get over with the fans. Feuds with The Godwinns and The Nation of Domination have elicited only an apathetic fan response, and when The LOD did win the belts in October of 1997, it was not the "event" win it should have been.

They lost the title one month later to The New Age Outlaws (Road Dog Jesse James and Billy Gunn), but in doing so Hawk and Animal finally found a rewarding storyline. Rematches, during which The Outlaws ridiculed The LOD for being past their prime (they rechristened the team "The OLD"), set up a veteran-vs.-upstart-newcomer scenario that clicked with fans. Hawk's familiar "Oooh — what a rushhhh!" call had magic again, and when Animal revived his favorite quote — "We dine on danger and snack on death!" — it sounded once again like he truly meant it.

Though the crowd was behind them at this point, the scriptwriters were not; The LOD was losing most of its battles, usually as a result of inter-ference from allies of The Outlaws in Degeneration X. After one particularly humiliating defeat in February of 1998, Hawk and Animal turned against each other. They disappeared for awhile, and it seemed a Warrior vs. Warrior match was imminent.

Instead, The Legion of Doom made a surprise return at 1998's WrestleMania billed as "LOD 2000" and accompanied by glamour-girl Sunny. They won a 15-team battle royal and received a huge pop from the sold-out arena crowd. But Sunny was gone a few months later, and all the heat generated by their "twisted steel with sex appeal" makeover quickly dissipated.

Paul Ellering returned, but he was no Sunny, and, even after he betrayed The LOD by joining forces with the tag team Disciples of Apocalypse, fans didn't care — probably because most of them weren't old enough to remember who Ellering was!

As 1998 drew to a close, The LOD found itself in a scenario inspired by the film *All about Eve*. After a moody, distraught Hawk began showing up drunk or on drugs for live television appearances, his place on the team was taken by Darren Drozdov, a former football player. On a November *Raw* broadcast, Hawk climbed to the top of the Titantron screen at the entrance to the arena and threatened to jump. Drozdov, in attempting a rescue, appeared to push him off.

The suicide angle was forgotten after Hawk returned claiming Drozdov had pushed drugs on him in an effort to trigger animosity between Hawk and Animal. Now clean and sober, Hawk has reclaimed his place in The LOD, and the reformed, original Legion of Doom will no doubt make yet another run at tag-team gold.

REAL NAME:
Lawrence Pfohl

ALSO KNOWN AS:
The Total Package, The Narcissist

BORN:
June 2, 1958, Chicago, Illinois

HEIGHT:
6' 4"

WEIGHT:
265 pounds

PROFESSIONAL DEBUT:
October 31, 1985

PROFESSIONAL AFFILIATIONS: The Four Horsemen, The Allied Powers,
The Dungeon of Doom, NWO Wolfpack, New World Order

FINISHING MOVE:
the torture rack, the flying forearm

TITLES HELD

NWA **Southern Heavyweight title**
Won: November 19, 1985, over Wahoo McDaniel
Lost: January 15, 1986, to Jesse Barr
Regained: February 14, 1986, over Jesse Barr
Lost: July 22, 1986, to The Masked Superstar
Regained: July 29, 1986, over The Masked Superstar
Lost: January 16, 1987, to Kevin Sullivan

NWA **United States Heavyweight title**
Won: July 11, 1987, over Nikita Koloff
Lost: November 26, 1987, to Dusty Rhodes
Regained: February 20, 1989, over Barry Windham
Lost: May 7, 1989, to Michael P.S. Hayes
Regained: May 22, 1989, from Michael P.S. Hayes
Lost: October 27, 1990, to Stan Hansen
Regained: December 16, 1990, from Stan Hansen
Title vacated July 14, 1991, after Luger wins the World Heavyweight title

NWA **World Tag-Team title**
(with Barry Windham)
Won: March 27, 1988, over Arn Anderson and Tully Blanchard
Lost: April 20, 1988, to Arn Anderson and Tully Blanchard

(with Sting)
Won: January 22, 1996, over Harlem Heat (Booker T and Stevie Ray)
Lost: June 24, 1996, to Harlem Heat and The Steiner Brothers (triangle match)

(with The Giant)
Won: February 23, 1997, over The Outsiders (Scott Hall and Kevin Nash)
Decision reversed on February 24, 1997

WCW **World Heavyweight title**
Won: July 14, 1991, over Barry Windham
Lost: February 29, 1992, to Sting
Regained: August 4, 1997, from Hulk Hogan
Lost: August 9, 1997, to Hulk Hogan

WCW World Television title
Won: February 17, 1996, over Johnny B. Badd
Lost: February 18, 1996, to Johnny B. Badd

Regained: March 6, 1996, over Johnny B. Badd
Lost: August 20, 1996, to Steve Regal

The popular line of thought on Lex Luger's wrestling persona is "million-dollar body, ten-cent brain." The Total Package, as he's often called, has always had the looks, the physique, and the athletic ability to hold any title, but in big matches he falls victim to every screwjob ending in the book of wrestling clichés — from being distracted by a manager outside the ring to turning his back at the wrong moment and getting clocked by a foreign object.

Of course, Luger really loses under orders from the booker, just like any other wrestler. So the real culprit is not stupidity but circumstance and simple bad timing. Whenever Luger is in the midst of a push, something or someone always comes along to force him out of the spotlight, whether it be Sting, or Hulk Hogan, or the NWO. And whenever he is actually allowed to win a belt, he usually holds it for less time than most people keep library books.

It was not always this way: in fact, Lex Luger burst onto the scene by pinning Ed Gantner on October 31, 1985. It was Luger's professional debut. Less than three weeks later, he defeated veteran Wahoo McDaniel to win the NWA Southern Heavyweight title. Luger had won Georgia's top belt before anyone even had a chance to ask, "Who is this guy?"

Born Lawrence Pfohl, in Chicago, Luger went on to become a scholarship football player at Penn State and the University of Miami. In 1978, he became the youngest offensive lineman in the history of the Canadian Football League. After one season with the Montreal Concord, Pfohl tried his luck in the NFL, but he could do no better than secure a spot on the Green Bay Packers reserve team.

So Larry Pfohl, turning to wrestling, became Lex Luger. He learned the basics from trainer Hiro Matsuda and debuted with NWA Florida before graduating to NWA Georgia and claiming his first title victory. Luger switched the Southern Heavyweight belt with Jesse Barr in 1986 and lost it again to The Masked Superstar before defeating Taskmaster Kevin Sullivan, who had won the belt in the interim.

When Jim Crockett bought out NWA Georgia in 1987, Luger and Sullivan became a part of WCW. Once again, Luger was placed on a fast track to main-event status. In less than three months, he had taken Ole Anderson's place in The Four Horsemen and defeated Nikita Koloff for the United States Heavyweight title. But, the storyline went, he still wasn't happy; Luger argued constantly with Horsemen manager James J. Dillon over his failure to be granted a World title shot. He finally got one, against Dusty Rhodes, in November of 1987, but he lost when Rhodes hit him with a chair that Dillon had hurled into the ring.

The bad blood between Luger and Dillon escalated until Luger eliminated Dillon from a battle royal during a January 1988 pay-per-view. He was fired from The Horsemen and immediately became a babyface. Luger formed a tag team with Ole Anderson, the man he had replaced in The Horsemen, to square off against founding Horsemen Ric Flair and Arn Anderson. At a March 1988 Clash of the Champions event, Luger and Barry Windham defeated Arn Anderson and Tully Blanchard for the NWA World Tag-Team titles. They lost the titles when Windham betrayed Luger to join The Horsemen.

At the 1988 Great American Bash, Luger wrestled his first pay-per-view main event, a singles match against Ric Flair for the World Heavyweight title.

(Photo Credit: Marko Shark)

Luger performed all his signature moves, including the devastating clotheslines and forearm shots that comprised the major part of his offense. He had Flair helpless in his torture-rack finisher (a submission hold that stretches the back), but the match was stopped by the Maryland State Athletic Commission because Luger was bleeding. The two met again six months later at Starrcade, where Flair won a 30-minute slugfest to hold onto his title.

Perhaps as a consolation prize, Luger beat Windham for the U.S. belt. Again, he started to campaign for a World title shot, and he did not disguise his frustration when Ricky Steamboat wrestled Flair for the belt at the next two pay-per-views. The fans sided with Steamboat, and Luger found himself a heel again. At the 1989 Great American Bash, Steamboat bashed Luger's swollen head with a chair, giving The Total Package the DQ win.

A feud with newcomer Brian Pillman had Luger treading water until he was given another shot at Flair's World title. He replaced an injured Sting at the main event of WrestleWar in February of 1990. Sting sat at ringside during the match. Luger was in command until, as the contest neared the 40-minute mark, The Horsemen emerged from backstage to attack Sting. Luger left the ring to make the save and lost the match by count-out. This made Luger one of the good guys again — by now fans needed scorecards to determine whether they should applaud or boo when he was announced.

The face turn put a stop to Luger's whining about the World title for awhile, and he happily defended his U.S. belt against all comers, including Sid Vicious, "Mean" Mark Callous, and Stan Hansen, with whom Luger switched the title near the end of 1990. Luger's rescue of Sting was not forgotten by the bookers, who teamed the two wrestlers in a series of tag matches. They didn't win the tag belts until 1996, but their styles obviously complimented each other, and the duo probably would have earned the title sooner had Luger not left to join the WWF.

Prior to his departure, however, Luger finally got the green light to realize his dream: a shot at the coveted Heavyweight title. When Ric Flair jumped to the WWF, his NWA and WCW titles were declared vacant. In a cage match between the top two contenders at the 1991 Great American Bash, Luger subjected Barry Windham to a piledriver and followed up with a pin to score the victory. Among Luger's first acts as WCW champ was to hire Harley Race as his manager, signaling yet another heel turn. He defended the belt against Rick Steiner and Ron Simmons but lost a title match to Sting in February of 1992 at Superbrawl. By then, he had informed the Turner organization of his intention to join the WWF, and he was effectively written out of the federation weeks before his actual departure.

Vince McMahon chose to debut Luger not as a wrestler but as the standard-bearer for his new World Bodybuilding Federation (WBF). The WBF never caught on with fans, and it lost its biggest name when Luger suffered a broken arm in a motorcycle accident. The federation folded, and when his arm had healed Luger debuted in the WWF at the 1993 Royal Rumble.

Billed as "The Narcissist," Luger played a vain prettyboy, a character very similar to one Shawn Michaels was already playing. He would bring a mirror to the ring during his entrance and pose in front of it before attacking his opponent. Luger and Michaels clearly had a ready-made gimmick to launch a feud, and it might have produced some spectacular matches, but since both wrestlers were heels at the time such a contest never materialized. Accompanied to the ring by a fawning Bobby Heenan, Luger spent his first few months in the WWF pitted against Curt Hennig and Tatanka. His flying-forearm finishing move was said to be especially lethal due to the steel plate that had been inserted in his arm during surgery.

Yokozuna, the 600-pound sumo wrestler, won the Rumble that year, but he was in a bad mood after losing the WWF World Heavyweight title to Hulk Hogan at WrestleMania IX. With his Japanese-flag-waving manager, Mr. Fuji, Yokozuna accused all American wrestlers of being wimps and challenged any one of them — or any American athlete from any sport — to body-slam him. To further embarrass the United States, the contest was held, on July 4, 1993, in New York City, on the deck of the aircraft carrier USS Intrepid.

A dozen athletes tried and failed to lift the huge Yokozuna, who exulted in his superiority to Americans on their day of independence. When all seemed lost, a helicopter appeared in the sky above and landed near the Intrepid. Lex Luger emerged to a huge cheer from the assembled fans, even though he was still supposed to be a heel. After a brief staredown, Luger hoisted the sumo star and slammed him onto the carrier deck. Sure, Yokozuna had worked with Luger to sell the move, but it was still undeniably impressive. And don't let any historical revisionists tell you it was a hip toss: the tape clearly shows Luger lifting, turning, and dropping Yokozuna. For Luger, it was a career highlight that may never be surpassed.

After his Fourth of July heroics, Luger was repackaged as "Made in the USA" Lex Luger and sent on a coast-to-coast bus trip (the Lex Express) to meet fans across America. At SummerSlam, Luger body-slammed Yokozuna again, winning the match by count-out. Luger should have won the title that night; he'd signed a contract granting him the opportunity to claim the Heavyweight belt. When he won by count-out, balloons the colors of the American flag were released from the ceiling in celebration. But, since a title cannot change on the basis of a count-out, Luger went home empty-handed.

Luger now wore red, white, and blue trunks and made his entrances to patriotic, military music. He had stepped into the American-hero role previously occupied by the recently departed Hulk Hogan, and he now found himself as over with the fans as anyone in the federation. He began 1994 by cowinning the Royal Rumble with Bret Hart after both men fell to the floor at the same time. But it was Hart who went on to beat Yokozuna for the title at WrestleMania X; Luger had fought Yokozuna earlier on the same card but lost by DQ courtesy of special referee Curt Hennig. Rumor had it that Luger was supposed to win, but he had bragged about his upcoming victory to some bar patrons a week before the match and word had gotten back to WWF officials, who promptly changed the storyline. If this is true, then that "ten-cent brain" line isn't entirely undeserved.

Hennig's departure scuttled a promising feud, and with Bret Hart now installed as a popular champion, Luger was reduced to wrestling Tatanka again. Though Tatanka was a heel at this point, there were uncomfortable historical overtones to a symbol of American strength beating up an Indian. Luger, now thoroughly out of the World-title contest, was shuttled into another political storyline: he was teamed with The British Bulldog to form The Allied Powers. The Powers opened WrestleMania XI (a sign of their dwindling status), by pinning Eli and Jacob Blu.

At a July 1995 In Your House pay-per-view, The Powers lost to Owen Hart and Yokozuna when Luger was pinned by Yokozuna after 10 uneventful minutes. Less than two months later, Luger shocked the wrestling world by appearing on the debut broadcast of WCW's *Monday Nitro*. There he launched a verbal assault on the WWF and fell back into his old habit of demanding an immediate title shot against WCW champ Hulk Hogan. One week later, Luger's title match with Hogan was interrupted by The Dungeon of Doom.

Fans still weren't sure which Lex Luger they were seeing, but after he hired Jimmy Hart as his manager and argued with the popular Randy Savage, they consigned him back to the heel camp. Sting, however, remained loyal to his former tag partner, which caused friction throughout WCW. Luger was now finding himself in higher-profile matches again; he forced Savage to submit at the 1995 World War III and teamed with Sting to wrestle The Road Warriors to a no contest at Superbrawl VI.

Sting tried to convince the rest of WCW that Luger was on the level, but it was only after the NWO storyline got underway that Luger's loyalty was proven. He joined Sting and Randy Savage to take on The NWO Outsiders (Scott Hall and Kevin Nash) and their mystery partner at the 1996 Bash at the Beach. The mystery partner turned out to be Hulk Hogan, and the chaos that resulted prevented the match from being decided.

Ironically, once Luger's status in WCW was established and he started hearing cheers again, Sting's loyalty was called into question because he attacked Luger prior to the Fall Brawl pay-per-view. The attack was later revealed to be a NWO ruse performed by a Sting look-alike, but Sting felt betrayed by the contention and walked away from Luger, Ric Flair, and Arn Anderson at the annual WarGames match.

While Sting brooded, Luger became one of WCW's most potent weapons against NWO, though most of his matches ended in outside interference that forced a DQ. In 1997, he teamed with The Giant, who had left NWO, to beat The Outsiders for the tag titles. Eric Bischoff, WCW/NWO boss, reversed the decision the following night. At Bash at the Beach, Luger and The Giant faced Hulk Hogan and Chicago Bulls star Dennis Rodman. Luger "racked" Hogan — forced him to submit to his torture-rack hold — and made himself the number-one contender for Hogan's World title.

Just one month later, Luger scored a surprise pin on Hogan in the main event of an otherwise standard *Monday Nitro* telecast. Every WCW wrestler in attendance charged the ring to congratulate the new champion, and the show ended with a locker-room celebration complete with flowing champagne. This being Luger, however, the new champ was forced to give the belt right back — at the Road Wild pay-per-view one week later.

Still a top contender, Luger feuded with Scott Hall during the fall, but his position on the depth chart dropped after the arrival of Rowdy Roddy Piper and the return of Sting to active competition. While Piper and Sting contended for the Heavyweight title, Luger had to settle for a dumb feud with Buff Bagwell to determine who was the real "total package."

In 1998, Luger drifted through skirmishes with Randy Savage and Scott Steiner until his career was revived by an invitation to join the red-hot NWO Wolfpack. Alongside Sting, Kevin Nash, and Konnan, Luger was now a crowd favorite, in line for a title match against Goldberg. Instead, he sold out again, joining Nash, Scott Hall, and Hulk Hogan in a reunion of the original New World Order. Some guys just never learn.

REAL NAME:
Dean Simon

ALSO KNOWN AS:
Dean Solkoff, The Iceman, The Man of 1,000 Holds

BORN:
August 4, 1960, Tampa, Florida

HEIGHT:
5' 9"

WEIGHT:
215 pounds

PROFESSIONAL DEBUT:
1979

PROFESSIONAL AFFILIATION:
The Four Horsemen

FINISHING MOVE:
the texas cloverleaf

TITLES HELD

ECW **Television title**
Won: November 4, 1994, over 2 Cold Scorpio
Lost: March 18, 1995, to 2 Cold Scorpio
Regained: July 21, 1995, over Eddy Guerrero
Lost: July 28, 1995, to Eddy Guerrero

ECW **Tag-Team title**
(with Chris Benoit)
Won: February 25, 1995, over Tasmaniac and Sabu
Lost: April 8, 1995, to Public Enemy and the team of Rick Steiner and Tasmaniac (triangle match)

wcw **Cruiserweight title**
Won: March 20, 1996, over Shinjiro Ohtani
Lost: July 8, 1996, to Rey Misterio Jr.
Regained: October 27, 1996, over Rey Misterio Jr.
Lost: December 29, 1996, to The Ultimo Dragon
Regained: January 21, 1997, over The Ultimo Dragon
Lost: February 23, 1997, to Syxx (Sean Waltman)
Regained: May 17, 1998, over Chris Jericho
Title surrendered over rule discrepancy on June 11, 1998

wcw **Tag-Team title**
(with Chris Benoit)
Won: March 14, 1999, over Barry Windham and Curt Hennig
Lost: March 29, 1999, to Kidman and Rey Misterio, Jr.

Most of the champions of wrestling from the 1940s to the 1960s don't have many positive things to say about the current state of their sport. It's too showbiz, they complain; too silly; too over the top. What a wrestler can do on the microphone is now seen as more important than what he can do in

DEAN MALENKO

the ring. So when Dean Malenko is praised for his wrestling acumen by the legendary Lou Thesz, as he was in a 1998 interview with the Hall of Famer, it means more than any championship belt. But if Malenko's that good, why hasn't he been more successful? Easy — he's not showbiz, he's not silly, and he's never over the top.

Malenko has been dubbed The Iceman because of his frozen facial expression. He looks angry all the time, and though this strategy has worked wonders for Stone Cold Steve Austin, it has not had the same effect on Malenko's career. His mike skills are nonexistent, and because he can't effectively promote his feuds, they don't generate much heat with the fans. Still, when he steps between the ropes, especially to face an opponent with above-average skills, Dean Malenko becomes a one-man wrestling clinic. There isn't a hold he cannot counter or a move he doesn't execute with textbook precision.

Dean Malenko is the youngest son of Professor Boris Malenko, a skilled grappler in his own right. The Professor's Tampa-based wrestling school was the training ground for Dean and his brother, Joe. In the early 1990s, they broke into the professional ranks and made their first big splash in New Japan. Dean was sometimes billed as Dean Solkoff, but then he settled on his father's wrestling name, which, in turn, Boris Malenko had actually chosen over the real family surname — Simon.

The Malenkos entered ECW as a tag team in 1994 and fought a losing match for the tag belts against Sabu and Tasmaniac. After Boris Malenko passed away, Joe returned to Tampa to run the wrestling school and Dean launched his singles career. He won the Television title from 2 Cold Scorpio and wrestled terrific matches against the likes of Shane Douglas and Eddie Guerrero.

In January of 1995, Malenko began teaming with Chris Benoit, and by February they were tag champions. For almost a month, Malenko held two of ECW's three championship belts. Both Benoit and Malenko remained among the federation's most popular and decorated stars until their departure for WCW late in the year. They entered as a tag team but the federation soon split them up, the first of several mistakes it made in handling both wrestlers' careers.

Malenko's somber demeanor branded him as a heel, even though he pinned the equally unpopular Shinjiro Ohtani to win the Cruiserweight title in March of 1996. He beat Brad Armstrong in his first pay-per-view title defense (at the May Slamboree) then confirmed his heel status by stealing Rey Misterio Jr.'s mask and pinning him with his feet elevated on the ropes. Misterio won the rematch in a classic display of aerial maneuvers vs. mat wrestling. Though Malenko will also climb the ropes on rare occasions, his natural style relies more on submission holds that wear down his opponent. It's a technically sound strategy, but not one that makes for an exciting match.

At the Hog Wild pay-per-view in August of 1996, Dean Malenko wrestled his former tag partner, Chris Benoit. The match, which was called a time-limit draw after 30 minutes and then extended, to the delight of the crowd, remains The Iceman's best moment in wcw. Benoit was the victor due to interference from Woman, but Malenko earned the respect of the fans.

For the next eight months, Malenko either reigned as Cruiserweight champ or was considered the number-one contender. He regained the title from Misterio in October then switched it in December and January of 1997 with The Ultimo Dragon before losing to Syxx and becoming another victim of illegal nwo tactics. But Malenko was not without a belt for long; he pinned Eddie Guerrero in March of 1997 for the United States title, only to lose it to Jeff Jarrett in June.

Storylines for Malenko had been underdeveloped ever since his arrival in wcw. For the most part, he wrestled whomever was available, and he would enter into revenge matches every time he or his opponent won through underhanded means. His alliances with Chris Benoit and Jeff Jarrett were shortlived.

But, in 1998, Malenko finally started to wrestle matches with a subtext. Old opponent Eddie Guerrero returned, and this time he was able to get under Malenko's skin, causing The Iceman to "snap" in the ring and struggle with his emotions. Malenko's next feud was with Chris Jericho, his polar opposite in terms of character/persona. Jericho taunted Malenko mercilessly; he wore trunks emblazoned with the figure "1,004," a reference to Malenko's "Man of 1,000 Holds" identity, and made derogatory remarks about Malenko's late father.

After being defeated by Jericho in a Cruiserweight title match, Malenko (now a crowd favorite) appeared emotionally devastated in the ring. The usually mild-mannered announcer Gene Okerlund interviewed Malenko after the match and berated him for losing. Malenko said he was going home, and walked silently out of the arena. His "retirement" lasted about six weeks, during which time Jericho continued his verbal assault on the Malenko family. The Iceman returned in May of 1998 and defeated Jericho for the Cruiserweight title. He soon lost it again, but then he set his sights on something more prestigious than any belt: membership in The Four Horsemen. Malenko was welcomed into the fold shortly after Ric Flair's return from an extended leave. The new Horsemen — Flair, Malenko, Chris Benoit, and Arn Anderson — became wcw's most potent weapon against the rule-breaking nwo Hollywood.

SHAWN MICHAELS

REAL NAME:
Michael Hickenbottom

ALSO KNOWN AS:
The Heartbreak Kid

BORN:
July 22, 1965, San Antonio, Texas

HEIGHT:
6'

WEIGHT:
235 pounds

PROFESSIONAL DEBUT:
October 16, 1984

PROFESSIONAL AFFILIATIONS:
USA Express (The American Force), The Midnight Rockers, Degeneration X

FINISHING MOVE:
standing side kick (sweet chin music)

TITLES HELD

Central States Television title
Won: 1985, over Art Crews
Title vacated when Michaels jumped to the Texas All-Star federation

Texas All-Star Tag-Team title
(with Paul Diamond as American Force)
Won: September 1, 1985 (tournament win)
Lost: September 21, 1985, to The Masked Hoods (Ricky Santana and Tony Torres)

NWA Central States Tag-Team title
(with Marty Jannetty as The Midnight Rockers)
Won: May 15, 1986 (tournament win)
Lost: May 22, 1986, to Brad and Bart Batten

AWA World Tag-Team title
(with Marty Jannetty as The Midnight Rockers)
Won: January 27, 1987, over Buddy Rose and Doug Somers
Lost: May 25, 1987, to Soldat Ustinov and Boris Zhukov
Regained: December 27, 1987, over The Midnight Express (Dennis Condrey and Randy Rose)
Lost: March 19, 1988, to Badd Company (Paul Diamond and Pat Tanaka)

AWA Southern Tag-Team title
(with Marty Jannetty as The Midnight Rockers)
Won: October 26, 1987, over The RPMS (Mike Davis and Tommy Lane)
Lost: November 16, 1987, to The RPMS
Regained: November 16, 1987, over The RPMS
Titles vacated when The Rockers won the AWA World Tag-Team titles on December 27, 1987

WWF Tag-Team title
(with Marty Jannetty as The Midnight Rockers)
Won: October 30, 1990, over The Hart Foundation (Bret Hart and Jim Neidhart)
Decision reversed on November 6, 1990

(with Diesel)
Won: August 28, 1994, over The

Headshrinkers
Titles vacated when team splits in November 1994
Regained: September 24, 1995, over Owen Hart and Yokozuna
Decision reversed on September 25, 1995, due to controversial finish

(with Stone Cold Steve Austin)
Won: September 20, 1997, over Owen Hart and Davey Boy Smith
Titles surrendered in June 1997, when Shawn Michaels is injured

WWF **Intercontinental title**
Won: October 27, 1992, over The British Bulldog
Lost: May 17, 1993, to Marty Jannetty
Regained: June 6, 1993, over Marty Jannetty
Title vacated when Shawn Michaels leaves the WWF, in September 1993

Regained: May 19, 1995, over Jeff Jarrett
Title surrendered to Dean Douglas on October 22, 1995, when Shawn Michaels is unable to defend

WWF **World Heavyweight title**
Won: March 31, 1996, over Bret Hart
Lost: November 17, 1997, to Sycho Sid
Regained: January 19, 1997, over Sycho Sid
Title surrendered on February 13, 1997, after Shawn Michaels is injured
Regained: November 9, 1997, over Bret Hart
Lost: March 29, 1998, to Stone Cold Steve Austin

WWF **European title**
Won: September 20, 1997, over Davey Boy Smith
Lost: December 11, 1997, to Hunter Hearst Helmsley

"The show . . . stopper, the main . . . eventer, The Heart . . . break . . . Kid!" Sounds like a ring introduction, but that tribute to Shawn Michaels was actually composed by . . . Shawn Michaels. He did it during one of his heel turns, which recur every few years like *Brady Bunch* reunions. However, there's really not much difference between a good "Kid" and a bad one; either way, Michaels is cocky, narcissistic, tremendously agile, and athletic, and one of the sport's best sellers. His ability to take a bump could make The Brooklyn Brawler look like championship material.

Born in San Antonio, Michaels grew up a fan of Tully Blanchard, Wahoo McDaniel, Ric Flair, and Bob Backlund. Mexico was just down the road, and he would cross the border to see wrestling shows where he could study the high-flying, breakneck style of the *luchadores*. These lessons were refined by his first trainer, Jose Lothario.

Michaels wrestled in high school but skipped college to turn pro at the age of 19. In the NWA Central States Federation, he won his very first match, pinning Art Crews. In 1985, his first year in the business, he beat Crews again for the Central States Television title then joined the Texas All-Star Federation and formed the tag team USA Express with Paul Diamond. The new team, sometimes called The American Force, was awarded the tag-team belts after tag champion Chavo Guerrero split with his partner, Al Madril. Though The Force reigned for only three weeks, the team joined with Dave Patterson to win the six-man belts shortly thereafter.

Late in the year, Shawn Michaels met another young up-and-coming talent named Marty Jannetty. Their styles were similar, and they began wrestling as a team, billing themselves as The Midnight Rockers. They made a deal that whichever team member was invited to join a major federation first would lobby to bring the other along. Surprisingly, it was Jannetty who got the call, from AWA, and he was as good as his word. The Rockers were an immediate hit and were invited to join the WWF; but they celebrated hard the night before their first scheduled television appearance and were fired for showing up late.

Back in the AWA, The Midnight Rockers defeated the Sherri Martel-managed team of Buddy Rose and Doug Somers for the tag belts. They held the title for five months then left to freelance in several Southern and Midwestern federations. The Rockers faced such legendary teams as the original Rock-n-Roll Express, then returned to the AWA for a second tag title reign.

In 1988, the WWF offered Michaels and Jannetty a second chance, and this time they showed up at the appointed hour. Before departing the AWA, Michaels happily lost the title to his old partner Paul Diamond, who had teamed with Pat Tanaka to form Badd Company.

After appearing in dark matches and house shows, The Midnight Rockers wrestled their first televised match, achieving a quick victory over The Conquistadors. Their brisk teamwork and side-by-side dropkicks, often executed after sliding through their opponents' legs, went over huge with the fans. A feud then erupted with The Brainbusters, a team comprised of Arn Anderson and one of Michaels's wrestling idols, Tully Blanchard. Their matches, including one classic *Saturday Night's Main Event* contest, pitted the speed and athleticism of The Rockers against the strength and rule-breaking tactics of The Brainbusters. Though Anderson and Blanchard soon made their way back to WCW, the unresolved feud had put The Rockers on the map.

At the 1989 Royal Rumble, Michaels lasted 14 minutes against the WWF's best, but there was still no sign of a singles career in his future. At their first WrestleMania, The Rockers lost to The Twin Towers (Akeem and The Big Boss Man) and then embarked upon a feud with The Fabulous Rougeau Brothers. Unofficially, The Rockers had already become the top contender for the tag belts held by The Hart Foundation, but in the WWF of the 1980s it was rare for two crowd favorites to be given the chance to square off. As a result, Michaels and Jannetty were stuck battling loser teams such as The Orient Express (Sato and Tanaka) and Power and Glory (Paul Roma and Hercules).

Michaels injured his knee in the summer of 1990 and was written out of the action via the storyline of Hercules damaging the knee with his trusty steel chain. After Michaels had undergone surgery and The Rockers had wrestled a lackluster revenge match against Hercules and Roma, the team defeated The Hart Foundation in a Fort Wayne, Indiana, house show that was never televised. Jim Neidhart had announced his intention to leave, so Vince McMahon ordered that the belts be lost to The Rockers. After Neidhart changed his mind, McMahon reversed his decision. The official story came from WWF President Jack Tunney, who ruled that the top rope had been loosened during the match, rendering The Rockers' victory invalid.

The team's one-week reign as champs was not acknowledged on television until years later, and a rematch was never scheduled. This incident marks the starting point of the nonmanufactured heat between Shawn Michaels and Bret Hart, which would continue to be fueled by professional jealousy until Hart's screwjob departure from the WWF.

It wasn't until the 1991 Royal Rumble, nearly two years since their WWF debut, that The Rockers finally scored a pay-per-view victory, against the "new" Orient Express (Tanaka and Paul Diamond). Rematches filled their touring schedule, but in the summer Michaels's knee gave out again, and he was sidelined for that year's SummerSlam. Jannetty wrestled The Rockers' matches with substitute partners, including Shane Douglas and Jim Powers.

(Photo Credit: Mitchell Levy/Globe Photos, Inc.)

When Michaels returned, something seemed to be missing from the old Rockers teamwork. Many fans figured it was just ring rust, but gradually a work was revealed that would pit Michaels against Jannetty and lead to the dissolution of The Rockers. The actual breakup, however, took more than six months.

After a series of typical mishaps and misunderstandings during which the team lost to such contenders as The Nasty Boys and The Legion of Doom, the final blow was struck one week before the 1992 Royal Rumble, when the team was interviewed by Brutus Beefcake for his "Barber Shop" segment. What appeared to be an attempt at reconciliation turned violent when Michaels threw Jannetty through the barbershop window. So much for Beefcake's Nobel Peace Prize.

When a popular tag team splits, what inevitably follows is a series of singles matches in which the former partners attempt to settle their dispute in the ring. The WWF tried to follow the pattern, but Jannetty soon disappeared, leaving Michaels free to begin his singles career.

On Valentine's Day, 1992, a new theme song was debuted in the WWF: "Boy Toy," performed by Shawn Michaels. He entered the ring, bumping and grinding like a male stripper, with new manager "Sensational" Sherri Martel at his side. The purple fringed costume of The Rockers was gone; Michaels was now clad in white tights decorated with red hearts — one big heart covered his derriere. Inside the ring, he slowly peeled off his mirrored sunglasses and leather chaps as Martel fawned over him, but it was clear that Michaels, now billed as The Heartbreak Kid (HBK), loved himself even more.

A streak of wins over opponents such as Virgil, Jimmy Snuka, and Tito Santana put Michaels in line for the Intercontinental title, at that point held by his old tag-team nemesis Bret Hart. Along the way, Michaels also fought a few matches against Randy Savage for the Heavyweight title but lost all of them due to Martel's bungled interference.

Clearly, there was gold in Michaels's future, and some sources assert that he was supposed to win the Intercontinental belt at SummerSlam 1992. But after the venue was switched to London's Wembley Stadium, Vince McMahon (with visions of rioting English soccer fans dancing in his head) opted instead to give The British Bulldog a title shot. The Bulldog won before one of the largest crowds in wrestling history. Michaels was relegated to an undercard match against Rick Martel in which the two battled for the affections of Sensational Sherri.

The upside for the WWF was that now Michaels could win the belt without beating Bret Hart; such a win would pave the way for a match between Michaels and Hart later on. But after Michaels pinned The Bulldog, Bret Hart won the Heavyweight title, resulting in a champion-vs.-champion match at the 1992 Survivor Series. After a superb exhibition by both wrestlers that lasted nearly half an hour, Michaels tapped out of The Hit Man's sharpshooter.

The Sherri Martel-Shawn Michaels alliance was dropped in 1993, though an attempt was made to generate heat by having Martel support Jannetty in his title shot against The Heartbreak Kid. Jannetty lost, and Martel joined forces with Michaels's next foe, Tatanka. At Wrestlemania IX, Tatanka lost to Michaels, who was accompanied to the ring by Luna Vachon.

A Michaels-Jannetty title switch in the summer of 1993 failed to revive Jannetty's struggling career; though one Michaels-Jannetty match, from the *Raw* broadcast of July 19, 1993, won Match of the Year honors from *Pro Wrestling Illustrated*. Jannetty remained with the WWF for another two years and had a very brief reign as tag-team champion with The 1–2–3 Kid in 1994. He later jumped to WCW, but he never again found the level of success that he had enjoyed as a member of the Rockers.

Apparently, the WWF still liked to have Michaels come to the ring with somebody, so after Martel's departure he was joined by bodyguard Kevin Nash (Diesel). The storyline had Shawn upset over several losses arising from outside interference, including one to Jannetty caused by Curt "Mr. Perfect" Hennig. It was Diesel's job to prevent intrusions, and if he occasionally tripped up one of HBK's opponents when the ref's back was turned, so much the better.

With Diesel guarding the ring area, Michaels embarked upon the longest WWF winning streak of his career. Tatanka, Crush, Randy Savage, Bob Backlund, Mr. Perfect, and Lex Luger all made unsuccessful attempts to take the Intercontinental title, which was then stripped from Michaels due to a lack of scheduled title defenses. There is no evidence inside or out the storyline to support that charge.

Following a classic ladder match with Razor Ramon at WrestleMania X (see The 10 Best Wrestling Matches of All Time, page 187), Michaels took much of the summer of 1994 off. He spent his time managing Diesel's flourishing career and hosting an interview segment on *Raw* called The Heartbreak Hotel. Michaels also interfered in a Diesel-Razor Ramon match, helping his former bodyguard to win the Intercontinental title. A few months later, in August of 1994, HBK and Diesel defeated The Headshrinkers to become tag team champions.

A storyline that saw Michaels and Diesel part company just like Michaels and Jannetty had was postponed after Michaels broke his right hand in a match against Fatu. Amazingly, after having a steel pin inserted in his hand he continued to make appearances. At Survivor Series Michaels "accidentally" leveled Diesel with his devastating side kick, but it wasn't until January of 1995 that HBK demonstrated he had fully recovered. He won the Royal Rumble despite being the second man in the ring and then set his sights on the Heavyweight title, now held by none other than Diesel. The match took place at WrestleMania XI; Diesel won, even though Michaels's new bodyguard, Sid Justice, lent HBK a hand.

Throughout this long heel phase, there were always some cheers in the arena for HBK. He could win over the toughest crowd with his work ethic. The time was right for Michaels to turn babyface again: it happened when he was betrayed by Sid Justice and sidelined with back injuries after being subjected to three straight powerbombs.

Michaels and Diesel renewed their friendship, and then Michaels claimed the Intercontinental title for the third time after pinning Jeff Jarrett. This set the stage for an Intercontinental ladder rematch with Razor Ramon, and once again the results were spectacular. The Heartbreak Kid's victory solidified his status as a champion, but then real life interfered with the storyline: Michaels was attacked by nine men outside the Club 37 nightclub in Syracuse, New York. According to the police report, Michaels, The British Bulldog, and The 1–2–3 Kid were in a car when the assailants approached. Michaels was the first to confront them and was beaten while the other two wrestlers were held back. He suffered multiple cuts and bruises and was later treated at St. Joseph's Hospital. Syracuse detectives had to close the case without making an arrest because Michaels checked himself out of the hospital and flew home to Texas without giving them a statement. He would not wrestle again until the 1996 Royal Rumble, which he won for the second year in a row.

The Rumble victory earned Michaels the right to face Bret Hart for the Heavyweight title at WrestleMania XII. Fans looked forward to a battle between two of the WWF's best technical wrestlers, and the federation did not disappoint; the event was booked as a 60-minute iron-man match (see The 10 Best Wrestling Matches of All Time, page 188), but after one hour of action, neither man had scored a single pin. A five-minute overtime was ordered; champion Bret Hart, believing he had managed to retain the title, reluctantly returned to the ring and was pinned after falling victim to HBK's "sweet chin music."

Shawn Michaels was now at the height of his technical expertise and his drawing power. Prior to the ascension of Stone Cold Steve Austin, and after Scott Hall and Kevin Nash left for WCW, Michaels was the WWF's franchise player. He defeated The British Bulldog Davey Boy Smith, amid the allegations of Smith's wife, Diana, that Michaels had tried to seduce her; he fought a tremendous match against Vader, then switched the title with Sycho Sid, winning it back before his hometown fans in San Antonio, Texas. One month later, however, he was forced to surrender the title because of recurring back and neck injuries. He addressed the fans during a *Raw* broadcast, telling them he was leaving for awhile to "find my smile." His speech became the wrestling equivalent of Sally Field's "You like me!" outburst at the Academy Awards ceremony, and it was much ridiculed in the months that followed.

During a rather chaotic 1997, Michaels won the tag belts when he was forced to pair up with Steve Austin. The team dissolved soon afterwards, and Michaels, again sidelined by injury, agreed to referee the Heavyweight title match between The Undertaker and Bret Hart. During the match, he inadvertently nailed The Undertaker with a chair. The fans turned on him for giving The Hit Man, who had just turned heel, the victory, and Michaels turned heel as well.

Bad blood between HBK and The Undertaker led to the first WWF Hell in the Cell match (see The 10 Best Wrestling Matches of All Time, page 190). After the match, Michaels, his face resembling ground beef, was carried from the cell by Hunter Hearst Helmsley and Chyna. This trio then went on to form the rule-breaking group Degeneration X (DX). Their sophomoric stunts were initially booed by fans but proved too funny to resist.

Michaels and DX were a perfect fit. Whether wrestling as a face or a heel, HBK already led the league in gratuitous buttshots, and now he had even more motivation to moon the crowd or play strip poker in the ring, as he did on one episode of *Raw*.

When Michaels defeated Davey Boy Smith for the European title, he became the WWF's first (and, to date, only) Grand Slam title winner. McMahon ordered HBK to give fellow DX member Helmsley a title shot, and Michaels obliged, rolling over after an uproarious fake match that gave Helmsley his first WWF gold.

At WrestleMania XV, Michaels entered the ring to face the red-hot Stone Cold Steve Austin for the WWF title. Guest referee Mike Tyson was alleged to be on the side of DX, but there were more rumors rampant among wrestling's informed fans that HBK was far from 100 percent when he entered the ring. The rumors were true, though you'd never know it from his performance. Despite crippling back pain, Michaels took several horrendous bumps, dropping the title while appearing to make every effort to hold onto it. Tyson, for all the buildup his guest shot had received, turned out to be more of a distraction than a selling point for this first-rate match.

With the exception of the occasional guest-announcer gig on *Raw*, Michaels did not return full time to the WWF until November of 1998, when

McMahon appointed him commissioner. His first act was to schedule a title match between The Rock and his old DX pal X-Pac. He then clocked X-Pac with a chair, thus reintroducing himself as a heel. Fans never stopped cheering, and HBK soon turned face again, but the condition of his back will ultimately determine whether he ever returns to the ring.

REY MISTERIO JR.

REAL NAME:
Oscar Gutierrez

ALSO KNOWN AS:
Super Nino, Colibri

BORN:
December 12, 1974, San Diego, California

HEIGHT:
5' 3"

WEIGHT:
150 pounds

PROFESSIONAL DEBUT:
1991

PROFESSIONAL AFFILIATION:
Latino World Order (LWO)

FINISHING MOVE:
hurancurana

TITLES HELD

Mexico AAA Welterweight title
Won: October 28, 1992, over Fantasma de la Quebrada
Lost: February 26, 1993, to Heavy Metal

WWA Light Heavyweight title
Won: 1993, from El Espanto Jr.
Lost: October 1993, to Juventud Guerrera
Regained: November 30, 1994, over Juventud Guerrera
Lost: March 2, 1995, to Juventud Guerrera
Regained: June 16, 1995
Title vacated September 22, 1995, when Misterio wins Welterweight title

Mexico AAA Lightweight title
Won: November 30, 1994, over Juventud Guerrera

WWA World Tag-Team title
(with Rey Misterio)
Won: 1995, from Villano IV and Villano V
Lost: March 2, 1995, to Fuerza and Juventud Guerrera

AAA Mexico Trios title
(with Octagon and Super Muneco)
Won: April 15, 1995, over Tony Arce, Vulcano, and Rocco Valente
Lost: July 6, 1995, to Fuerza Guerrera, Psichosis, and Blue Panther

WWA World Welterweight title
Won: September 22, 1995, over Psichosis
Lost: September 28, 1995, to Psichosis
Regained: September 29, 1995, over Psichosis
Lost: April 28, 1996, to Juventud Guerrera
Regained: July 20, 1996, over Juventud Guerrera
Lost: February 21, 1997, to El Hijo del Santo

WCW Cruiserweight title
Won: July 8, 1996, over Dean Malenko
Lost: October 27, 1996, to Dean Malenko
Regained: October 26, 1997, over Eddie Guerrero
Lost: November 10, 1997, to Eddie Guerrero
Regained: January 15, 1998, over

Juventud Guerrera
Lost: January 24, 1998, to Chris Jericho
Regained: July 13, 1998, over Chris Jericho
Decision reversed on July 14, 1998, due to outside interference from Dean Malenko
Regained: March 15, 1999, over Kidman
Lost: April 19, 1999, to Psichosis
Regained: April 26, 1999, over Psichosis

It's hard to surprise a wrestling fan anymore. The search for a new, imaginative gimmick or a new angle between two familiar characters constantly challenges the creativity of wrestling's promoters. But the encyclopedia of holds and counterholds and moves is rarely supplemented with new entries — what more can be done inside the ring that hasn't been done already?

One of the few wrestlers now attempting to answer that question is Rey Misterio Jr., who, by the time he had turned 22, had already introduced a medley of innovative, high-flying combinations to the sport that left even the most jaded fan breathless. Misterio has done more to promote the *lucha libre* style of Mexican wrestling in the United States than anyone else. No wrestler has ever worked above the ropes more skillfully, but his fearless aerial acrobatics have already caused him to be grounded more than once by serious injury.

One can only wish Misterio a long and healthy career, but considering the degree of risk involved in every one of his matches, it's hard to imagine his back, knees, and ankles holding out for two more decades. "The adrenaline of the people makes you do crazy things," he once said. "They're high risk moves, but sometimes you don't care. You just try to have a good match and show the people what you've got. After you get hurt, that's when you realize, 'oh, man, I shouldn't have done that!'"

The first wrestler known as Rey Misterio ("King of Mystery") performed in Mexico and southern California during the 1970s and 1980s. His nephew, Oscar Gutierrez, grew up watching Uncle Rey perform and was mesmerized by the adulation he received. Before he was 10 years old, wrestling had become Oscar's only career choice. While being trained by his uncle, he spent long after-school hours learning the *lucha libre* style. His size — 5' 1" and 120 pounds — was cause for concern, but he was strong and fast and fearless when it came to launching himself off the top rope, whether his opponent was in the ring or on the concrete floor below.

Mexican law requires that any wrestler be 18 years old before he is granted a professional license. But by the time Oscar had turned 15 he was ready. He dropped out of high school and wrestled pickup matches on non-sanctioned cards, some of which were held in farmhouses. He donned a mask like his uncle and called himself Colibri (Spanish for "hummingbird").

For the next three years, Oscar Gutierrez worked steadily to little acclaim. And then, one night before he was scheduled to perform, Rey Misterio came to the ring and introduced Colibri as his nephew. "From now on, his name, Colibri, will no longer be used. I now authorize him to use my name, Rey Misterio Jr."

From that moment on, Oscar strove to be worthy of his uncle's endorsement, and with the Misterio name as his calling card, he was soon wrestling in Mexico's major promotions. When his friend Konnan formed AAA Wrestling in 1992, Rey Misterio Jr. was among the first to join the new organization. Now 18 and a licensed professional, he captured several titles — the most gratifying being the tag belts he earned alongside his uncle.

From 1993 to 1996, he would exchange WWA Welterweight and Light Heavyweight belts with Juventud Guerrera, another mercurial masked wrestler, young Misterio's equal in speed and daring. Misterio was among the first of the Mexican wrestlers to popularize *lucha libre* in Japan, where he worked for the WAR Association. He and his most frequent WAR opponent, Psichosis, put on a display of *planchas*, flying dropkicks, and midair flips that garnered standing ovations.

The Psichosis-Misterio feud was renewed when both wrestlers joined ECW in September of 1995. Together they introduced the *lucha libre* style to American audiences. Misterio became a fan favorite, even though he never participated in the bloodletting that had made the federation infamous. Both he and Psichosis also continued to wrestle in Mexico. There Misterio first won the Welterweight title from Psichosis, only to lose and regain the belt within seven days.

Rey Misterio Jr. joined WCW in the spring of 1996, once again following in his uncle's footsteps (Rey Misterio Sr. had appeared at Starrcade 1990). Eric Bischoff first spotted him at Antonio Inoki's World Wrestling Peace Festival in Los Angeles and signed him up soon afterwards. His size made him the underdog in every match, and WCW fans soon took the diminutive *luchadore* to their hearts.

Misterio was reunited with both Psichosis and Juventud Guerrera, and their acrobatic battles quickly became a *Nitro* highlight. In July of 1996, Misterio defeated Dean Malenko for the Cruiserweight title and regained the WWA Welterweight title from Guerrera a few days later.

Then Misterio became one of the first WCW victims of the NWO invasion: he was picked up and hurled into a trailer outside an arena by Kevin Nash. And NWO interference prevented Misterio from defeating Syxx (Sean Waltman) in several matches. Frustrated, Misterio challenged Nash to a one-on-one match and was powerbombed with bone-jarring authority. He suffered minor injuries, which were aggravated in subsequent matches with NWO member Konnan.

Despite the pain, Rey continued to thrill the crowds with his high-flying maneuvers and spinning *hurancaranas* that snapped an opponent into a pin position with lethal precision. He defeated Eddie Guerrero for the Cruiserweight title, putting his mask on the line in the contest. His reign was brief, but Misterio picked up the belt yet again after beating Juventud Guerrera in January of 1998.

And, just as quickly, he lost it again — this time to Chris Jericho. Misterio suffered torn anterior cruciate and meniscus ligaments in the match, and he required six months of rehab before returning to the ring at the July Bash at the Beach. During the hiatus, Misterio not only gave his legs some much-needed rest, but he also built up his upper body. Bolstered by a few extra pounds of muscle, Misterio exacted his revenge on Jericho by regaining the Cruiserweight title. Jericho managed to have the result thrown out, but by now Misterio was used to short title reigns.

Late in 1998, Misterio joined Eddie Guerrero's Latino World Order (LWO), though he's been working to reform their rule-breaking tactics ever since. His matches with Billy Kidman rank among the best cruiserweight exhibitions of the 1990s.

On February 21, 1999, Rey wrestled alongside Konnan in a tag-team match against The Outsiders — Scott Hall and Kevin Nash. Misterio put his mask on the line against the hair of The Outsiders' companion, Miss Elizabeth. Shockingly, Misterio's team lost, and Misterio unmasked for the first time in his career. How this will affect his identity and his popularity remains to be seen.

KEVIN NASH

REAL NAME:
Kevin Nash

ALSO KNOWN AS: Master Blaster Steele, Oz, Vinnie Vegas, Diesel, Big Daddy Cool, Big Sexy — The Giant Killer

BORN:
July 9, 1959, Detroit, Michigan

HEIGHT:
7'

WEIGHT:
356 pounds

PROFESSIONAL DEBUT:
September 14, 1990

PROFESSIONAL AFFILIATIONS:
The Master Blasters, New World Order, NWO Wolfpack, The Outsiders

FINISHING MOVE:
jackknife powerbomb

TITLES HELD

WWF **Intercontinental title**
Won: April 19, 1994, over Razor Ramon
Lost: August 29, 1994, to Razor Ramon

WWF **Tag-Team title**
(with Shawn Michaels)
Won: August 28, 1994, over The Headshrinkers
Titles vacated November 1994
Regained: September 24, 1995, over Owen Hart and Yokozuna
Decision reversed September 25, 1995

WWF **World Heavyweight title**
Won: November 23, 1994, over Bob Backlund
Lost: November 19, 1995, to Bret Hart

WCW **Tag-Team title**
(with Scott Hall as The Outsiders)
Won: October 27, 1996, over Harlem Heat
Lost: January 26, 1997, to The Steiner Brothers

Regained: January 27, 1997 (decision of January 26 reversed)
Lost: February 23, 1997, to Lex Luger and The Giant
Regained: February 24, 1997 (decision of February 23 reversed)
Lost: October 13, 1997, to The Steiner Brothers (Sean Waltman substituted for an injured Kevin Nash)
Regained: January 12, 1998, over The Steiner Brothers
Lost: February 9, 1998, to The Steiner Brothers
Regained: February 22, 1998, over The Steiner Brothers
Lost: May 17, 1998, to Sting and The Giant

WCW **World Heavyweight title**
Won: December 27, 1998, over Goldberg
Lost: January 4, 1999, to Hulk Hogan
Regained: May 9, 1999, over Diamond Dallas Page

A convincing argument can be made for Kevin Nash as the most talented "big man" in wrestling. Certainly he's the most charismatic, though it took some time before his frat-boy attitude could be worked into a character capable of putting him over with the fans. Nash's triumph over three of the lamest alter egos ever foisted upon a wrestler is a study in tenacity; but it's his ring skills, his unwillingness to rely solely on the basic power moves utilized by other men in his weight class, that separates Nash from wrestling's other giants.

Growing up in Detroit, Kevin Nash was always the tallest kid in class, and so he was marked for basketball stardom early on. After slam-dunking over the heads of his hapless high-school opponents for four years, the seven-footer became a standout center at the University of Tennessee. At one time, only Earvin "Magic" Johnson was thought to have more NBA potential among Michigan natives. Nash played professionally in Europe for awhile but changed careers in 1990. While he was working as a doorman and bouncer at a nightclub frequented by NWA wrestlers, several of them suggested he try out for the squared circle. A natural performer and comedian, Nash liked the idea of a career that combined athletics and showbiz.

He debuted in the NWA as a bodyguard for Nancy Sullivan (Woman). His role was limited to the odd cheap shot in support of the tag team Doom. The gig lasted only a few weeks, until Woman lost control of Doom and vanished. Nash disappeared too, only to reemerge a few months later as Steele, half of the tag team known as The Master Blasters. The team's gimmick was obviously inspired by The Road Warriors — even their name was taken from the same source material (Master Blaster was a character in the 1985 film *Mad Max beyond Thunderdome*). Relegated to the undercard for most of their brief existence, The Master Blasters only earned title shots when the belt holders had early dinner reservations.

As NWA morphed into WCW, The Blasters were morphed out of existence; this supposedly came after a particularly embarrassing incident in which Nash's partner, Master Blaster Blade (Al Green), attempted a diving head butt and missed by a distance that even wrestling fans considered ludicrous.

At the time, WCW owner Ted Turner was on a movie-buying spree, having purchased the rights to the MGM library. Similarly inspired, talent-bookers Jim Herd and Dusty Rhodes introduced a slew of movie-themed wrestlers, including Kevin Nash, reborn as a wizard named Oz. If Big Daddy Cool hasn't yet burned all the tapes from this phase of his career, try to find one, because the getup was hilarious. His long hair dyed a glittery silver, Nash would stroll to the ring in a green robe and matching tights. He would usually be accompanied by a "munchkin" known as Wizard.

The "unbeatable" Oz competed throughout 1991 until Ron Simmons kicked him off the yellow brick road on his way to the WCW Heavyweight title. Away from the ring, Nash played the only slightly less embarrassing role of Super Shredder in *Teenage Mutant Ninja Turtles 2: The Secret of the Ooze* (1991).

A new year, 1992, brought yet another new character: Nash next assumed the role of rough-and-tumble bouncer Vinnie Vegas. A vision in his pink vest and tights, Vegas joined Diamond Dallas Page's Diamond Mine stable and would often team with Page in midcard matches. His finishing move, lifting his opponent high above the ring and dropping him face first into the turnbuckle, was dubbed "snake eyes." But Vinnie crapped out almost as fast as Steele and Oz, and it was then that Kevin Nash decided to try his luck in the WWF.

In the summer of 1993, Vince McMahon introduced Nash in the familiar role of bodyguard, this time to Shawn Michaels. Why a former Intercontinental champion would need a bodyguard is a question no one bothered to ask. Dressed in black leather and answering to the name Diesel, Nash suddenly seemed more menacing than ever before, though he didn't actually wrestle for several months.

Diesel's coming-out party was the 1994 Royal Rumble. As the seventh man to enter the ring, he quickly eliminated everyone who was still there when he arrived, including Bart Gunn, Scott Steiner, and Owen Hart. Bob Backlund, Billy Gunn, and Virgil then entered the fray, and one by one they were tossed right back out. Nash stood alone in the ring, waving out each victim. "Believe it or not, a lot of the fans are actually cheering!" said McMahon from the commentator's position. Nash was eliminated after 20 eventful minutes, but a star was born.

The heel had turned face overnight, and he dominated the WWF throughout 1994. He beat Razor Ramon for the Intercontinental title, won the tag titles alongside Shawn Michaels, and beat Bob Backlund in eight seconds to win the Heavyweight belt. In doing so, he became the first wrestler to win the top-three WWF titles in the course of one year.

Throughout this rise to prominence, a series of "inadvertent" standing side kicks that Michaels landed in Diesel's face resulted in the dissolution of the team. The tag titles were vacated, and Diesel lost his Intercontinental belt to Razor Ramon due to interference from Michaels. But Diesel, now also introduced as Big Daddy Cool, held onto the Heavyweight belt for an impressive 358 days. By this time, he had become the most significant figure in the WWF's "New Generation" advertising campaign.

In 1995, Diesel and Shawn Michaels reconciled and regained their tag belts, though the decision was reversed the next day because they didn't beat the reigning champs (Davey Boy Smith subbing for Owen Hart alongside Yokozuna). The WWF deployed their other big men against Nash, but these guys — like Sycho Sid and King Mabel — did not have the mobility or the technical skills to sell a match. Diesel, unlike every other wrestling titan, wrestled his best matches against smaller opponents, such as Shawn Michaels and Bret Hart.

Diesel's two matches with Bret Hart, at the 1995 Royal Rumble and the 1995 Survivor Series, were outstanding confrontations. He won the first but lost the second — and with it his title. The plan was for Diesel to turn heel again, but his announcement that he would no longer be the WWF's "corporate puppet" was not enough to turn off the applause. (The same gimmick actually played much better when Steve Austin employed it in 1998.) It was only after Nash began interfering in The Undertaker's matches and attacking Shawn Michaels that he was able to achieve the desired level of fan contempt.

After costing The Undertaker the Heavyweight title at the 1996 Royal Rumble, Diesel made one of the more memorable exits from the ring during his own title match with Bret Hart. The Undertaker, emerging from a hole in the canvas, grabbed Diesel and pulled him below the surface. The scenario was all too symbolic of Kevin Nash's declining status in the WWF.

Diesel was trounced by The Undertaker at WrestleMania XII and, on May 19, 1996, he wrestled his final WWF match, at Madison Square Garden. Nash was pinned by Michaels, and afterwards Nash, Scott Hall, Hunter Hearst Helmsley, and Michaels all broke character and announced to the fans that Hall and Nash were leaving the WWF.

Two weeks after Hall's debut in WCW, he was joined by Nash, appearing under his own name for the first time. Calling themselves The Outsiders, they claimed superiority over every wrestler in WCW. The duo became a trio when Hulk Hogan executed his astonishing heel turn, and thus the New World Order (NWO) was born. The Outsiders won the WCW Tag titles from Harlem Heat in October of 1996 and formed The Wolfpack after recruiting Sean Waltman (Syxx).

The rise to prominence of the NWO was exciting, groundbreaking stuff. Nash found himself at the heart of the most unique wrestling angle of the 1990s. Though he had followed the familiar pattern of rising from WCW obscurity to attain WWF stardom, Nash didn't stop there: he returned to WCW and actually became bigger than ever, staying over with WCW fans even as he trashed their longtime heroes, including The Four Horsemen. "I'll stay over no matter what," he said. "I'm just too damn funny to stay on the back burner."

A Nash-Giant feud started promisingly but lost steam after injuries to both wrestlers delayed the payoff. Nash pulled a last-minute no-show at the 1997 Starrcade, incurring the wrath of WCW executives. He claimed he had missed his plane, though rumors circulated that he had suffered a minor heart attack. When the match finally took place, at the 1997 Souled Out, Nash powerbombed The Giant right into the hospital with a neck injury. The powerbomb was outlawed, but Nash kept doing it, racking up fines and jail time according to the storyline.

Away from the ring, Nash was causing trouble that was not in the script. Eric Bischoff, WCW boss, fired Sean Waltman to send a message to

"Diesel"

Nash and Hall, both notorious locker-room troublemakers. Nash asked to be released. He later recalled Bischoff's response as, "Are you crazy? You're not going anywhere! You're locked for four years — I'll send you to Poland before I send you to Vince [McMahon]." Nash replied, "They love me in Poland!"

Cooler heads prevailed, though Nash's rebel streak still resurfaced on occasion. At a 1998 outdoor Spring Break event, he announced to the inebriated college crowd that "Fat girls need lovin' too!" and was suspended for a week. Tensions between Nash and Hulk Hogan were manufactured so that Nash could form a splinter NWO group, NWO Wolfpack. This move allowed WCW to sell twice as many NWO T-shirts (Wolfpack shirts carry the same NWO logo, dyed red).

After Sting, Lex Luger, and Randy Savage joined NWO Wolfpack, Nash's group became the hottest property in WCW. Nash became a sought-after commodity in Hollywood as well, appearing in episodes of ABC's *Sabrina, The Teenage Witch* and Nickelodeon's *Weinerville*.

Nash's greatest performance, however, may be the one that followed his stunning victory over Goldberg in the contest for the WCW Heavyweight title at the 1998 Starrcade. He feigned outrage at Scott Hall, who had knocked Goldberg out with a tazer during the match. Nash demanded a rematch in January of 1999, but instead of wrestling Goldberg he challenged Hulk Hogan, then rolled over for him and awarded Hogan the belt. The original New World Order was back and ready to wreak havoc on WCW once again.

THE NEW AGE OUTLAWS

NAME:

The Road Dog Jesse James
Bad Ass Billy Gunn

PROFESSIONAL DEBUT:

1997

PROFESSIONAL AFFILIATION:

Degeneration X

TITLES
HELD

WWF **Tag-Team title**
Won: November 24, 1997, over The
Legion of Doom (Hawk and Animal)
Lost: March 29, 1998, to Cactus Jack and
Chainsaw Charlie (Terry Funk)
Regained: March 30, 1998, over Cactus
Jack and Terry Funk
Lost: July 13, 1998, to Kane and Mankind
Regained: August 30, 1998, over Kane
and Mankind
Lost: December 13, 1998, to The Big Boss
Man and Ken Shamrock

REAL NAME:

Brian James

ALSO KNOWN AS:

The Dark Secret, Brian Armstrong, The Roadie, Jesse James Armstrong, Double J Jesse James

BORN:

May 20, 1965, Marietta, Georgia

HEIGHT:

6' 4"

WEIGHT:

240 pounds

PROFESSIONAL DEBUT:

1992

OTHER TITLES HELD

USWA **Southern Heavyweight title**
Won: September 11, 1995, over Brian Christopher
Lost: October 23, 1995, to Brian Christopher

USWA **Tag-Team title**
(with Tracy Smothers)
Won: October 28, 1995, over PG-13 (Wolfie D and Stevie Ice)
Lost: January 3, 1996, to Tommy Rich and Doug Gilbert
Regained: February 14, 1996, over PG-13

Lost: February 17, 1996, to PG-13

USWA **Television title**
Won: April 13, 1996 (tournament win)
Lost: May 4, 1996, to Tony Falk
Regained: May 19, 1996, over Tony Falk
Title vacated when Jesse James is defeated in a loser-leaves-town match by Jeff Jarrett on June 10, 1996

WWF **Intercontinental Title**
Won: March 15, 1999, over Val Venis
Lost: March 29, 1999, to Goldust

REAL NAME:
Monte "Kip" Sopp

ALSO KNOWN AS:
Kip Winchester, Rockabilly

BORN:
November 11, 1970, Austin, Texas

HEIGHT:
6' 5"

WEIGHT:
255 pounds

PROFESSIONAL DEBUT:
1992

PROFESSIONAL AFFILIATION:
The Smoking Gunns

WWF **Tag-Team title**
(with Bart Gunn as The Smoking Gunns)
Won: January 23, 1995, over Bob Holly and The 1–2–3 Kid
Lost: April 2, 1995, to Owen Hart and Yokozuna
Regained: October 25, 1995, over Owen Hart and Yokozuna
Titles vacated in March 1996, due to injury
Regained: May 26, 1996, over Henry and Phineas Godwinn
Lost: September 22, 1996, to Owen Hart and The British Bulldog

Oh, you didn't know? In 1997, The New Age Outlaws became the WWF's hottest tag team, but their popularity had more to do with their microphone skills than with anything they did in the ring. The Road Dog Jesse James and Bad Ass Billy Gunn had worked steadily in and out of the WWF, but it was their alliance with Degeneration X and one magical catchphrase that vaulted them into the ranks of tag-team royalty.

"Oh, you didn't know? Your ass better call somebody!" James exclaims as they make their entrance, holding the last syllable until the fans join in. Once inside the ring, James provides the team's introduction himself: "Ladies and gentlemen, boys and girls, children of all ages: Degeneration X proudly brings to you its WWF Tag-Team champions of the world! The Road Dog Jesse James, The Bad Ass Billy Gunn, the New . . . Age . . . Outlaws!" By the summer of 1998, the entire speech was being recited verbatim by everyone in the arena and written out on signs that stretched the length of a whole seating section.

Billy Gunn, a man of fewer words, then grabs the mike and announces,

"And if you're not down with DX, we got two words for ya!" — to which the fans yell, "Suck it!" After all that, the match itself is practically an anticlimax.

Of the two, Billy Gunn had enjoyed the most success prior to taking on Outlaw status; he'd done so as a member of The Smoking Gunns tag team. There was always a cowboy/western identity to his characters, a by-product, perhaps, of his Texas upbringing. In the early 1990s, he wrestled in Florida's IWA promotion as Kip Winchester and formed a tag team and friendship with Bret Colt. The WWF liked what they saw in the young, attractive team and repackaged them for their debut as "brothers" Billy and Bart Gunn, The Smoking Gunns. They wore jeans and cowboy boots to the ring, and they fired caps in the air with their six-shooters.

The duo was promoted right away as a contender, though there was no shortage of tag teams in the WWF at the time. For their first pay-per-view appearance, The Gunns joined The Steiner Brothers in a six-man tag match against The Headshrinkers and Money, Inc. Billy Gunn was allowed to end the match by pinning Ted DiBiase, an indication that The Smoking Gunns were going to get a quick push. Billy's solo career was not given the same support; he wrestled jobber extraordinaire Steve Lombardi, a.k.a. The Brooklyn Brawler, at the 1993 Survivor Series in the only match that was not broadcast on pay-per-view.

The Smoking Gunns defeated Bob Holly and The 1–2–3 Kid (Sean Waltman) to win the Tag titles in January of 1995, just one day after Holly and The Kid won the belts in a tournament at the Royal Rumble. Except when they pulled a title switch with Owen Hart and Yokozuna, The Gunns reigned as champions for the rest of 1995, staving off challenges from Public Enemy, Razor Ramon and Sean Waltman, and Jacob and Eli Blu.

At the 1996 Royal Rumble, Billy and Bart defeated Skip and Zip, The Bodydonnas, to retain the belts. Sunny, the sexy, blond gold-digging manager of the Bodydonnas, began a flirtation with Billy Gunn. The storyline would have continued had Billy not been sidelined with an injury. While he recuperated, Sunny allied herself with new champs The Godwinns, then dumped them to manage The Gunns back to tag-team gold.

As the WWF gravitated towards darker, nastier angles, the squeaky-clean Smoking Gunns began to look like Boy Scouts in a strip club. So, the storyline went, they were tarnished by Sunny, whose affection for Billy triggered jealousy and dissent between him and brother Bart. The Gunns lost the title to Owen Hart and The British Bulldog. They disbanded soon after. On a *Raw* broadcast in December of 1996, The Gunns faced each other in a singles match, and Billy supposedly suffered a serious neck injury at the hands of his "brother." The storyline was never revived after that; Billy recouped and faced Flash Funk at the WrestleMania XII preshow, while Bart became a jobber whose career would not be revived until he participated in the WWF Brawl for All boxing competition in 1998.

Billy's future partner, Brian "Jesse" James, was born into a wrestling family. His father, Bob Armstrong, was a mainstay on the Southern regional circuits, and his brothers, Brad, Scott, and Steve, all went into the business. Bob schooled all four of his sons in the sport's finer points, and they all set out to seek their fortunes with varying degrees of success.

After serving in the military and seeing action during Operation Desert Storm, Brian James debuted on the Smoky Mountain circuit in 1993 as The Dark Secret. He then opted for the less exotic name of Brian Armstrong for subsequent forays into Smoky Mountain, the USWA, and WCW, where his brother Brad was approaching midcard status. Wrestling fans speak often of the "Armstrong Curse," which has prevented every member of the family, talent notwithstanding, from becoming a superstar.

In 1994, Jeff Jarrett was primed for a major push in the WWF as the country-music-singing Double J. Brian signed up to play The Roadie, Double J.'s accomplice and competitive edge in close matches. He interfered in several of Jarrett's matches with Razor Ramon and nearly cost his boss the title at WrestleMania XI. They began working as a tag team in 1995, and The Roadie received a minor push by winning solo matches against Bob Holly and The 1–2–3 Kid.

Jarrett never went over as well as the WWF had hoped, so he and The Roadie both left the federation. Jarrett went to WCW and The Roadie worked in the USWA as Jesse James Armstrong. In the space of a year, he held the Southern Heavyweight title, the Television title, and the Tag titles (with Tracy Smothers).

Despite his success, James agreed to return to the WWF to revive an earlier storyline that had been plotted but never performed. Before leaving the federation, Jarrett had lip-synched to a catchy country tune called "Alone with My Baby Tonight," and it had been played on a few *Raw* telecasts. When James came back into the fold, he revealed that the vocals were actually his own, proving his assertion with a live performance. Though the fans responded well to the song, they didn't really care about the Milli Vanilli angle.

When the singing-wrestler bit bombed, James was approached by The Honky Tonk Man, who offered him his services as manager. James responded by taking The Honky Tonk Man's balsa-wood guitar and smashing it over his head. Outraged, Honky Tonk recruited Billy Gunn, changed his name to Rockabilly, and went after James. The Gunn-Rockabilly alliance was shortlived, however. James beat Gunn in a singles match on the April 20, 1997 In Your House pay-per-view, but shortly thereafter James, now calling himself The Road Dog, convinced Gunn to drop the Rockabilly gimmick and join him in a tag team. In their first match they defeated The Headbangers (Mosh and Thrasher) by breaking a boom box over Mosh's head.

At first, they were billed as themselves, though Billy added "Bad Ass" to his introduction. Taunting The Legion of Doom by calling the team "OLD," they won a surprising number of matches against The LOD, the most decorated team in wrestling history; the upstart duo even humiliated its veteran opponents by shaving off their Mohawk haircuts. In November of 1997, The Outlaws defeated The LOD to become WWF Tag-Team champs.

The highlight of the team's heel antics occurred during a *Raw* episode that aired during the summer of 1998: The Outlaws trapped Cactus Jack and Terry Funk inside a dumpster and pushed the dumpster off a ten-foot rise onto a concrete floor. It was a horrendous bump, and it stopped the show temporarily, eventually prompting a rare apology from the perpetrators for stepping over the line. The incident led to a dumpster match at WrestleMania XIII. Cactus Jack and Terry Funk snared the victory, but they did not win the belts due to a technicality (they had purportedly trapped The Outlaws in the wrong dumpster).

Shortly after being drafted by Degeneration X, Billy Gunn and Jesse James became The New Age Outlaws. While DX was a rule-breaking organization of heels, The Outlaws also earned their fair share of fan hostility. But under the leadership of Shawn Michaels and Hunter Hearst Helmsley, the group began winning over fans with their outrageous behavior and frequent slams at WCW. In the process, two men with singles careers that were going nowhere became the most popular WWF tag team since The Hart Foundation.

The Outlaws reigned during 1998, but when Shawn Michaels returned to the WWF after an extended injury leave and allied himself with Vince McMahon's new Corporation team, there were rumors that the man who had recruited The Outlaws into DX might try to recruit them into his new organization. On a November 1998 *Raw* telecast, The Outlaws appeared in three-piece suits alongside Michaels and McMahon, and the fans' worst fears seemed about to be realized. But in the final match, pitting DX member Sean Waltman (X-Pac) against Corporation member Ken Shamrock, Billy Gunn nailed Shamrock with a chair shot. They then stripped off their suits to reveal their old, familiar DX costumes and gave Michaels the famous DX crotch-chop salute.

Retaliation was not long in coming; after a hilarious skit on the December 13, 1998, *Raw* in which DX performed a parody of McMahon's Corporation members, McMahon ordered The Outlaws to defend their title against Shamrock and The Big Boss Man. During the match, Michaels knocked Billy Gunn unconscious with The Boss Man's nightstick and The Outlaws lost their belts.

One week later, Gunn faced Shamrock in singles competition for the Intercontinental title, and The Road Dog defeated Mankind for the WWF's Hardcore title. Both men now seem primed for successful singles careers, but it would be a shame if they didn't also continue their tag-team pursuits.

REAL NAME:
Page Joseph Falkinburg

BORN:
April 5, 1956, Tampa, Florida

HEIGHT:
6' 5"

WEIGHT:
260 pounds

PROFESSIONAL DEBUT:
1991

PROFESSIONAL AFFILIATIONS:
Badd Company, The Freebirds (both as manager)

FINISHING MOVE:
the diamond cutter

TITLES HELD

wcw **Television title**
Won: September 17, 1995, over The Renegade
Lost: October 29, 1995, to Johnny B. Badd

wcw **United States Heavyweight title**
Won: December 28, 1997, over Curt Hennig
Lost: April 19, 1998, to Raven
Regained: October 26, 1998, over Bret Hart

Lost: November 30, 1998, to Bret Hart

wcw **World Heavyweight title**
Won: April 11, 1999, over Ric Flair, Hulk Hogan, and Sting (four-corners match)
Lost: April 26, 1999, to Sting
Regained: April 26, 1999, over Goldberg, Kevin Nash, and Sting (four-corners match)
Lost: May 9, 1999, to Kevin Nash

The transition from wrestler to manager happens so often that it's hardly newsworthy. Former competitors Bobby Heenan, Freddie Blassie, and Ted DiBiase have all traded in their tights for business suits and traded on their years of experience in outside interference. What's unique about Diamond Dallas Page is that he made the reverse transition. The former manager of such wrestlers as Dick Slater, Bam Bam Bigelow, and Badd Company, Page now ranks as one of wcw's most bankable stars, and he can lay claim to one of the most devastating finishing moves in the business.

His "people's champion" persona was quickly embraced by wwf converts — the fans who were not watching wcw when Page was strutting around in his frilly outfits, flaunting his millionaire's income, calling fans "scum," and verbally abusing his wife, Kimberly, then billed as The Diamond Doll. Such a character is a far cry from the working-class hero Page now plays, a regular guy in stonewashed jeans, denim vest, and "Diamond Cutter" T-shirt (available at the concession stand).

Page claims this guy's a lot closer to his own personality and that's why the fans are responding. "What really works in wrestling is when there is the element of doubt and, in the same breath, realism," he has said. "I know that everything started coming together when I started to make Diamond Dallas Page more Page Falkinburg. I'm the same guy in person that I am on TV now, which wasn't the case a few years ago."

At the age of seven, young Page Falkinburg received his "Dallas" nickname from his father, with whom he lived after the divorce of his parents. The moniker derived from Page's devotion to the Dallas Cowboys football team, which took hold despite his being raised in New Jersey.

In high school, Page was a popular kid who played basketball and once got expelled for mooning a girl in a locker room. When he was 17, he began working in a bar on the Jersey Shore and was quickly promoted from broom jockey to bouncer. After graduation, Page earned a full athletic scholarship to Coastal Carolina University, but he dropped out after only six weeks.

Back in Jersey, he continued to work the bar scene at such hot nightspots as the Stone Pony, Montego Bay, and Club Xanadu. He also indulged his lifelong interest in wrestling by learning some basic moves from former pro Tito Torres. But a knee injury, dating back to when he was hit by a car at the age of 12, flared up every time he tried to exert himself in the ring. Still, he hung around wrestling venues as often as he could, befriending many of the competitors — including Jake Roberts and Dusty Rhodes — and watching the action from backstage. At WrestleMania III, in fact, Page could be seen driving a pink Cadillac.

Page desperately wanted to enter the wrestling world, and, after watching Bobby Heenan fire up a crowd with his usual brand of confrontational stand-up comedy, he decided to try his luck as a manager. He made a videotape of himself spouting off the type of tough rhetoric he saw Heenan and Jesse Ventura use on television. He mailed the tape to the AWA, and one week later he was asked to fly to Las Vegas for an interview. In 1988, Page became the new manager of Badd Company (Paul Diamond and Pat Tanaka), replacing the recently departed Paul E. Dangerously. In March of 1988, Badd Company won the Tag titles and held them for more than a year.

For the next two years, Page expanded his stable to include Johnny Ace, Dick Slater, Scott Hall, and Bam Bam Bigelow. He also did television commentary for Championship Wrestling in Florida alongside announcer Gordon Solie. But the desire to wrestle still burned inside him.

In 1991, Dallas Page joined WCW as the manager of The Freebirds (Jimmy Garvin and Michael P.S. Hayes) and continued to represent Scott Hall, then known as The Diamond Studd. In November of 1991, Page finally succumbed to the temptation to enter the ring. He became The Diamond Studd's tag-team partner, "Diamond" Dallas Page. Outside the ring, on

December 1, he married Kimberly, his girlfriend of three years.

When Hall joined the WWF as Razor Ramon, Page feuded with Johnny B. Badd and joined forces with Hall's future fellow Outsider, Kevin Nash, who was still working under his embarrassing alias of Vinnie Vegas. Page found another ally in Scotty Flamingo, with whom he would later have a celebrated feud, after Flamingo stopped taking baths and became the Bowery-born Raven.

In 1993, although his knee was still holding up, Page was sidelined for almost a year after tearing a rotator cuff during a match against Tex Slazinger and Shanghai Pierce. When he

(Photo Credit: Jill Kokesh/AP Photo)

Diamond Dallas Page arm-locks "Hollywood" Hogan during a WCW match while Jay Leno looks on.

returned, he began playing a frustrated, filthy-rich, would-be superstar who wasn't getting the title shots he believed he deserved. He filled a fishbowl with slips of paper inscribed with his opponent's names and he'd draw one out at random; he'd then issue a challenge to that wrestler. It was a great gimmick that led to a feud with Terry Taylor and helped put Page over as an arrogant jerk.

It was at about this time that Kimberly Page started to use her master's degree in advertising to help sell her husband. As The Diamond Doll, Kim accompanied DDP to the ring and more than once was offered up as the prize in a challenge match. Dave Sullivan beat Dallas in an arm-wrestling match at the 1995 Great American Bash and won a date with Kim. At Fall Brawl in September of 1995, Page won the Television title from The Renegade but dropped it the next month to Johnny B. Badd. Badd, who also won Kimberly's "services" as a result of the victory, dearly hoped this was one of those rare instances when a wrestling-world gimmick was based on something real.

Apparently, Kim enjoyed her time with the Badd guy, or so the story went. Page lost a rematch for the title at World War III as a result of The Doll's interference and lost again at Superbrawl. What had become Page's most significant feud to date was scheduled to end with a loser-leaves rematch, but Johnny B. Badd bolted for the WWF before the matter could be settled. Ed Leslie, The Booty Man, wrestled in his place alongside Kim, the newly christened "Booty Babe." Page was pinned, but returned within weeks, citing a loophole he had found in the retirement contract.

By this time, he had also developed a finishing move he called "the diamond cutter." It had been inspired by a maneuver called the ace crusher, which had been used by his friend and former "employee" Johnny Ace. After learning that maneuver at WCW's Power Plant, Page applied to it some elements of the cravat, a hold used by Lord Steven Regal. And, influenced by Jake Roberts's ability to deploy his DDT move coming out of several different maneuvers, Page worked out more than 50 different ways to unleash his diamond cutter. The four-fingered "diamond" sign that precedes the move was suggested by wrestler Ron Reis, who used the same sign to set up the diamond defense on his college basketball team.

Page's return from "retirement" was punctuated by his victory at the 1996 Battlebowl. He was no longer the wealthy elitist, his previous incarnation. The new storyline had Page losing his six-million-dollar fortune and selling off his wrestling attire to jobbers. Then, WCW reported that Page had been "discovered" sitting on a curb by a passenger in a mysterious limo, who stopped and picked Page up. His benefactor was rumored to be Ted DiBiase, but the truth was never revealed.

Whatever storylines were in development for Page changed when Scott Hall and Kevin Nash returned to WCW, ushering in the era of the New World Order. After Hulk Hogan pledged his allegiance, Page was asked to join. He refused, contending that, as his former tag partners, Hall and Nash should have asked him to come on board first.

Page's rejection of NWO, despite the flimsy reason he offered, marked the beginning of his rise as a face. Now reunited with Kimberly, he was praised for his integrity and work ethic. His reward was replacing Randy Savage as the target of weekly NWO butt-kickings at the end of every *Monday Nitro*.

Savage, at that point the most recent convert to NWO Black and White, ignited a feud with DDP by holding up samples from Kimberly's *Playboy* pictorial. Page named The Macho Man as his toughest opponent as well as the one he most despised. "Certain things are angle and entertainment-based, (but) sometimes people start stretching the boundaries which make you step into the real world," he said. "At times, Savage and I are in the real world."

Page and Savage fought all through 1997. Both sustained injuries that were half-work, half-genuine. For a tag match against The Macho Man and Scott Hall, Page chose a "mystery partner," thus introducing Curt Hennig to WCW. Hennig wound up ditching DDP and joining the NWO. At the 1997 Starrcade, Page won the United States title by pinning Hennig.

By 1998, Diamond Dallas Page was getting bigger ovations than anyone else in WCW with the exception of Ric Flair. He was also fighting some of his best matches ever, against Chris Benoit and Raven, to whom he lost the United States title. A memorable triangle match involving DDP, Benoit, and Raven (at Uncensored 1998) was followed by another impressive showing in a Heavyweight title match against Sting.

After the NWO split into two factions, DDP seemed poised to join the Wolfpack group until he was attacked by Hulk Hogan and Chicago Bulls star Dennis Rodman. The attack was avenged in July of 1998 at Bash at the Beach;

Hogan and Rodman teamed up against DDP and Utah Jazz great Karl Malone. Though the heat was generated by Rodman and Malone, who had clashed during the NBA playoffs just one month earlier, the main-event, pay-per-view match was unquestionably the biggest of DDP's career. Unfortunately, Hogan was off his game that night and Rodman, looking drunk, botched several basic moves. Malone gave an enthusiastic effort and even executed a diamond cutter on the referee, but by then the fans were chanting "bor-ing," and they were right.

Page, who seemed lost in the crowd at his first main event, was sent directly into another guest-celebrity grouping, this one even more bizarre than the first. At Road Wild, he teamed with comedian Jay Leno against Hogan and Eric Bischoff (see The 10 Most Embarrassing Wrestling Matches/ Gimmicks, page 203). But a victory at WarGames earned Page a Heavyweight title match against Goldberg at Halloween Havoc. It was to be his third pay-per-view main event in six months — and his first chance to wrestle without having to babysit a guest star. Page lost a competitive match, though most of the country didn't get to see it because of a cable snafu at WCW.

In 1999, Page enjoyed two brief title reigns as Heavyweight champ, and embarked upon a heel turn that should secure his main event status for the forseeable future. His knee still threatens to go at any time, but Diamond Dallas Page still loves what he's doing and enjoys each day, knowing it could be his last in the squared circle.

ROWDY RODDY PIPER

REAL NAME:
Roderick George Toombs

ALSO KNOWN AS:
The Masked Canadian, Roddy the Piper, Piper Machine, Hot Rod, The Icon

BORN:
April 17, 1951, Glasgow, Scotland

HEIGHT:
6' 2"

WEIGHT:
250 pounds

PROFESSIONAL DEBUT:
1966

PROFESSIONAL AFFILIATIONS:
None

FINISHING MOVE:
the sleeper

TITLES HELD

NWA **Americas Tag-Team title**
(with Crusher Verdu)
Won: February 28, 1976, over Gory
Guerrero and Chavo Guerrero
Lost: March 1976, to Butcher Vachon and
Chavo Guerrero
Regained: June 1976, over Butcher
Vachon and Chavo Guerrero
Lost: August 13, 1976, to Porkchop Cash
and Frank Monte

(with The Hangman)
Won: October 29, 1976, over Carlos and
Raul Mata
Lost: January 21, 1977, to Victor Rivera
and Cien Caras

(with Keith Franks)
Won: July 22, 1977, over Tom Jones and
Mando Guerrero
Lost: July 29, 1977, to Tom Jones and
Mando Guerrero

(with Chavo Guerrero)
Won: September 1977 over Black
Gordman and Goliath

Lost: November 2, 1977, to Black
Gordman and Goliath

(with Ron Bass)
Won: April 21, 1978, over Chavo Guerrero
and Black Gordman
Lost: May 26, 1978, to Hector Guerrero
and Black Gordman

(with Pak Choo)
Won: September 1, 1978, over Black
Gordman and Ryuma Go
Lost: October, 1978, to The Twin Devils

NWA **Americas Heavyweight title**
Won: March 12, 1976, over Chavo
Guerrero
Lost: April 23, 1976, to Chavo Guerrero

NWA **United States Heavyweight title**
(San Francisco)
Won: June 24, 1978, over Moondog
Lonnie Mayne
Lost: July 14, 1978, to Moondog Lonnie
Mayne

NWA Pacific Northwest Tag-Team title (with Killer Brooks)

Won: November 21, 1978, over Dutch Savage and Jonathan Boyd
Lost: April 3, 1979, to Adrian Adonis and Ron Starr

(with Rick Martel)

Won: March 29, 1980, over Bruce Miller and Luke Williams
Lost: May 12, 1980, to Bruce Miller and Luke Williams
Regained: August 5, 1980 (awarded titles when Bruce Miller and Luke Williams left the circuit)
Lost: August 10, 1980, to Buddy Rose and Ed Wiskosi
Regained: August 15, 1980, over Buddy Rose and Ed Wiskosi
Lost: September 12, 1980, to Rip Oliver and Fidel Cortez
Note: Mike Popovich replaced Rick Martel after Martel lost a loser-leaves-town match on August 16, 1980

NWA Pacific Northwest Heavyweight title

Won: February 17, 1979, over Jonathan Boyd
Lost: June 30, 1979, to Stan Stasiak
Regained: September 13, 1980, over Buddy Rose
Lost: September 20, 1980, to Buddy Rose

NWA Mid-Atlantic Television title

Won: November 1, 1980, over Paul Jones (tournament final)
Title vacated on January 27, 1981, when Piper wins the United States Heavyweight title
Regained: March 27, 1983, over Dick Slater
Lost: May 1, 1983, to Greg Valentine

NWA Mid-Atlantic Heavyweight title

Won: January 27, 1981, over Ric Flair
Lost: August 8, 1981, to Wahoo McDaniel
Regained: November 1, 1981, over Ricky Steamboat
Lost: May 10, 1982, to Jack Brisco
Regained: July 7, 1982, over Jack Brisco
Lost: August 3, 1982, to Jack Brisco

NWA United States Heavyweight title (Mid-Atlantic)

Won: April 16, 1983, over Greg Valentine
Lost: May 1, 1983, to Greg Valentine

WCW United States Heavyweight title

Won: February 8, 1999, over Bret Hart
Lost: February 21, 1999, to Scott Hall

WWF Intercontinental Heavyweight title

Won: January 19, 1992, over The Mountie
Lost: April 5, 1992, to Bret Hart

Long before he starred in John Carpenter's sci-fi action film *They Live* (1988), Roddy Piper was already an actor of tremendous range and intensity. When wrestling first got big in the 1980s, Piper was the sport's foremost heel; his performances in the ring and on the microphone could incite a crowd to heights of hatred previously reserved for South American dictators.

When Hulk Hogan was wrestling's superhero, Roddy Piper was his arch-nemesis. He was The Joker in a red kilt — a dangerous psycho with an evil, twisted grin, who lived only to destroy Hogan and to taunt every man, woman, and child who cheered when he performed.

In interviews, whether he was giving or receiving, Piper would work himself into such a manic state that he seemed only seconds away from a straitjacket. But for all his crazed tantrums, he was also a formidable adversary. Hey, any guy who could wear a kilt to the ring *had* to be pretty tough.

Though you may have hated Piper if you were a Hogan fan, you also kinda looked forward to his appearances, knowing he would bring out the best in your hero. From 1984 to 1986, these two men rode the crest of the biggest wave of popularity that wrestling had ever seen.

Since he doesn't have a Scottish accent, some fans might think the claim that Piper's birthplace is Glasgow, Scotland, is merely an invented detail of his professional persona. But Piper, whose real name is Roderick Toombs, actually *was* born in Glasgow — and he really does play the bagpipes. His family moved to Toronto when Roddy was five years old. His home life wasn't a very happy one, and young Roddy ran away at the age of 13, spending several weeks sleeping on the streets, or in youth hostels when he could afford the 25¢ admission.

An uncle of a friend of Piper's promoted fights in Manitoba, and through him Piper entered an open tournament offering a $25 purse. "I wasn't fighting for sport, I was fighting for my life — for a decent place to sleep and warm clothes to wear and something to eat," he has explained. "I learned to hide all my emotions under a mask of aggression." Piper won his first match and went on to compete in both boxing and wrestling matches throughout his teenage years.

When he was 15 years old, Piper earned another $25 by wrestling Larry "The Axe" Hennig, a veteran grappler who disposed of Piper in about 10 seconds. But wrestling offered paychecks that were steady, albeit small, and Roddy continued to work as a jobber in Winnipeg, Toronto, and various other centers across Canada. He used his real name at first, since it wasn't important that anyone remember it. In the early 1970s, however, he decided to make wrestling a career and, inspired by his Scottish heritage, began calling himself Roddy the Piper.

By 1975, when he entered the NWA's Los Angeles territory as the new heel in town, he'd shortened the name to Roddy Piper. At the same time, and often on the same card, he would also appear in the more popular persona of The Masked Canadian. In 1976, he won his first belt, the NWA Americas Tag-Team title alongside Crusher Verdu over the father-son team of Gory and Chavo Guerrero. Titles changed hands frequently back then: from 1976 to 1978, Piper enjoyed brief reigns as both United States champion and Heavyweight champion. He also held the Tag titles seven times with six different partners, most notably Keith Franks, with whom he would later feud in the WWF under Franks's new name, Adrian Adonis.

After wrestling countless matches in California against such greats as Mil Mascaras, Victor Rivera, and almost every member of the Guerrero family, Piper moved north to the NWA Pacific Northwest territory. He became a fixture at Portland, Oregon, events and liked the area so much that he later built a home there. He pinned Jonathan Boyd for the circuit's Heavyweight title and teamed with Rick Martel to win the Tag belts; after Martel lost a loser-leaves-town match in August of 1980, Piper teamed with Mike Popovich. The two did not get along, however, and in less than a month they had dropped the belts to Rip Oliver and Fidel Cortez.

Playboy Buddy Rose did a one-week switch of his Heavyweight title with Piper, further polishing Piper's reputation before he graduated to the more prestigious NWA Mid-Atlantic division. Piper's brawling style again proved successful right away, even against the much-improved competition. He won a tournament for the vacant Television title, then beat Ric Flair in January of 1981 for the Heavyweight title. After holding the belt for more than six months — quite an accomplishment at a time when reigns usually survived just days or weeks — Piper lost to Wahoo McDaniel. Two months later, Piper regained the title over Ricky Steamboat.

Piper and Ric Flair, arguably the two most charismatic heels in wrestling history, formed a close friendship that was tested under fire when they toured the Dominican Republic together in 1982. Upon defeating local favorite Jack Vonino in the capital city of Santo Domingo, they were attacked by fans and suffered a variety of injuries. Some witnesses also reported that shots were fired by soldiers; whether this was done to disperse the crowd or to finish off Piper and Flair is still open to debate.

(Photo Credit: Marko Shark)

Before leaving the NWA ranks for good, Piper switched his Heavyweight title with Jack Brisco, the United States title with Greg Valentine, and the Television title with Dick Slater. In the summer of 1983, he fought a dog-collar match with Valentine, a contest that, due to its brutality, has since passed into wrestling legend. According to *Wrestling World*, the pair "left the ring flooded in blood."

In January of 1984, Rowdy Roddy Piper joined the World Wrestling Federation. The same month, Hulk Hogan pinned The Iron Sheik to win the WWF World Heavyweight title. Almost immediately, Piper was pushed to the forefront of the heel rankings and began feuding with Hogan. Hogan won almost every match, though many ended in DQ after one of Piper's allies — usually Paul Orndorff or Cowboy Bob Orton — joined the attack.

Piper and Hogan were ideal adversaries because they were two sides of the same coin. Both could bring 20,000 fans to their feet simply by talking, but on the technical side neither could do more than execute rudimentary holds and moves. Something in the clash of their personalities captivated not only longtime wrestling fans, but also people who had never watched a match before. Celebrities such as Mr. T and Cyndi Lauper joined them in their battles, and MTV broadcast *The War to Settle the Score* on February 18, 1985. In the main event, Hogan defeated Piper by DQ after Lauper and Mr. T interfered.

Hogan and Mr. T defeated Piper and Paul Orndorff in the main event of the first WrestleMania, held on March 31, 1985. He beat Piper again in November at the Wrestling Classic pay-per-view.

Rowdy Roddy Piper had become one of wrestling's most familiar faces, but his days as a champion were over. The man who had won multiple titles in every circuit he'd joined did not win a single belt in his first four years with the WWF. In fact, after his feud with Hogan cooled, he didn't even wrestle very often, though he appeared on every federation telecast with his "Piper's Pit" show — almost every week from 1983 to 1987 Piper would "interview" different wrestlers, though these exchanges would usually end in a challenge or a fight.

Some of the WWF's most memorable moments happened on "Piper's Pit." Among the highlights were Piper's horrible (but hilarious) roasting of living legend Bruno Sammartino and his attack on Jimmy "Superfly" Snuka, which involved bopping the islander on the head with a coconut. It was also in the Pit that Andre the Giant ripped the crucifix from Hulk Hogan's chest, setting the stage for their title match at WrestleMania III.

Mr. T was the favorite when he met the rowdy Scot in a boxing match at WrestleMania II. Piper promised to give up boxing and wrestling — "and even tiddly winks!" — if he lost. The match deteriorated into a comedic slugfest reminiscent of The Three Stooges, ending in the fourth round when Piper reverted to wrestling. He was disqualified, but nobody held him to his promises.

By now, Piper's uproarious antics had begun to win over the fans. When he announced his retirement in 1987, even the most fervent Hulkamaniac acknowledged that the WWF would not be as much fun without the man they now called "Hot Rod." Piper left the federation in appropriately grand style — before 90,000 screaming fans at WrestleMania III. He defeated Adrian Adonis with a sleeper hold in a hair-vs.-hair match and shaved Adonis bald with help from Brutus Beefcake, who thereafter billed himself as "The Barber."

In 1988, Roddy Piper starred in the critically acclaimed science-fiction film *They Live*. He played John Nada, a transient construction worker who uncovers an alien plot to infiltrate the planet Earth. His performance was well received, but other good roles did not follow. Like most wrestling retirements, Piper's proved less than permanent.

Piper made a surprise appearance at WrestleMania IV in 1989, hosting a "Piper's Pit" segment with talk-show loudmouth Morton Downey Jr. He joined the announcing team a few weeks later but gave no indication that he would return to the ring until SummerSlam, when he helped The Ultimate Warrior win the WWF Intercontinental title from Ravishing Rick Rude. Piper's first match after his return was at the November Survivor Series: he captained a team comprised of himself, The Bushwhackers, and Jimmy Snuka in a losing effort against Rick Rude, Curt Hennig, and The Rougeau Brothers.

Early in 1990, Piper coasted through a brief feud with Bad News Brown; it was all part of a failed effort to get Brown over better with the fans. The feud ended at WrestleMania VI in an inconclusive double count-out. After that, Piper returned to the broadcaster's table, where he stayed for over a year, until his old drinking buddy Ric Flair arrived. At the 1991 Survivor Series, Flair and Piper captained opposing teams. Flair, the only wrestler not disqualified after the ensuing brawl, was declared the winner.

In 1992, eight years after he had first joined the WWF, Rowdy Roddy Piper finally won a title. At January's Royal Rumble, he put The Mountie to sleep and won the Intercontinental belt. He was challenged by former champ Bret Hart, and their match was set for WrestleMania VIII. Though his feud with Hogan had already become legend, his match with Hart may have been Piper's finest WWF performance.

He was now a face, but still Piper could not resist reverting to street-fighting form during the match: he gouged Hart's eyes and even bit him; The Hit Man was left dazed and bloodied. When the referee became incapacitated, Piper went for the bell, planning to use it on his opponent. The 62,000 fans rose and protested; Piper hesitated, and then dropped the bell to a huge pop. The match continued, and Hart got the pin. Piper, in a rare moment of good sportsmanship, shook Hart's hand and raised it in victory.

It was a good note on which to retire (again), and Piper knew it. He stayed away from the ring for nearly two years, though he did serve as special referee in the Bret Hart-Yokozuna title match at WrestleMania X. Hip-replacement surgery in January of 1995 put on hold any plans for another comeback. Piper again played special WrestleMania referee, this time for the bizarre "I quit" match between Bret Hart and Bob Backlund.

In 1996, when WWF interim president Gorilla Monsoon was injured by Vader, Piper stepped in and immediately found himself drawn into a feud with Goldust. The result was a Hollywood-backlot brawl at WrestleMania XII, which started as a wrestling match but ended up like one of those stunt shows performed for tourists at movie studios. At one point, Piper tried to run Goldust down with a car!

Piper still seemed happy in his on-again, off-again affiliation with the WWF, which is why his walk-on at the end of a WCW pay-per-view in October of 1996 came as such a surprise. At the end of Halloween Havoc, after Hulk Hogan had pinned Randy Savage and crowned himself the true icon of wrestling, fans at the MGM Grand in Las Vegas heard the sound of bagpipes; it heralded the entrance of another icon, who begged to differ. The Hogan-Piper staredown in the ring was their first in 11 years, and Piper milked the moment for all it was worth. He chastised Hogan for his new attitude and worked in a few cheap shots about Hogan's receding hairline just for old time's sake.

A match between Hogan and Piper was set for Starrcade in December. Tony Schiavone and the other WCW announcers claimed that Piper was the one man Hogan had never defeated, which wasn't even close to being true. Still, the renewal of their classic feud drew impressive pay-per-view numbers. Piper, now the crowd favorite, controlled the nontitle match most of the way and put Hogan in the sleeper to win it.

Several follow-up appearances on *Nitro* ended with Piper being attacked by the entire NWO, a ploy to entice him into agreeing to a rematch. He accepted, and had Hogan beaten again at the February 1997 SuperBrawl until interference from new NWO member Randy Savage spoiled the victory. Piper then teamed up with The Four Horsemen (at the urging of an injured Ric Flair) to battle an NWO team at the March pay-per-view. The NWO team won, and Flair and Piper had a falling out not long afterwards that led to a singles match at Bash at the Beach. The match was not properly set up by a good storyline, and this suggested that WCW had already run out of ways to use Piper.

A few months later, Eric Bischoff borrowed a page from the WWF's playbook and made Piper interim president (Chairman J.J. Dillon had been assaulted by Hulk Hogan). His first act was to arrange a cage match between himself and Hogan at Halloween Havoc. The match, by far the most disappointing of their meetings, quickly became a sad spectacle: the two veterans were gasping for air within minutes of the bell. Piper won again with his sleeper, though both he and Hogan looked like they could use a nap.

A worked injury at the end of that cage match allowed Piper some time off, but, even after J.J. Dillon's return, the WCW still used Piper to arrange special matches and reverse screwjob decisions. In May of 1998, he ruled that Randy Savage could keep the WCW Heavyweight title after Hogan pinned him with help from Bret Hart. At the July Bash at the Beach, Piper participated in a chaotic cage match in which he was supposedly teamed with Savage against Hogan and Hart. The match ended with Piper pinning his own partner for the victory.

Currently, Piper turns up in WCW every few months, to arrange a match or take on an opponent who runs his mouth too much. Though he managed to win the United States title from Bret Hart in 1999, his reign was brief and his working of subsequent matches showed little of the fabled Hot Rod magic. But enjoy his appearances while they last, for when Roddy Piper does leave wrestling for good, the sport will have lost one of its most memorable characters.

REAL NAME:
Duane Johnson

ALSO KNOWN AS:
Rocky Maivia, Flex Cavana

BORN:
May 2, 1972, Honolulu, Hawaii

HEIGHT:
6' 4"

WEIGHT:
272 pounds

PROFESSIONAL DEBUT:
1995

PROFESSIONAL AFFILIATIONS:
The Nation of Domination, The Corporation

FINISHING MOVES:
the people's elbow, the rock bottom

USWA **Tag-Team title (with Bart Sawyer)**
Won: June 17, 1996, over Brickhouse Brown and Reggie B. Fine
Lost: July 15, 1996, to Brickhouse Brown and Reggie B. Fine

WWF **Intercontinental title**
Won: February 13, 1997, over Hunter Hearst Helmsley
Lost: April 28, 1997, to Owen Hart
Regained: December 8, 1997 (title surrendered by Stone Cold Steve Austin)
Lost: August 30, 1998, to Hunter Hearst Helmsley

WWF **World Heavyweight title**
Won: November 15, 1998, over Mankind (tournament victory)
Lost: January 4, 1999, to Mankind
Regained: January 24, 1999, over Mankind
Lost: January 31, 1999, to Mankind
Regained: February 15, 1999, over Mankind
Lost: March 28, 1999, to Stone Cold Steve Austin

Second-generation wrestlers are abundant in the two major federations; Curt Hennig, Randy Savage, Dustin Runnels, Dean Malenko, and Brian Christopher all learned the finer points from their fathers. But no other wrestler can claim a closer lineage to the sport than Duane Johnson, a.k.a. The Rock.

Johnson's grandfather was High Chief Peter Maivia, who competed in the NWA and the WWWF. His father, Rocky Johnson, held the WWF Tag-Team belts with Tony Atlas in 1983. His cousin is Jimmy "Superfly" Snuka. Even his grandmother was in on the action, working as a wrestling promoter in Hawaii. As Rocky Maivia, a name he fashioned to honor his father and grandfather, Johnson is the only third-generation wrestler in the WWF.

"My father wasn't adamantly against it, but he was against it," says Maivia of the idea that he might become a wrestler. At first it didn't seem to matter, since he was actually more interested in a career in football. He played defensive end and defensive tackle at the University of Miami from 1990 to 1995, but he injured his back prior to his senior year. Playing his final season despite the injury, his numbers suffered accordingly. "My stock went into the toilet," he recalls. "I wasn't even drafted."

He recovered sufficiently to play one season for the Calgary Stampeders in the Canadian Football League, wrestling during the off season under his real name. Unhappy on the Canadian gridiron, Duane Johnson finally made the commitment to wrestling. Putting aside his reservations, Rocky Johnson trained his son for six months. In 1996, Duane debuted in the USWA under the awful name of Flex Cavana. He won the Tag belts with Bart Sawyer, but when it became clear the USWA was headed for bankruptcy he jumped to the WWF. With his buffed physique, clean-cut look, and illustrious family heritage, he seemed a natural face, and that's how Rocky Maivia was introduced to WWF fans when he debuted at Madison Square Garden in November of 1996.

Though he proved an exceptionally talented wrestler, crowd response to early Maivia matches was indifferent at best. The announcers heaped praise upon young Rocky, touting him as one of the sport's brightest new stars even before he had managed to accomplish anything. He was permitted to defeat both Goldust and Crush at the Survivor Series — another federation attempt to bestow blue-chip status upon him. But it's the fans who make the final decision as to whether a wrestler will be put over, and in this case they weren't buying the hype.

In February of 1997, Maivia won the Intercontinental title, defeating Hunter Hearst Helmsley. This was the last straw for WWF fans, who resented Maivia's rapid rise to a title shot. The cheers sounded forced, and there were boos amidst the applause. Maivia lost the title to Owen Hart two months later and was then sidelined with a knee injury.

When Maivia returned that summer, he replaced Ahmed Johnson in the Nation of Domination, a collection of heels. Now the fans no longer had to restrain their derision, and they chanted "Rocky sucks!" with joyful abandon. When he squared off against Stone Cold Steve Austin, Maivia became the wrestler WWF fans most loved to hate.

The Rock (as he was now introduced), proved a natural villain; during interviews he would raise his eyebrow in comically sinister fashion and declare himself "the people's champion" while the arena echoed with jeers. He introduced three catchphrases, "Lay the smack down," "Know your role and shut your mouth," and "Smell what The Rock is cookin'," all of which are now part of his entrance soundtrack.

The Rock regained the Intercontinental belt when Austin decided he no longer wanted it. As The Nation's only titleholder, he began to assert his authority, much to the dismay of Nation leader Farooq. While he feuded with

Ken Shamrock, tensions between The Rock and Farooq escalated. The day after WrestleMania XIV, The Rock ousted Farooq and assumed control of The Nation. Owen Hart joined the new team at The Rock's request after an April 1998 pay-per-view.

Through the summer of 1998, The Nation and Degeneration X engaged in a series of battles, including a bloody streetfight in August that set the stage for SummerSlam. At SummerSlam, later that month, The Rock faced Triple H in a ladder match for the Intercontinental belt. Though the resulting action was not in the same league as that seen in the ladder matches between Shawn Michaels and Razor Ramon, Helmsley's victory over The Rock was the highlight of the pay-per-view.

And then, while almost no one was looking, The Rock became the superstar he'd hoped to become three years earlier. Seemingly overnight, the boos were transformed back into cheers. He still plays the same arrogant character, promising to flex the "people's eyebrow" before dropping the people's elbow on a stunned opponent. The move is certainly among the dumbest ever devised — it's a simple elbow drop — but when The Rock removes his elbow pad with a dramatic flourish the crowd loves it. It doesn't seem to matter that every opponent recovers immediately from the move.

The WWF, however, seemed to prefer him as a villain, and so The Rock joined Vince McMahon's stable of heels right after he won the Heavyweight title. Though "the people's elbow" is now called "the corporate elbow," it still brings a tremendous pop, and though The Rock dropped the title to Mankind in January of 1999, and to Stone Cold Steve Austin two months later, it's safe to say he won't be without it for long . . . if you smell what The Rock is cookin'.

RANDY SAVAGE

REAL NAME:
Randy Poffo

ALSO KNOWN AS: The Spider, The Executioner, The Destroyer, The Macho Man, Macho King, The Madness

BORN:
November 15, 1952, Sarasota, Florida

HEIGHT:
6' 2"

WEIGHT:
237 pounds

PROFESSIONAL DEBUT:
November, 1973

PROFESSIONAL AFFILIATIONS:
The Megapowers, New World Order, NWO Wolfpack

FINISHING MOVE:
the flying elbow drop

TITLES HELD

NWA **Southeastern Tag-Team title (with Lanny Poffo)**
1977

NWA **Mid-America Heavyweight title**
Won: January 3, 1978, over Dutch Mantell
Lost: April 1978, to Dutch Mantell
Regained: November 11, 1978, over Dutch Mantell
Lost: March 2, 1979, to Bobby Eaton
Regained: December 26, 1983, over Terry Taylor
Lost: April 1984, to Humongous

ICW **Heavyweight title**
Won: March 13, 1979, over Lanny Poffo
Lost: July 21, 1979, to Lanny Poffo
Regained: 1981, over Lanny Poffo
Lost: 1981, to Lanny Poffo
Regained: 1982, over Lanny Poffo
Lost: November 26, 1983, to Paul Christy

AWA **Southern Heavyweight title**
Won: March 17, 1985, over Jerry Lawler
Lost: May 7, 1985, to Jerry Oske
Regained: May 13, 1985, over Jerry Oske
Lost: June 3, 1985, to Jerry Lawler

WWF **Intercontinental title**
Won: February 8, 1986, over Tito Santana
Lost: March 29, 1987, to Ricky Steamboat

WWF **World Heavyweight title**
Won: March 27, 1988, over Ted DiBiase
Lost: April 2, 1989, to Hulk Hogan
Regained: April 5, 1992, over Ric Flair
Lost: September 1, 1992, to Ric Flair

USWA **Unified Heavyweight title**
Won: November 11, 1993, over Jerry Lawler
Vacated November 20, 1993, when USWA and WWF ended copromotion

WCW **World Heavyweight title**
Won: November 26, 1995 (tournament win)
Lost: December 27, 1995, to Ric Flair
Regained: January 22, 1996, over Ric Flair
Lost: February 11, 1996, to Ric Flair
Regained: April 19, 1998, over Sting
Lost: April 20, 1998, to Hulk Hogan

Randy Savage is to Hulk Hogan what The Rolling Stones are to the Beatles. Fans who discovered wrestling in the heyday of Hulkamania find it impossible not to think of the two stars in relation to each other. They rose to prominence in the WWF at the same time, they went to WCW at about the same time, and for more than a decade they remained two of the sport's most popular and successful draws. They have been tag-team partners and bitter rivals, but, in the final analysis, it will be Hogan's legacy that defines wrestling's second golden age, with Savage a candidate for first runner-up.

Yet, like The Rolling Stones, Savage can look back with pride on a career studded with accomplishments. He won championship belts in six different federations, something even Hogan never achieved. He developed his own greatest-hits medley of gimmicks — from his raspy-voiced "Ooooh, yeah!" exclamation to his glittery capes, cowboy hats, and wraparound goggles — which will all eventually find their way into the Wrestling Hall of Fame. Perhaps most impressive, he called himself "The Macho Man" 10 years after the Village People song came out and nobody laughed.

He was born Randy Poffo, the son of Hall of Fame wrestler Angelo Poffo. Randy's brother, Lanny, set out to follow his father's example, but baseball was Randy's sport. He played first base and outfield in the minor leagues for such franchises as the Chicago White Sox, Cincinnati Reds, and St. Louis Cardinals. One year he finished third in the league for home runs and runs batted in, but he never took a pitch in the majors.

A shoulder injury brought his big-league dreams to an end, so Randy packed away his baseball glove and gave the family business a go. In 1973, calling himself The Spider, he made his debut in the Florida State Heavyweight Federation. During his first match he pinned opponent Paul Christy. He bounced around various Southern circuits, primarily the Mid-South and the Kentucky-based International Championship Wrestling (ICW), taking the name Randy Savage in 1976.

Savage wrestled under his real name when he entered the NWA Southeastern circuit as tag-team partner to brother Lanny. Though they won the Tag titles, Savage didn't stay with the team for long. In 1978, as The Executioner, he won the NWA Mid-America Heavyweight belt from Dutch Mantell. At the same time, he continued to work the smaller circuits as both Randy Savage and The Destroyer. When Lanny Poffo jumped to ICW, Savage followed, switching the federation's World title with his brother in 1979.

It was in ICW that Randy Savage first began to build a reputation and a following. Though he continued to tour, he stayed with ICW until 1983. He held the World title three times, pinning his brother to win the belt at the beginning of every reign. He fought the great Ricky Starr and the odd Gypsy Joe and then lost his ICW title to Paul Christy, the man he had pinned at his pro debut 10 years earlier. In December of 1983, Savage took the NWA Mid-America Heavyweight title for the third time.

After an uneventful stint in the AWA in 1985, Savage entered the WWF and began developing the persona that he still uses. He was a heel early on

— one who preferred inflicting injuries on his opponents to simply pinning them. In the Wrestling Classic tournament of 1985, Savage disposed of Ivan Putski, The Dynamite Kid, and Ricky Steamboat before losing to The Junkyard Dog. His strong showing after just a few months in the federation was indicative of his rapid rise to featured matches.

In 1986, The Macho Man was joined on his walks to the ring by his wife, the lovely Miss Elizabeth (Elizabeth Heulette). She was, supposedly, a manager, but no one was going to confuse her with Bobby Heenan or Mr. Fuji. She didn't interfere in matches, and she didn't run smack on the microphone; in fact, she rarely spoke at all. Savage treated her more like a valet; Elizabeth would remove his cape and hold the ring ropes open for his entrance. When Savage lost a match, he would yell at Elizabeth and she would meekly try to calm him down.

Fans sympathized with the subservient Elizabeth, which increased Savage's heat as a heel. At the same time, Savage became more popular that ever, especially among the teenage boys in the arena, who couldn't wait to see his drop-dead gorgeous manager in her short, sexy dresses.

The Macho Man won the Intercontinental title from Tito Santana in February of 1986. It was Elizabeth, however, who was mainly responsible for his first good storyline. George "The Animal" Steele developed a crush on Miss Elizabeth; the slow-witted, hairy, turnbuckle-eating wrestler began to follow her around, and Savage lost several matches by leaving his opponent to attack Steele. But Steele was no real match for the athletic Savage, so The Macho Man took to wrestling Ricky Steamboat, a more worthy opponent, while The Animal went back to grazing outside the ring.

The Savage-Steamboat feud produced a classic series of matches, famous for their frequent momentum shifts, high-flying offense, quick reversals, and multiple near-falls. Most ended with Savage being disqualified for attacking Steele outside the ring. One of the first instances of Savage's "macho madness" occurred when he drove the ring bell into Steamboat's throat, leaving Steamboat gasping for air. The injury was supposed to be a work — a stunt to generate more interest in their upcoming WrestleMania III match — but Steamboat was actually hurt by the impact of the bell. Savage was unfazed: while Steamboat was being carried out of the arena on a stretcher he attacked him a second time.

WrestleMania III was a milestone in the history of the WWF and of wrestling in general, mostly because of its main-event match featuring Hulk Hogan and Andre the Giant. But those two titans were overshadowed that night by their opening act; Randy Savage and Ricky Steamboat electrified the 90,000 faithful in attendance with a tremendous wrestling exhibition (see The 10 Best Wrestling Matches of All Time, page 184). After a grueling 15-minute match, Steamboat pinned Savage and captured the Intercontinental title.

The Macho Man was still playing the heel, but his talent in the ring and the growing popularity of his manager compelled bookers to tinker with his image. A new storyline unfolded after Steamboat lost the Intercontinental belt to The Honky Tonk Man, who Savage then faced on a *Saturday Night's Main Event* telecast. When he was on the verge of victory, Savage was triple-teamed by The Honky Tonk Man and The Hart Foundation and subjected to one of Honky Tonk's balsa-wood guitar shots. A distraught Elizabeth dashed to the backstage area and emerged a few seconds later with Hulk Hogan, who made the rescue.

From this simple event emerged The Megapowers, a Hogan-Savage alliance comparable in its magnitude to a Superman-Batman team-up in a DC comic. The Macho Man also developed a new appreciation for Miss Elizabeth. When he waved her away from the ropes so he could hold them open for her, there were tears in her eyes; as I watched, I began to think announcer Gorilla Monsoon would start blubbering as well.

Savage's singles career also benefited from the partnership. Now second only to Hogan on the WWF depth chart, he drew a tremendous pop when he entered the ring to the classical strains of Elgar's "Pomp and Circumstance." The Macho Man may be the only person ever to march to that music without being en route to pick up a diploma.

(Photo Credit: Seth Poppel Yearbook Archives)

"Randy Poffo" as he appeared in his high school yearbook

It is interesting to note that Lanny Poffo also joined the WWF around this time but never rose above midcard status. He first played "Leapin'" Lanny Poffo and then tried out two more characters: as the poet laureate of the WWF, he would open each match with four lines of insulting verse about his opponent; when that didn't work, he became "The Genius," a heel who won by outthinking his rivals. But even a surprise victory over Hulk Hogan on a *Saturday Night's Main Event* could not ignite his career. His relation to Savage was never mentioned, and the brothers rarely faced each other in the ring.

Hogan dropped the Heavyweight title to Andre the Giant in 1988; Andre's attempt to give the belt to manager Ted DiBiase resulted in the title being declared vacant. A tournament to find a new champion was set for WrestleMania IV. After Hogan and Andre eliminated each other in a first-round double-DQ match, it was Macho Man Randy Savage who took center stage, defeating Butch Reed, Greg Valentine, The One Man Gang, and Ted DiBiase to capture the Heavyweight title.

Hogan seemed elated at his partner's victory, and they continued to wrestle as The Megapowers while Savage defended the title against all comers. The big tag match of summer 1988 was Hogan and Savage vs. Ted

DiBiase and Andre the Giant. At SummerSlam, Elizabeth played a more substantial role than usual by removing her skirt to distract DiBiase, which allowed Savage to roll him up for the pin.

Since Elizabeth always accompanied The Megapowers, it made sense for her to start managing Hogan in his singles matches as well. The ever-gallant Hulkster always treated her like a lady, but those hugs after his victories stirred jealousy within The Macho Man, and thus began a tale of romance and heartbreak that became the WWF's answer to *Knot's Landing*. The love triangle turned violent on *Friday Night's Main Event*, a primetime broadcast in which The Megapowers faced The Twin Towers (Akeem and The Big Boss Man). During the match, Hogan was hurled out of the ring and directly into Elizabeth. Since the diminutive beauty had never taken a bump before, the incident stunned the crowd. Elizabeth was knocked unconscious, and a tearful Hogan carried her backstage for medical treatment. Savage, left alone in the ring, lost the match and blamed Hogan. While Elizabeth was tended to by paramedics, Savage attacked his partner, finalizing the heel turn that had been brewing for weeks.

The main event for WrestleMania V was Hogan vs. Savage, and the question on every fan's mind was which wrestler would receive Elizabeth's support. When she announced her allegiance to Hogan, Savage hired a new female manager, "Sensational" Sherri Martel. Hogan pinned The Macho Man to regain the Heavyweight title, and the belt remained with Hogan for the rest of the year. Savage feuded with Brutus Beefcake, who referred to Martel as "Scary Sherrie." He also teamed with Zeus (Tiny Lister), Hogan's costar in the 1989 film *No Holds Barred*, but it didn't boost ticket sales.

After defeating Hacksaw Jim Duggan for the King of the Ring title, Savage temporarily changed his billing to "Macho King" Randy Savage. The first feud of his royalty phase was against Dusty Rhodes, but it only got interesting when the WWF staged a rare mixed-tag match at WrestleMania VI. Savage and Sherri faced Rhodes and his female manager, Sapphire. Distraction in the form of a surprise appearance by Elizabeth cost Savage's team the match.

At the 1991 Royal Rumble, Savage asked The Ultimate Warrior for a shot at his Heavyweight title and was turned down. He retaliated later that night by interfering in The Warrior's match with Sgt. Slaughter. Savage broke his royal sceptre over The Warrior's head, allowing Slaughter to get the pin and win the title.

Savage and Elizabeth had been apart for more than a year, and the time had come for them to reunite in some dramatic fashion. At WrestleMania VII, The Macho Man lost a classic retirement match to The Ultimate Warrior. Sherri lit into the beaten Savage, but Elizabeth emerged from the crowd to make the save, and she and her man left the arena together. Honoring the retirement stipulation of the match, Savage became a commentator for the WWF, and during a summer telecast he proposed to the woman who was already his wife in real life.

The wedding of Randy Savage and Elizabeth, the "match made in heaven," was presented on SummerSlam. It was a surprisingly straightforward affair; Elizabeth looked radiant in her bridal gown, and Savage went formal, though he still wore a white cowboy hat. The Undertaker and Jake "The Snake" Roberts disrupted the reception, and Savage was given permission to wrestle Roberts. One of their matches escalated into a feud, and by 1992 everyone had forgotten that Savage was supposed to be in retirement.

The arrival of Ric Flair in 1992 provided The Macho Man with a fresh feud, which was triggered by Flair's claim that he'd had intimate knowledge of The Macho Man's wife. Flair's threat to display pictures of their affair proved empty, and Savage defeated him in a title match at WrestleMania VIII. He lost the title back to Flair a few days later. In subsequent matches, Savage was victimized by outside attacks from Flair and Curt Hennig. Savage lost in a summertime title match after passing out as a result of Flair's figure-four leglock. He continued to wrestle until the Royal Rumble, and then he retired once again.

The Macho Man returned to his commentator duties for the better part of the next two years. He became a last-minute replacement for the departed Curt Hennig at the 1993 Survivor Series and had a brief feud with Crush that ended in a falls-count-anywhere match at WrestleMania X. In late 1994, he followed the money — and Hulk Hogan — to WCW, where he was again paired with his old partner in The Megapowers against The Dungeon of Doom.

The WWF feud between Savage and Ric Flair was renewed when Flair attacked Savage's 80-year-old father, Angelo Poffo. Matches with Flair dominated the rest of 1995. Savage won the World War III battle royal for the vacant WCW World title but lost it to The Nature Boy one month later at Starrcade.

Some confusion arose as to how best to utilize Randy Savage in WCW, and though he's remained a prominent player since his arrival, the fans were unsure at that point whose side he was on or how long he would stay there. The return of Elizabeth — who had since become Savage's ex-wife — seemed a step in the right direction, but the reunion turned out to be a ploy: Elizabeth set up Savage for an attack by Flair and The Four Horsemen. After Hogan and Elizabeth revealed their loyalty to New World Order, Savage was promoted as the one man who could withstand their invasion and fight for WCW. He was attacked every week on *Nitro* — the telecast usually ended with The Macho Man face down in the ring, the calling card "NWO" spray painted on his back. At the 1996 Halloween Havoc, Savage lost to Hogan in the main event and then disappeared for the rest of the year.

With Savage gone, Diamond Dallas Page became the WCW's last best hope — and the NWO's favorite whipping boy. When The Macho Man came back, he fought alongside Sting, then he joined the NWO and attacked Page, none of which made any sense. Still, some of the Savage-Page matches had their moments, especially after Elizabeth and Page's wife, Kimberly, got caught up in the war.

Savage quickly tired of his NWO membership and jumped to NWO Wolfpack, though he never played a clearly defined role in either organization. He enjoyed another reign as World champion after pinning Sting in April of 1998, but he lost to Hogan one month later. Injuries have kept him out of commission lately, but when Randy Savage is healthy he can still electrify a crowd with his speed and daring. During an otherwise dull cage match at the 1998 Great American Bash, he brought the fans to their feet when he performed a flying axe handle from the top of a ten-foot cage.

RANDY SAVAGE

REAL NAME:	Kenneth Wayne Kilpatrick (later legally changed to Shamrock)
ALSO KNOWN AS:	Vinnie "Mr. Wrestling" Torelli, The World's Most Dangerous Man
BORN:	February 14, 1965, Warner Robins, Georgia
HEIGHT:	6'
WEIGHT:	220 pounds
PROFESSIONAL DEBUT:	1989
PROFESSIONAL AFFILIATIONS:	The Corporation, The Union
FINISHING MOVE:	the ankle-lock submission

TITLES HELD

wwf **King of the Ring 1998**

wwf **Intercontinental title**
Won: October 12, 1998, over Hunter
Hearst Helmsley
Lost: February 14, 1999, to Val Venis

wwf **Tag-Team title**
(with The Big Boss Man)
Won: December 14, 1998, over The New
Age Outlaws
Lost: January 25, 1999, to Owen Hart and
Jeff Jarrett

Ken Shamrock has been called the epitome of the modern gladiator. His specialty is pankration, a form of hand-to-hand combat first practiced by the ancient Greeks. When the modern Olympic Games were inaugurated in 1906, boxing and wrestling were revived as events but pankration was not because it was deemed too barbaric. Shamrock plied his trade instead in bar fights and streetfights and in the Japanese Pancrase circuit. He has defeated the world's best fighters and martial artists, including Masami Funaki, Bas Rutten, Royce Gracie, and Dan "The Beast" Severn.

Shamrock brought his skills to the wwf in 1996, though he won't be using all of them. "No one in the wwf could even come close to Shamrock in a legitimate match," says wrestling historian Mike Chapman. "Once he has an opponent in the ankle-lock submission, it's curtains; he'd either tap out or kiss his Achilles tendon goodbye."

But Chapman, who has studied the greatest wrestlers of the twentieth century, does not cap his praise there. "Ken Shamrock," he states, "is a guy who could have survived during the Frank Gotch era. He would have been a huge star in wrestling in the 1920s, '30s, and '40s. He's tough mentally and physically, he has incredible strength, he's extremely well-conditioned, he has a fierce pride, but he'd do a title switch if the money was right."

Kenneth Wayne Kilpatrick was born in Warner Robins, Georgia. He grew up in a hostile environment as the youngest of three boys, all of whom had a penchant for getting into trouble. After his parents separated, Ken went to live with his mother and brothers in a Savannah housing project, where fights were an everyday occurrence.

One of Shamrock's earliest memories, according to his fascinating 1998 autobiography, *Inside the Lion's Den*, was of being pulled out of his kindergarten class and dragged to the principal's office by his earlobe. He punched his teacher in the stomach then broke away and locked himself in an empty classroom. His new stepfather, an ex-army aviator who revered discipline, had little tolerance for such behavior. Every infraction committed by the Kilpatrick boys would result in a severe belt-lashing.

The family moved to Napa, California, when Ken was five years old, but the change of surroundings did nothing to change his attitude. His stepfather tried to steer the three boys into sports, hoping that such activity would provide them with a positive outlet for their aggression. Ken excelled at Little League baseball and Pop Warner football, but he would still join his brothers to fight and commit petty theft. He ran away from home for the first time at the age of 10 and wound up in the hospital after being stabbed by a teenage boy.

In 1977, the brothers were thrown out of their home. Ken was 13. The boys went their separate ways, and all of them landed in juvenile lockups; one eventually did time in the state penitentiary. Ken began to turn his life around after meeting Bob Shamrock, proprietor of the Shamrock Ranch, a facility for troubled boys in Susanville, California. Finding himself in a loving and caring environment for the first time, Ken responded by returning to school and rekindling his interest in sports. Bob Shamrock saw something special in the boy and encouraged him to make the right choices for his future.

In high school, Ken was the captain of his football team and an undefeated wrestler who seemed destined to win a state championship belt. But during a practice session he lost his balance while hoisting an opponent on his shoulders. He suffered a fractured vertebrae, and after surgery his doctors cautioned him against engaging in any strenuous activity for one year; they also advised him never to attempt contact sports again. Two months later, Ken was back at it, more determined than ever to succeed. When he turned 18, he was legally adopted by Bob Shamrock and took his benefactor's last name.

Ironically, the fighting skills that had brought Ken Shamrock so much trouble as a youth were the same skills that now furnished him with a career. Jobs as a bouncer, a bodyguard, and even a male dancer came and went, but then Shamrock began to distinguish himself in "toughman contests," informal tournaments in which the last man standing would win a small purse, usually one thousand dollars. He tried unsuccessfully to make the US Olympic Wrestling Team in 1988; the experience inspired him to attend professional wrestling academies in California and North Carolina.

In the spring of 1989, Shamrock made his wrestling debut on the South Atlantic circuit as a heel named Vinnie "Mr. Wrestling" Torelli. The pay wasn't great, so Shamrock supplemented his income by entering toughman contests — he won nearly every one he entered. At the suggestion of Dean Malenko, Shamrock tried out for Japan's Universal Wrestling Federation (UWF). He spent the next two years in Japan, wrestling for UWF and its Pancrase offshoot. In 1995, Ken Shamrock won the first Pancrase tournament and earned himself the title "King of Pancrase."

A form of pancrase, or pankration, came to America in 1993 with the Ultimate Fighting Championship (UFC). Unlike the events held by the WWF and WCW, UFC is shoot-fighting in its purest form, a no-holds-barred battle between two warriors. Shamrock competed in UFC between 1993 and 1996; he held the tournament's Superfight belt from July 14, 1995, until May 17, 1996, and won many more fights than he lost.

Though he would have preferred to remain with the UFC, Shamrock received an offer from the WWF that was too lucrative to pass up. He signed with the federation in February of 1997 and made his first significant WWF appearance as a guest referee at WrestleMania XIII for a match between Bret Hart and Stone Cold Steve Austin. When Hart refused to release his sharpshooter hold on Austin, Shamrock intervened. Thus began a series of unofficial confrontations between Shamrock and various WWF stars, all of which ended with the challenger tapping out of Shamrock's ankle-lock submission hold.

Ken Shamrock's first actual WWF match took place on April 6, 1997, against Vernon White, one of the students at Shamrock's Lodi, California, training facility, dubbed the Lion's Den. The match was a borderline shoot, which explains why Shamrock fought an opponent of his own choosing and not an established WWF wrestler. However, Shamrock found it hard to leave shoot-fighting behind. When he wrestled Vader one month later on a pay-per-view, Shamrock broke Vader's nose and temporarily disabled him — the Masked Mastodon was unable to walk for a week.

At SummerSlam 1997, Shamrock lost to The British Bulldog in a screwjob match. He "snapped" in the ring, attacking The Bulldog, the referee, and anyone who dared approach him. The fans roared, and Shamrock's rampages became a part of his character. The gimmick also allowed him to dominate more established WWF talent and then lose by disqualification so his opponents could keep their titles.

Shamrock was the crowd favorite in a series of matches against The Rock in early 1998. He then teamed with Steve Blackman for a few matches against The Nation of Domination. But it was the arrival of Dan "The Beast" Severn, Shamrock's UFC nemesis, that set the stage for a potentially classic feud. Severn, a Greco-Roman wrestling specialist, defeated Shamrock in

1996 and took his UFC Superfight belt after a controversial split decision. The rematch was supposed to take place not in UFC but in the WWF. Would the two veteran shoot-fighters stick to the script or fall back into old habits?

As it turned out, Severn was sidelined with a neck injury in the summer of 1998, leaving Shamrock's status unclear. He feuded with Owen Hart and looked impressive in a lion's-den match in which he and Hart battled in a round steel cage. The fans began turning against Shamrock, however, when he was sent into a three-way feud with Mankind and The Rock, both of whom were in the midst of face turns. Shamrock couldn't compete with their rising popularity, so he became the bad guy. He cemented his heel status by winning the Intercontinental title from Hunter Hearst Helmsley and joining Vince McMahon's corporation. Alongside The Big Boss Man, he helped defeat The New Age Outlaws for the Tag-Team titles.

REAL NAME:
Steve Borden

ALSO KNOWN AS:
Flash, The Stinger

BORN:
March 20, 1959, Venice Beach, California

HEIGHT:
6' 2"

WEIGHT:
260 pounds

PROFESSIONAL DEBUT:
1985

PROFESSIONAL AFFILIATIONS:
PowerTeam USA, The Blade Runners, The Four Horsemen, NWO Wolfpack

FINISHING MOVES:
stinger splash, scorpion deathdrop, scorpion deathlock

TITLES HELD

UWF **Tag-Team title**
(with Eddie Gilbert)
Won: July 20, 1986, over The Fantastics
(Tommy Rogers and Bobby Fulton)
Titles held up in dispute on August 17, 1986
Regained: August 31, 1986, over The Fantastics
Lost: September 27, 1986, to The Fantastics

(with Rick Steiner)
Won: April 12, 1987, over Terry Taylor and Chris Adams
Lost: May 17, 1987, to The Lightning Express (Brad Armstrong and Tim Horner)

NWA **Television title**
Won: March 31, 1989, over Mike Rotunda
Lost: September 3, 1989, to The Great Muta

NWA **Heavyweight title**
Won: July 7, 1990, over Ric Flair
Lost: January 11, 1991, to Ric Flair

WCW **United States Heavyweight title**
Won: August 25, 1991, over Steve Austin
(tournament win)
Lost: November 19, 1991, to Rick Rude
Regained: June 18, 1995, over Meng
(tournament win)
Lost: November 13, 1995, to Kensuke Sasaki

WCW **World Heavyweight title**
Won: February 29, 1992, over Lex Luger
Lost: July 12, 1992, to Big Van Vader
Regained: March 11, 1993, over Big Van Vader
Lost: March 17, 1993, to Big Van Vader
Regained: December 28, 1997, over Hulk Hogan
Title declared vacant on January 8, 1998, due to a controversial decision
Regained: February 22, 1998, over Hulk Hogan
Lost: April 19, 1998, to Randy Savage
Regained: April 26, 1999, over Diamond Dallas Page
Lost: April 26, 1999, to Diamond Dallas Page

WCW International Heavyweight title
Won: April 17, 1994, over Rick Rude
Lost: May 1, 1994, to Rick Rude
Regained: May 22, 1994, over Vader
Lost: June 23, 1994, to Ric Flair

WCW Tag-Team title
(with Lex Luger)
Won: January 22, 1996, over Harlem Heat (Booker T and Stevie Ray)
Lost: June 24, 1996, to Harlem Heat

(with The Giant)
Won: May 17, 1998, over The Outsiders (Scott Hall and Kevin Nash)
Sting pinned The Giant in a singles match for control of the titles on June 14, 1998; he then chose Kevin Nash as his new partner
Lost: July 20, 1998, to The Giant and Scott Hall

Call Sting "the franchise," because that's what he's been to World Championship Wrestling before and after its separation from the NWA. While Ric Flair, Lex Luger, The Steiner Brothers, Arn Anderson, and Dusty Rhodes all defected to the brighter spotlight of the WWF in its heyday, Sting remained WCW's most loyal company soldier.

Through good storylines and bad, Sting was almost always the crowd favorite. His speed and athleticism were his greatest weapons in the ring, but what put Sting over with the fans were his unbridled enthusiasm and the joy he seemed to manifest in performing. His smile disappeared in 1996, as did his colorful ring garb and blond buzzcut. The new Sting was a dark avenging angel who never talked and hardly ever wrestled. Inexplicably, he became more popular than ever. I guess Sting is destined to be a face, no matter what type of face paint he wears.

College basketball star Steve Borden received his first wrestling training from Hall of Famer Red Bastien. In 1985, he began wrestling in his native California as a member of PowerTeam USA, a four-man outfit that also included Jim Hellwig, later known as The Ultimate Warrior. After PowerTeam dissolved, Borden and Hellwig remained together as the tag team Rock and Flash, a.k.a. The Blade Runners.

Flash became Sting when the young team joined the UWF promotion, but The Blade Runners didn't last long. Hellwig, after the first of what would be many disputes with federation presidents and promoters, left to join the World Class promotion. Sting won the UWF Tag belts alongside Blade Runner allies Eddie Gilbert and Rick Steiner, but his career didn't take off until he went solo in mid-1987.

By then, the UWF were booking cards with the more prominent NWA, and Sting started getting noticed after he feuded with Lex Luger, then the NWA's United States champion. Promoters noticed the heat generated by this relative newcomer and put Sting on the fast track to stardom by allowing him to challenge the already legendary Ric Flair.

After weeks of Sting and Flair taunting one another, the match was set for World Wide Wrestling in February of 1988. The Nature Boy won but had to be carried out on a stretcher after Sting applied his scorpion hold, a Boston-crab variation, and refused to break it for nearly three minutes.

STING

The rematch, held at Clash of the Champions on March 27, 1988, ranks right up there on the list of Sting's career highlights. Flair brought his ring savvy, his figure-four leglock, and his bag of dirty tricks; Sting countered with his quickness, the scorpion, and stinger splashes, high-impact dives into Flair's chest. The 45-minute time limit expired, and both men left the ring knowing they had fought in a war.

Less than two years into his NWA career, Sting was already a headliner. He joined with Luger to fight The Road Warriors during their brief heel turn and won the NWA World Television title over Mike Rotunda in March of 1989. But it was his battles with The Horsemen that occupied most of Sting's time until the much-heralded arrival of The Great Muta.

Already a sensation in Japan, Muta combined martial arts with daring aerial maneuvers and the unique gimmick of shooting colored mist from his mouth to blind or disorient his opponent. Sting's title match with Muta took place at the January 1989 Great American Bash and more than lived up to the advance hype. Sting won, but due to extenuating circumstances (the referee caught Muta's spray and had to be replaced) the title was held up. Later on the same card, Muta interfered in the World title match between Ric Flair and Terry Funk. Sting also returned to the ring, and by the time the dust had settled Flair and Sting had forgotten their past conflicts and joined forces.

By Halloween Havoc 1989, Sting had lost his title to Muta and Flair had been on the receiving end of numerous Terry Funk attacks. A tag match was held inside a steel cage so that Sting and Flair could exact revenge. After Muta was taken out with a crotch shot, hardcore vet Terry Funk found himself disabled by a vicious double-team effort; Flair put Funk in the figure four while Sting attacked him from above.

Outside of The Horsemen, however, no alliance between Flair and another wrestler tends to last very long. There was talk of Sting becoming a Horseman, but that lasted only until the NWA scheduled a Flair-Sting title match at WrestleWar 1990. Sting was urged to forfeit the match to show "Horsemen loyalty." Instead, he attacked Flair and suffered knee injuries that kept him out of the match and out of action for six months.

Lex Luger was granted the title shot instead. A common enemy, The Horsemen, revived the friendship between Luger and Sting, and Sting stationed himself ringside to witness the action. "Come on and kick his you-know-what!" Sting yelled as Luger subjected The Nature Boy to his torture-rack finisher. But when Arn and Ole Anderson attacked Sting on the sidelines, Luger dropped Flair to rescue his friend. This led to a loss by count-out.

In July of 1990, Sting was finally given the kind of title match against Flair that he needed. Horsemen interference was neutralized by a no-DQ stipulation: Sting would be awarded the belt if they tried anything. If only this rule had been in place to counter those endless NWO interferences of the past few years!

The rematch lived up to its potential and ended when Sting fought off a figure four and caught Flair with an inside cradle for the pin. In a memorable postmatch interview, Sting paid tribute to his opponent: "Ric Flair is the greatest World champion of all time. I am a champion for one night and one night only, because I have some big shoes to fill."

Sting held the title through rematches with Flair and a new feud with Sid Vicious but faced an intriguing new challenger in September of 1990. The Black Scorpion, a mysterious masked wrestler who claimed to know Sting from his days in California, issued a title challenge. The storyline went over huge with the fans, who eagerly tried to guess the identity of the man behind the mask. Was it Flair? Arn Anderson? Sting's old tag partner, The Ultimate Warrior?

During a Clash of the Champions event, Sting grabbed at the mask. It appeared the mystery would end there, but then a second Black Scorpion appeared in the arena. The NWA had several wrestlers wear the Scorpion garb at house shows; usually he was played by Ole Anderson, though Sting's opponent that night was Al Perez. Of course, the fans were supposed to believe it was always the same guy, and a few marks probably did.

The story climaxed at Starrcade 1990 when Sting faced his masked opponent in a steel cage surrounded by four additional masked Scorpions. The number proved to be a tip-off as Sting got the pin and pulled away the mask of his pinned adversary to reveal the face of Ric Flair (though this was the first and only time Flair had worn it). Less than a month later, Flair defeated Sting without a mask to regain the title.

Alongside Lex Luger, Sting participated in a classic tag match with The Steiner Brothers at the 1991 SuperBrawl that ended in a loss due to interference from Nikita Koloff. A feud with Koloff ensued that lasted through the summer, by which time Sting had won his first United States championship belt. He then began receiving giant gift boxes out of which would appear other wrestlers, such as Cactus Jack and Abdullah the Butcher. The sender was later revealed to be The Dangerous Alliance, which had been formed by Rick Rude and Paul E. Dangerously. Rude got a shot at Sting's United States title and won it with help from Heavyweight champion Lex Luger, who had just turned heel.

A victory at the BattleBowl battle royal put Sting first in line to challenge Luger. At SuperBrawl, a surprisingly one-sided match between former friends ended when Sting nailed Luger with a flying body-press and won the title.

The next challenge came from Vader; the usual feud was inaugurated, but it turned nasty after Vader power-slammed Sting with a little extra authority. Sting suffered broken ribs and a bruised spleen, which put him out of action until May of 1992. Two months after his return, Sting again faced Vader, this time at the July Great American Bash. Fans familiar with the storyline would've bet the mortgage on a Sting victory, but Vader won again after Sting mistimed a stinger-splash attempt and whacked his head on the ringpost.

A rematch was lined up, but Sting was forced to forfeit after being attacked by Jake "The Snake" Roberts, who made a memorable WCW debut by landing two DDTs on the federation's franchise player. Ron Simmons stepped in for Sting and defeated Vader, becoming the first African American Heavyweight champion in wrestling history. Sting vs. Jake Roberts was wrestling's summer of 1992 draw. The feud culminated in a match at that year's Halloween Havoc; Jake got bit by his own snake and slithered out of WCW, never to return.

Sting then resumed his feud with Vader, one of the longest of his career. At one point, he won the title back only to lose it again three days later. Along the way, he was distracted by Vader's occasional tag partner, Sid Vicious. Throughout 1993, Sting had his hands full with the two giants, but both feuds faded out with little fanfare. He went through the motions again with Rick Rude, then with Vader, and finally with Ric Flair after The Nature Boy returned from his WWF sabbatical. By this time, however, it was clear that Sting, and indeed WCW, was in a rut.

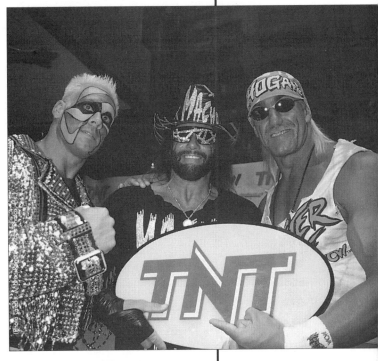

Sting, Randy Savage, and Hulk Hogan

That would all change in 1994 with the arrival of Hulk Hogan. As soon as the signing was announced, what the fans began to anticipate most was a Sting-vs.-Hogan match, a first-time battle between two of the most recognized wrestlers of the era. Since both were faces, however, it would take awhile before they could hook up under convincing circumstances.

Instead, Hogan immediately went after Ric Flair and was soon holding Heavyweight gold. Sting competed in a triangle match with Vader and The Guardian Angel to become the number-one contender, but he lost due to outside interference. It seems that WCW still wasn't ready for Hogan vs. Sting. At the 1994 Halloween Havoc, Hogan's cage match with Ric Flair ended in chaos when Hogan was attacked by The Butcher, Kevin Sullivan, and Avalanche. Sting raced to Hogan's rescue and would continue to help out in Hogan's war with Sullivan's "Faces of Fear." At the very least, it got them in the ring together.

In 1995, however, while Hogan usurped Sting as WCW's most prominent performer, the wrestler who had helped sustain the federation for a decade wasted his time in nickel-and-dime feuds with the likes of Avalanche and Big Bubba. In the fall, Lex Luger returned from his WWF stint and was allowed to get a title shot at Hogan by jumping the contenders line. Hogan achieved a tainted victory that again brought half the locker room rushing to the ring.

Fall Brawl was the scene of an uneasy alliance between Hogan, Randy Savage, Sting, and Luger, who defeated the team of Dusty Rhodes, Nikita

Koloff, and The Road Warriors. Meanwhile, there was apparent trouble within the ranks of The Horsemen: Flair appealed to Sting for help after being attacked by Arn Anderson and Brian Pillman. Flair pulled out all the stops in his amusing attempt to recruit his old foe; at one point, he even brought out a band of children to beg for Sting's help.

Ever the good guy, Sting agreed. But in the tag match pitting Sting and Flair against Anderson and Pillman, The Four Horsemen reunited and beat the gullible Stinger into a battered heap. The Nature Boy had put one over again.

Revenge was inevitable, because enough time had passed — a Flair-Sting match could once more generate some heat. The two veterans did not disappoint. This time, it was Sting scoring a convincing victory, after which he applied the scorpion deathlock to Flair, holding it for what seemed like several minutes. When Sting walked off with Lex Luger, whose association with The Dungeon of Doom was called into question, Hogan called Sting a traitor and (finally!) challenged him to a match.

On November 20, 1995, during a *Monday Nitro* telecast, Hulk Hogan wrestled Sting for the first time. One year of preparation was not enough for wcw to create a compelling storyline leading up to this historic clash, but most fans didn't care. For Hogan, it was the biggest match since the one he lost to The Ultimate Warrior and the first in which a clean pin on either side would mean something more than it usually did.

Sting walked to the ring garbed in red-and-yellow tights with matching face paint; whether this was a tribute to Hogan or an insult is open to debate. Hogan's music played but it was Randy Savage who emerged from backstage, drawing boos from the crowd. Hogan then came out of the crowd and the staredown began. The match pitted Hogan's power against Sting's finesse, and it appeared to be over when Sting trapped his opponent in the scorpion. "He's breaking my leg!" Hogan screamed in an atypical display of weakness, but the match ended in a DQ after The Dungeon of Doom interfered.

In January of 1995, Sting and Lex Luger won the wcw Tag titles from Harlem Heat, but their six-month reign was marred by confusion over whose side Luger was on. All wcw infighting stopped, however, after the arrival of the NWO and the revelation that Hogan had joined the upstart organization. As the NWO's declared purpose was the destruction of "wrestling tradition," Sting ranked high on the NWO enemy list. But as wrestler after wrestler sold out to the New World Order a wave of paranoia swept wcw, and even Sting did not remain above suspicion.

Two weeks before the 1996 WarGames, Sting attacked Lex Luger and there was speculation that he had joined the NWO. It was later proven that the "Sting" who had done the deed was a doppelgänger, but the real Sting found the accusations that had been hurled at him before the ruse was revealed impossible to forgive. At WarGames, he turned his back on wcw. The following night, on *Monday Nitro*, a new Sting appeared. He was dressed in black, with a painted-on white mask, and carried a plastic bat. The look was so reminiscent of Brandon Lee in *The Crow* (1994) that WCW was lucky not to be hit with a lawsuit.

Sting's new identity, in which he never showed emotion and rarely spoke, became an unlikely hit with the fans. He didn't even wrestle. For almost a year, Sting's television appearances would follow a standard pattern: just before the close of the three-hour *Nitro* telecasts (during which announcer Tony Shiavone would ask "Where is Sting?" about 50 times), Sting would lower himself on a cable from the roof of the arena, whack a few NWO members with his bat, and then fly back up into the rafters. Taking time off from house shows also gave Sting — or Steve Borden — the opportunity to star in a feature film, *The Real Reason*.

Ironically, by not wrestling, Sting restored the luster to his reputation. *Crow*-style Sting T-shirts became WCW's best-selling concession-stand items, and Sting once again found himself viewed as a larger-than-life persona who could match skills with anybody. As the countdown to Starrcade 1997 began, excitement escalated over Sting's return to the ring. The occasion was to be a climactic WCW-vs.-NWO battle with Hulk Hogan.

The WCW promotion department was pushed into overdrive; even the prematch press conference was aired live. The effort paid off: this would be the biggest pay-per-view broadcast in the federation's history. Sting, a little slower and heavier than he used to be, still showed few signs of ring rust during the battle. He dominated in the early stages, but Hogan responded with cheap shots and power moves — at one point it looked as if he had scored a clean pin. But Bret Hart, who had been appointed special referee for an earlier match, charged the ring and accused referee Nick Patrick of a quick count. He ordered the match to continue, and Sting scored the victory to claim the Heavyweight title.

Replays showed that Patrick's count wasn't that fast, but fans expected Sting to win his comeback match and WCW wasn't about to disappoint them. A jubilant Sting smiled for the first time in a year after the victory and then won a rematch the following night on *Monday Nitro*. In April of 1998, Sting lost the title to Randy Savage, who was helped by Bret Hart. He won the Tag-Team titles with The Giant, but after The Giant rejoined the NWO, Sting defeated him in a singles match for control of the belts. He followed Luger into the NWO Wolfpack and chose Kevin Nash as his new partner.

The Wolfpack Sting still dresses in black, but he's displaying all of his old zest and enthusiasm. An oft-delayed feud with Bret Hart is in the works for 1999, which — if handled right — could be the best angle both men have had in years.

THE ULTIMATE WARRIOR

REAL NAME:
Jim Hellwig (later legally changed to Warrior Jim Hellwig)

ALSO KNOWN AS:
The Rock, The Dingo Warrior

BORN:
June 16, 1957, Queens, New York

HEIGHT:
6' 3"

WEIGHT:
280 pounds

PROFESSIONAL DEBUT:
1985

PROFESSIONAL AFFILIATIONS:
PowerTeam USA, The Blade Runners, One Warrior Nation

FINISHING MOVE:
the warrior splash

TITLES HELD

WCWA **World Tag-Team title**
(with Lance Von Erich)
Won: November 17, 1986, over Matt Borne and Buzz Sawyer
Lost: December 1, 1986, to Al Madril and Brian Adias

WCWA **Texas Heavyweight title**
Won: February 2, 1987, over Bob Bradley
Lost: April 2, 1989, to Rick Rude

WWF **Intercontinental title**
Won: August 29, 1988, over The Honky Tonk Man
Lost: April 2, 1989, to Rick Rude
Regained: August 28, 1989, over Rick Rude
Vacated title after winning WWF Heavyweight title

WWF **World Heavyweight title**
Won: April 1, 1990, over Hulk Hogan
Lost: January 19, 1991, to Sgt. Slaughter

Most wrestlers leave their characters in the ring when the show is over, but The Ultimate Warrior blurs the line between fiction and reality. Jim Hellwig, the man who created the Warrior persona, often spouts the same quasimystical philosophy as his character even when he's not wearing face paint and spandex. Between his WWF glory days and his much-publicized comeback in WCW, he actually had his name legally changed to Warrior Jim Hellwig.

In keeping with the air of mystery that envelops the Warrior myth, Hellwig has released few details of his life prior to the establishment of his wrestling career. The Ultimate Warrior would prefer to have sprung from a bolt of lightning onto a Southwestern desert mountaintop and to have been raised by Native Americans who would train his body and spirit for a higher purpose. In the real world, though, Jim Hellwig was born in Queens, New York. He later divided his time between Atlanta, where he attended college, and Venice Beach, California, where he pursued his passion for weightlifting and competitive bodybuilding. At his peak, he could bench-press 500 pounds and deadlift 700 pounds. In 1985, Hellwig entered the Junior Mr. USA contest, but he was not pleased with where he placed in the competition. He returned to Atlanta, planning to complete the clinical requirements for a chiropractic degree.

Fate intervened via a phone call from Ed Connors, one of the owners of the Venice Beach Gold's Gym, where Hellwig often trained. Connors had a friend in Memphis who was looking for a bodybuilder type to complete a quartet of professional wrestlers called PowerTeam USA. Hellwig was a wrestling fan who fondly remembered following the exploits of The Crusher and Dick the Bruiser as he was growing up. He accepted the offer and made his wrestling debut as Jim "The Rock" Hellwig.

PowerTeam didn't last long, but two of its members, Hellwig and Steve "Flash" Borden, remained together and formed a tag team called The Blade Runners. They entered the UWF in 1986, and there Borden changed his ring name to Sting. Hellwig did not get along with Mid-South UWF boss Bill Watts, and so he moved on to the Texas-based World Class promotion, where he debuted as The Dingo Warrior.

He wore a variation of the face paint that he would later use as The Ultimate Warrior, but his hair was cut short and his style was more aggressive. Introduced by Gary Hart, a heel manager in the federation, The Warrior was a bad guy for his first few appearances, but soon he became a face and a close friend of The Von Erichs, the first family of Texas wrestling. With Lance Von Erich, he won the World Class Tag titles from Matt Borne and Master Gee, though their reign barely lasted one month.

The Warrior defeated Bob Bradley to become Texas Heavyweight champion and then received a call from Vince McMahon. He lost the title to Al Perez in June of 1987 to begin preparation for his WWF debut. In the autumn, he joined the sport's top federation as The Warrior and was being introduced as The Ultimate Warrior before the year's end.

The character was an immediate sensation, though the other wrestlers didn't know quite what to make of this wild man who would sprint to the ring, grab the ropes, and pump them furiously as though he was trying to tear them from the ring-post. "When I first came to the WWF all the veterans would constantly pull me aside and tell me to 'quit shaking the ropes, it looks stupid and weird,'" Hellwig recalled in an interview with Mike Tenay. "That became just another incident, out of hundreds, in my life, where I learned it's never stupid to go with what your intuition tells you, and it's always good to be a little weird."

The Warrior's rapid rise to prominence was marked by his being assigned a featured match in the following year's WrestleMania; there he defeated Herculez Hernandez. Just five months later, at SummerSlam, The

Ultimate Warrior pinned The Honky Tonk Man (a last-minute replacement for the injured Brutus Beefcake) in 28 seconds to win the Intercontinental title.

In 1989, The Warrior won a "posedown" over Ravishing Rick Rude, but then lost his Intercontinental belt to Rude with an assist from Bobby Heenan. He regained the title over Rude at SummerSlam that year and then scored some rare victories over Andre the Giant, usually by count-out after Andre was knocked out of the ring.

Early in his WWF career, The Warrior seldom did interviews, but champions still had to talk in the pre-Goldberg era, and gradually The Warrior developed one of the most unique raps in the business. He would launch into long, rambling, sometimes barely coherent sermons on his personal philosophy. "Warriorism is the living of life by realizing one is great by birth, and this greatness is inherent in one's being as a human," he once said. "One who strives to live as a warrior does so by utilizing his greatness, constantly developing the complete capabilities of it, both physically and mentally." Sometimes his interviews lasted longer than his matches!

Though the WWF was still reveling in Hulkamania, 1990 was truly the year of The Ultimate Warrior. He eliminated the mighty Hogan at the Royal Rumble and then faced the Heavyweight champion at WrestleMania. There was some animosity between the two — they had been tag partners at a *Saturday Night's Main Event* match and come to blows over a misunderstanding — but the match was a first of its kind for the WWF. When the federation's two most popular faces squared off, there was no way to predict who would win (see The 10 Best Wrestling Matches of All Time, page 186).

The match was dead even most of the way, but after each wrestler survived his opponent's finishing move, Hogan felt The Warrior splash for a second time and lost the title. "I will never forget that," Hellwig maintains. "It will be the highlight of The Ultimate Warrior's career." Jack Tunney, president of the WWF, declared that there would not be a rematch and that The Warrior's Intercontinental belt must be surrendered. The Warrior successfully defended the Heavyweight title in a cage match against Rick Rude then reteamed with Hogan at Survivor Series.

He lost the Heavyweight belt to Sgt. Slaughter at the 1991 Royal Rumble due to interference from Randy Savage, who was then in his "Macho King" heel phase. But it was Hulk Hogan, not The Warrior, who beat Slaughter and reclaimed the gold for the good guys of WWF at that year's WrestleMania; on the same card, The Warrior defeated Savage in a retirement match. Ironically, Savage's retirement proved much shorter than Hellwig's. After a lackluster feud with The Undertaker, The Ultimate Warrior vanished from the WWF.

He made a brief return in 1992 to beat Papa Shango and take on the unretired Savage for the WWF title at SummerSlam. Rumors circulated that the real Warrior had died and had been replaced by a look-alike. These rumors would haunt Hellwig for the remainder of his career. At WrestleMania VIII, he appeared again, to save Hogan from an attack by Shango. But on November 9, 1992, The Ultimate Warrior disappeared — this time, apparently, for good.

The reasons for The Warrior's departure vary depending on who's telling the story. Jim Hellwig had talked of his plans to take The Warrior into other media, including comic books, and of his desire to embark on a film career. Vince McMahon, however, expected The Warrior to maintain the same touring schedule as his other wrestlers, which left little time for side projects.

Hellwig and McMahon clashed again in 1993, over the ownership of the Warrior character. Hellwig filed a six-million-dollar lawsuit against the World Wrestling Federation, claiming that The Ultimate Warrior was his own creation, a variation of the Dingo Warrior character he had played prior to joining the WWF. The suit was settled by way of an agreement that allowed Titan Sports (the WWF's parent company) to utilize The Ultimate Warrior as a live wrestling persona and Hellwig to use the federation's marketing system for his other pursuits.

(Photo Credit: Tom Buchanan/Photofest)

He started Project Warrior, a company that would market the character through "Warrior Wear" and other products. He also established Warrior University, a wrestling school located near the Grand Canyon in northern Arizona. The facility functions as a multipurpose gym and learning center for the area's youth as well. Then Hellwig tried his hand at acting again by playing The Swordsman in *Firepower* (1997), a martial-arts/action film that has yet to be released.

It was not until July 22, 1995, that The Ultimate Warrior returned to the ring. The venue was an unlikely one: the Silver Nugget Casino in Las Vegas. He beat The Honky Tonk Man. From there he went on to participate in a show in Boston and a tour of Germany before making his first televised appearance back with the WWF. The Warrior destroyed Hunter Hearst Helmsley at the 1996 WrestleMania after kicking out of Helmsley's pedigree finisher. He defeated Intercontinental champion Goldust two months later but was then replaced by Sycho Sid for a full schedule of summer appearances. Hellwig contended that he missed a few appearances because his father was ill, but the WWF claimed he didn't inform the federation in advance of his no-shows and demanded he put up a performance bond. Hellwig refused to sign the bond contract and departed once again.

Rumors of The Warrior's return were never far from the surface in subsequent years, though Hellwig usually answered any inquiries with typically enigmatic comments. On August 17, 1998, Hulk Hogan stood in the ring during a WCW *Monday Nitro* broadcast and boasted that no wrestler, and no warrior, had ever defeated him. Suddenly, the lights dimmed and a familiar silhouette appeared at the entrance to the arena. Still in possession of a chiseled physique and an ability to deliver long diatribes on Warrior philosophy, Hellwig entered to a tumultuous ovation. He spoke for more than 15 minutes, and then he disappeared in a cloud of smoke.

After two months of speech making, Hogan and The Warrior finally had their rematch at Halloween Havoc. But the match, eight years in the making, did not live up to its advance publicity. A screwjob ending instigated by Hogan's nephew, Horace, helped The Hulkster avenge his earlier defeat. The Warrior vowed revenge 24 hours later on *Nitro*, but he apparently opted, instead, to return to the Arizona desert. His stock as a main-eventer dropped after that disappointing WCW stunt, but it's a good bet he'll turn up again, somewhere, to compete for a major title.

REAL NAME:
Mark Calloway

ALSO KNOWN AS: The Master of Pain, Texas Red, The Punisher, Mean Mark Callous, Cain the Undertaker

BORN:
March 24, 1962, Houston, Texas

HEIGHT:
6' 9"

WEIGHT:
328 pounds

PROFESSIONAL DEBUT:
1989

PROFESSIONAL AFFILIATIONS:
The Corporate Ministry, The Ministry of Darkness

FINISHING MOVE:
tombstone piledriver

TITLES HELD

USWA **Heavyweight title**
Won: April 1, 1989, over Jerry Lawler
Lost: April 25, 1989, to Jerry Lawler

USWA **Texas Heavyweight title**
Won: October 5, 1989, over Eric Embry
Lost: November, 1989, to Kerry Von Erich

WWF **World Heavyweight title**
Won: November 27, 1991, over Hulk Hogan

Lost: December 3, 1991, to Hulk Hogan
Regained: March 23, 1997, over Sycho Sid
Lost: August 3, 1997, to Bret Hart

WWF **Tag-Team title**
(with Stone Cold Steve Austin)
Won: July 26, 1998, over Kane and Mankind
Lost: August 10, 1998, to Kane and Mankind

Has there ever been a more dynamic, provocative wrestling character than The Undertaker? From his first WWF appearance in 1990, he has been one of the most recognizable faces in the sport and one of its most intimidating forces, even though he has rarely held a title. Though he seemed to emerge fully-developed from his debut, the passing years have added more layers to his mythos, resulting in one of the most detailed histories ever created for a character.

His ritual is as familiar to fans as the glare that bounces off Hulk Hogan's hairless dome. A bell tolls; the arena goes dark; fog fills the entrance as the somber first notes of Chopin's *Funeral March* (actually, his Sonata for Piano no. 2 in B-flat Minor) are heard. Out of the purple haze steps a tall figure dressed in a black, western-style costume, his face obscured by the brim of his hat and his long red hair.

His walk to the ring is impossibly slow. On special occasions, he is accompanied by an equally slow-moving band of druids, who carry torches to light his path. At the ring, the arena lights respond to the gesture of his outstretched arms. "You . . . will . . . rest . . . in . . . peace," he growls in a basso-profundo voice. During a match, The Undertaker seems virtually indestructible; he has been subjected to DDTs, ferocious clotheslines and flying forearms; and he will lie motionless in the center of the ring and then rise up, like Michael Myers in *Halloween*, to renew his assault, which culminates in a piledriver finishing move dubbed "the tombstone."

Everything about the persona screams "bad guy," but The Undertaker was quickly embraced by WWF fans, even after he scored an astonishing upset victory over Hulk Hogan to begin his first title reign as Heavyweight champion. This was one of the earliest instances in the modern wrestling era in which fans overruled a federation's choice of heroes.

Avid wrestling fans can recite The Undertaker's fictional history, but few know the identity of the person behind "the man from the dark side." Mark Calloway has kept a low personal profile since he debuted as The Undertaker, though reliable sources report that he is nowhere near as somber as his famous alter ego. Calloway was born in Houston, Texas (it's The Undertaker, of course, who's from Death Valley). He's married, he's a father, he likes motorcycles, and his favorite movie is *Night of the Living Dead* — which explains his character choice. To see Calloway without his Undertaker garb, rent the 1991 Hulk Hogan film *Suburban Commando*. (I know — that's a lot to ask.)

Calloway entered professional wrestling in 1989 as "The Master of Pain," a masked heel who was given a big buildup as an invincible monster and who went on to defeat Jerry Lawler for the Unified USWA World title. Lawler won the title back less than one month later, and The Master of Pain moved to USWA Texas. Still wearing a mask, he wrestled a few times as Texas Red then changed his name to The Punisher. Once again, he ascended to the Heavyweight title only to lose it within weeks.

But WCW scouts liked what they saw, and in 1990 Calloway became one of several new faces in the federation. Unfortunately, most of these wrestlers were hired to help put the established stars over, and Calloway, billed as "Mean Mark Callous," seemed stranded at the midcard level. When Sid Vicious suffered an injury, however, Calloway was invited to join Dan Spivey in The Skyscrapers, an up-and-coming tag team. When Spivey left, Calloway returned to singles competition. His equation for success was "MM + HP = WC," which meant "Mean Mark + heart punch = World champ." The heart punch, his first finishing move, was later outlawed. Just before Calloway's contract expired (later in 1990), he pinned Lex Luger at the Great American Bash. It was his most impressive showing to date.

When WCW declined to pick up his contract, Calloway was invited to join the World Wrestling Federation. He debuted at dark shows as "Cain the Undertaker," and was managed by Brother Love. But by the 1990 Survivor Series, his "official" debut, "Cain" had been dropped, and "The Undertaker" was introduced as an associate of The Million Dollar Man, Ted DiBiase.

(Photo Credit: Rich Freeda/Photofest)

He was the baddest of bad guys early on, a force of nature whose slow, methodical attack decimated the WWF's roster — he defeated Superfly Jimmy Snuka, Hacksaw Jim Duggan, and the portly Tugboat. Chair shots bounced off him like nerf balls; his walk across the top ring rope, the precursor to a devastating blow to an opponent's back, demonstrated a balance and grace never before seen in a wrestler the size of The Undertaker. And though Calloway wasn't exactly a barrel of laughs in any of his previous personas, as The Undertaker he buried his emotions along with his opponents, rendering the psychological strategies and intimidation techniques of others completely useless.

A supernatural quality was added to the character when The Undertaker was joined by aptly named manager Paul Bearer, who carried an urn to the ring that supposedly contained the ashes of The Undertaker's parents. According to the fiction, The Undertaker lived in his family's funeral home. After his parents died in a fire, he had been raised by Paul Bearer. The Undertaker drew strength from the urn; his power was sapped when it was stolen, as it was on numerous occasions. Bearer — real name William Moody — was a friend of Calloway's who played a cross between Peter Lorre and Dom DeLuise.

After scoring a pin, The Undertaker and Paul Bearer would stuff the beaten opponent into a body bag — a memorable gimmick, to say the least. They initiated a feud with The Ultimate Warrior until his departure from WWF and then set their sights on champion Hulk Hogan. During his "Funeral Parlor" interview segment, The Undertaker yanked off the cross Hogan wore on a chain around his neck, thereby earning himself megaheel status. After a few inconclusive televised matches, The Undertaker scored a stunning pin on Hogan at the 1991 Survivor Series, albeit with the assistance of Ric Flair. Hogan regained the belt a few days later, but such a victory so early in his WWF career propelled The Undertaker to a stature level from which he has never slipped.

In December 1991, The Undertaker prevented his occasional ally Jake "The Snake" Roberts from hitting Randy Savage's manager, Elizabeth. Thus began his face turn, which culminated in a victory over Roberts at the 1992

WrestleMania. His brief feud with Kamala that year led to the very first "casket match," which would become an Undertaker specialty. The object is to roll a dazed opponent into a coffin just outside the ring and shut the lid.

Harvey Whippleman, then Kamala's manager, embarked upon a crusade to destroy The Undertaker. He brought in a new wrestler billed as The Giant Gonzalez. The guy was huge, but in terms of agility he made Andre the Giant look like Rey Misterio. However, he did score a screwjob victory over The Undertaker by knocking him out with chloroform. The Undertaker took the rematch and then set his sights on the WWF's new Heavyweight champion, Yokozuna.

Though the two faced off in The Undertaker's favorite type of contest — the casket match — Yokozuna was able to retain his title by depositing The Undertaker in the casket with help from his manager, Mr. Fuji, Jim Cornette; and a gathering of heel wrestlers. The Undertaker's mystique was revived after he supposedly vanished from the casket — this also allowed Calloway to take some much-needed time off.

"Where is The Undertaker?" was a question asked for months during every WWF broadcast. Finally it seemed that he had returned as part of Ted DiBiase's Million Dollar Corporation. In reality, the character was a fake Undertaker played by Brian Harris, a.k.a. Brian Lee, who later played Chainz in the WWF's Disciples of the Apocalypse. Paul Bearer then reintroduced the "real" Undertaker, and the two Undertakers squared off at the 1994 SummerSlam. Calloway's Undertaker won, of course, and then went on to take revenge on Yokozuna by winning a second casket match. This time, he stationed martial-arts movie star Chuck Norris at ringside to ward off any outside interference.

The victory should have been the start of something big, but 1995 saw The Undertaker stalled in feuds with the likes of IRS, Mabel, and King Kong Bundy. The low point came when Kama, an unheralded newcomer, stole The Undertaker's urn and melted it down to make a chain. By the end of the year, however, The Undertaker had vanquished every opponent, reclaimed his urn, and been declared the number-one contender for the WWF title.

At the 1996 Royal Rumble, The Undertaker was denied a victory over WWF champion Bret "The Hit Man" Hart due to interference from Diesel, who was next in line for a shot and figured he had a better chance against The Hit Man. Since his title shot was set to take place in a cage, Diesel also figured he was safe from The Undertaker's interference. But after the match began, The Undertaker rose from a hole in the middle of the ring and dragged Diesel down "into Hell," as the announcers described it.

Though his chilling entrances always brought a pop from the fans, and though he had consistently been considered a top contender since his defeat of Hogan five years earlier, The Undertaker had fallen into a rut. But that shocking, horror-movie-inspired 1996 appearance during the Bret Hart-Diesel cage match signaled his return to prominence. At WrestleMania, he pinned Diesel and began his second reign as WWF champion. Feuds with

Mankind and Goldust became borderline hardcore matches; the WWF had begun its shift away from family entertainment.

The Undertaker's battles with Mankind grew progressively more bizarre. They pummeled each other through the basement of an arena in a boiler-room Brawl (SummerSlam 1996); in October, The Undertaker was dropped into an open grave during a buried-alive match. Paul Bearer, who had accompanied The Undertaker to every match for more than six years, suddenly switched his allegiance to Mankind for no apparent reason.

The Executioner (Terry Gordy) began to interfere in The Undertaker's battles with Mankind. At the 1996 Survivor Series, The Undertaker returned from another hiatus and defeated The Executioner in a Texas death match. Paul Bearer then sent Vader after his former charge at the 1997 Survivor Series. The Undertaker lost after being hit with his urn and had to forfeit his WWF title.

In 1997, The Undertaker gained and lost the WWF title again, and his war with Paul Bearer intensified. Bearer, whose tortured monologues about betrayal and sinister secrets had fans hitting the mute button in droves, claimed that The Undertaker's younger brother, Kane, had survived the funeral-home fire and that he, Paul Bearer, had raised Kane separately from The Undertaker. Meanwhile, The Undertaker fought a series of outstanding matches against Bret Hart, which culminated in a loss due to interference from special referee Shawn Michaels.

The two storylines came together at the October In Your House pay-per-view when the WWF introduced its first Hell in the Cell match (see The 10 Best Wrestling Matches of All Time, page 190). The Undertaker dominated that match, but he was denied a victory after the lights went out in the arena and a fiery explosion heralded the arrival of Kane (Glenn Jacobs). Shawn Michaels won, but he didn't look like a winner when he was practically carried out of the cage, his face beaten to a bloody pulp.

Kane continued to harass The Undertaker in the weeks that followed, though The Undertaker vowed that he would never fight his "brother." At an Undertaker-Michaels casket match, Kane appeared, rolled the casket containing The Undertaker into the arena entryway, and set it on fire. After the flames were extinguished, the casket was opened. The Undertaker had disappeared. Say this for Mark Calloway: no one makes more dramatic exits before taking time off!

The Undertaker returned in February of 1998 to take on Kane. But the first match between the "brothers," at the 1998 WrestleMania, did not live up to its hype. In April, Paul Bearer revealed that he was Kane's father. All this melodrama wasn't generating much response from the fans, and it seemed as if the feud was ready to fizzle out. At a pay-per-view dubbed *Unforgiven*, the Kane-Undertaker heat was rekindled — literally — in the first-ever "inferno match." The combatants were positioned within a ring of fire; each time one of them landed hard on the canvas, the flames intensified.

Granted, the fire was the type used by magicians, and the match was not as intense or as dangerous as the fire matches held in Japan, but some of the visuals were stunning, and as entertainment it was first-rate. The Undertaker won by diving over the burning ropes and onto Kane. He then beat up Paul Bearer, to the delight of the thousands of fans who were sick of the manager's high-pitched, whining voice.

In June of 1998, The Undertaker won what was perhaps the most brutal contest ever staged by the WWF — Hell in the Cell II — against Mankind (see The 10 Best Wrestling Matches of All Time, page 192). During July, the signs of a tenuous alliance were evident between The Undertaker and Kane, and, with Stone Cold Steve Austin, The Undertaker enjoyed a brief Tag title reign. The Undertaker lost a Heavyweight title shot to Austin in August then battled Kane for the belt after Austin lost a handicap triple-threat match to The Undertaker and Kane.

As 1998 drew to a close, The Undertaker drifted through on-again, off-again alliances with Kane and Paul Bearer and changed his entrance music to a Gothic heavy-metal dirge that was not as menacing as the funeral march. In 1999, he created the Ministry of Darkness, later rechristened the Corporate Ministry after the Undertaker joined forces with Vince McMahon's treacherous son, Shane. The new storyline has shifted traditional WWF alliances in unfamiliar ways, and promises to play out toward a cataclysmic conclusion.

REAL NAME:
Leon White

ALSO KNOWN AS:
Baby Bull, Bull Power, Big Van Vader, Super Vader

BORN:
October 15, 1956, Denver, Colorado

HEIGHT:
6' 5"

WEIGHT:
450 pounds

PROFESSIONAL DEBUT:
1986

PROFESSIONAL AFFILIATIONS:
None

FINISHING MOVE:
the vader bomb

TITLES HELD

CWA **Heavyweight title**
Won: March 1987, over Otto Wanz
Lost: July 1987, to Otto Wanz
Regained: August 1989, over Otto Wanz
Lost: June 30, 1990, to Otto Wanz
Regained: December 22, 1990 (tournament win)
Lost: July 6, 1991, to Mark Rambo

IWGP **Heavyweight title**
Won: April 24, 1989 (tournament win)
Lost: May 25, 1989, to Salman Hashimikov
Regained: August 10, 1989, over Riki Chosu
Lost: August 19, 1990, to Riki Chosu
Regained: January 17, 1991, over Tatsumi Fujinami
Lost: March 14, 1991, to Tatsumi Fujinami

UWA **Heavyweight title**
Won: November 22, 1989, over El Canek
Lost: December 9, 1990, to El Canek

IWGP **Tag-Team title**
(with Bam Bam Bigelow)
Won: March 1, 1992, over Hiroshi Hase and Keiji Mutoh
Lost: June 26, 1992, to The Steiner Brothers

WCW **Heavyweight title**
Won: July 12, 1992, over Sting
Lost: August 2, 1992, to Ron Simmons
Regained: December 30, 1992, over Ron Simmons
Lost: March 11, 1993, to Sting
Regained: March 17, 1993, over Sting
Lost: December 27, 1993, to Ric Flair

UWFI **Heavyweight title**
Won: August 18, 1994, over Nobuhiko Takada
Lost: April 20, 1995, to Nobuhiko Takada

WCW **United States Heavyweight title**
Won: December 27, 1995, over Hacksaw Jim Duggan
Stripped of title on April 23, 1995

The thing about Vader is he's just plain big. Standing inside the ropes with this 6' 5", 450-pound behemoth, a wrestler must understand how the U.S. army felt every time it ran into The Incredible Hulk. Vader is tall, wide, heavy, strong, and usually in a bad mood. Is it any wonder that his opponents have been known to fake injuries rather than face him in the ring?

Vader has always been portrayed as a monstrous force of nature, and so little information has ever been divulged about the man behind the character: Leon White. Before becoming a wrestler, White was a lineman for the Los Angeles Rams in the seasons before they moved to St. Louis. He received his early mat training from Brad Rheingans and in 1986 made his debut in the AWA billed as Baby Bull. He toured Austria and Germany (sometimes billed as Bull Power) and, in 1987, he defeated former AWA Heavyweight champion Otto Wanz to win the CWA title.

White dropped the belt just three months later then departed for the first of what would become many tours of Japan. During that tour, while wrestling for New Japan, he began billing himself as Big Van Vader. The *Star Wars* influence is obvious, but White also chose the name because he owned a big van. It's a good thing he didn't drive a Beetle.

On December 27, 1987, Vader made his Japanese debut in the main event of a Sumo Hall card. He pinned the great Antonio Inoki in less than three minutes, and the decision incited a riot in the auditorium. This caused New Japan to be banned indefinitely from its home arena.

Vader spent the next two years in Japan, competing for the IWGP title against such local favorites as Tatsumi Fujinami, Masa Chono, and Riki Chosu. In April of 1989, Vader vanquished three opponents in a tournament held to fill the vacated title. He switched the IWGP belt once more that summer then resumed his globetrotting by touring Mexico for the UWA. When he pinned El Canek for that federation's World title, Vader became the first wrestler to hold World titles on three continents simultaneously.

For almost a year, Vader reigned as IWGP champion. His most memorable title defense took place before nearly 64,000 fans in a sold-out Tokyo Dome, where he faced Stan Hansen and held onto the belt after a double-count-out decision. When he finally did lose, in August of 1990, it was to Chosu, the same wrestler he had pinned in August of 1989.

Vader's feud with Hansen continued after he made his WCW debut in July of 1990. After he destroyed Tom Zenk in two minutes in his first WCW match (at the 1990 Great American Bash), Vader wrestled several matches against Hansen, almost all of which ended in one or both of them being disqualified. Among their best encounters was their battle to a double-DQ at WrestleWar 1991.

In between brawls with Hansen, Vader lost and regained his North American, Asian, and European titles, and by 1991 he was working more or less full time for WCW. After he joined forces with manager Harley Race, Vader earned his first title shot against Sting. The turning point of the match was when Sting attempted a flying body-press from the top rope; Vader caught him in midair and power-slammed him into the canvas. The title was in jeopardy, but Vader was disqualified when he punched the referee. It was later revealed that Sting had suffered broken ribs and a bruised spleen.

In July of 1992, Vader defeated a still-sore Sting in the rematch. While Sting took time off to recuperate, Vader feuded with Nikita Koloff and was then sidelined himself after undergoing knee surgery. At Halloween Havoc, Vader stepped in for Rick Rude to defend Rude's United States title — successfully — against Nikita Koloff. He then lost to Sting in the King of Cable finals at Starrcade.

Though he was a guy who never looked like he needed much help, Vader wrestled frequently as part of a tag team — with Mr. Hughes in WCW and Bam Bam Bigelow in Japan. He held the IWGP Tag straps with Bigelow, but his tag career was short-lived. By 1993, he had returned to concentrating solely on singles matches, with the exception of a few tag bouts alongside Sid Vicious; he had also dropped the "Big Van" from his name and was being billed simply as Vader.

At Slamboree in May 1993, Vader defeated Sting in a "white castle of fear" strap match; it was the first of eight straight pay-per-view main events for Vader, an achievement matched only by Hulk Hogan in the days before pay-per-views went monthly. He switched the title with Sting and feuded with Dustin Rhodes, The British Bulldog, and Mick Foley as Cactus Jack. He also took up shoot-fighting in the UWFI, quickly working his way up to a title match against champion Nobuhiko Takada. On December 5, 1993, in front of more than 46,000 fans at Tokyo's Jingu Baseball Stadium, Vader was forced to submit to a Takada cross-arm-breaker.

Many scores were settled by the man called Vader in 1994: he won the UWFI title over Takada (thereafter calling himself Super Vader in that federation), he avenged an earlier loss to Sting, and he defeated Hacksaw Jim Duggan for the United States title. He was also Cactus Jack's opponent in an infamous match held in Germany, during which two-thirds of Jack's ear was severed after he became tangled in the ropes.

The one man Vader could not beat, however, was Ric Flair, who had pinned Vader for the Heavyweight title in a classic December 1993 match. Vader appeared to have the rematch won until The Boss, who had been appointed special referee, declared Flair the winner after Vader had supposedly given up. Vader then beat up on The Boss, who changed his moniker to The Guardian Angel, at house shows throughout the year.

Given his size and strength, Vader was a guy who could probably have won any match he wanted to. Some WCW house shows, in fact, were called "Vader's Roadkill Spree" because Vader would destroy all jobbers deployed against him. But after being forced to lose to Ric Flair, and to Hulk Hogan in 1995, Vader began taking his frustration out on various wrestlers and officials, and at times the brutality of his attacks went beyond what was called for in the storyline. These outbursts led to him being stripped of his United States title in April of 1995 amid rumors that the disciplinary action was more than a work.

He calmed down for awhile but, on August 29, Vader was suspended and then dismissed from WCW following a locker-room brawl with Paul Orndorff at Atlanta's Center State Theater. He was set to fight alongside Hogan in a WarGames pay-per-view match, but what was to have been the first-time pairing of two of wrestling's most dominant superstars never happened. Lex Luger took Vader's place.

Vader was injured in the brawl with Orndorff and stayed out of wrestling for the rest of 1995. When he did return, in January of 1996, it was to New Japan, where he lost to Antonio Inoki. The WWF decided to take a chance on the temperamental Vader and debuted him at the 1996 Royal Rumble with Jim Cornette as his manager. Two days after his arrival, he received his first suspension, for attacking federation president Gorilla Monsoon.

Though he displayed the same repertoire that was so successful in WCW — including a ring-shaking moonsault and the Vader bomb splash, with which he'd won many a match — Vader didn't earn a single title in three years with the WWF. He'd been given chances, but he lost to Shawn Michaels at the 1996 SummerSlam and to his former tag partner Sycho Sid at Survivor Series.

Vader's biggest WWF splash, in fact, didn't occur in the ring at all. During a 1997 tour of the Middle East, he appeared on the television show *Good Morning Kuwait* and attacked the host, Bassam Al Otham. Vader's justification was that he objected to the host's questions about the authenticity of wrestling. He stormed off the set but was detained by Kuwaiti authorities for more than a week before he was allowed to leave the country. After landing back in America, and landing in hot water with WWF brass, a defiant Vader claimed he'd do it all over again.

Coming out of yet another suspension, Vader feuded with Ken Shamrock, who was not about to stand for any extracurricular abuse. In their first match, Shamrock broke Vader's nose and left him unable to walk for a week. Vader, or "The Mastadon," as announcer Jim Ross called him, was glad to move on to other opponents, though in September he exacted some revenge on Shamrock in an ultimate-fighting-style rematch, held for FMW in Japan. Vader not only won but also left his opponent with internal injuries.

Back in the WWF, a Vader-Paul Bearer alliance was dissolved, and Vader turned good guy after he got in the face of Bret Hart during one of Hart's "America sucks!" diatribes. Vader subsequently teamed with The Patriot (Del Wilkes) for a series of matches against members of The Hart Foundation.

In April of 1998, after a brief feud with Goldust, Vader appeared in his biggest WWF match yet, against The Undertaker's "brother" Kane, who was at that point considered virtually unstoppable. Vader was pinned, and thus began his steady slide to jobber status, a first for the mighty man from Colorado. He lost to Al Snow, and to Marc Mero, and even to perennial doormat Jeff Jarrett. Towards the end of the year, he limped away from the WWF, probably just before he would have been pinned by the diminutive Taka Michinoku.

Though one wrestling mag called Vader "a human atlas of damaged body parts," he opted to resume his career after a few months off: he took his act back to Japan, where he won his first match before a large and appreciative crowd.

SEAN WALTMAN

REAL NAME:
Sean Waltman

ALSO KNOWN AS: The 1–2–3 Kid, The Kamikaze Kid, The Cannonball Kid, The Lightning Kid, Syxx, X-Pac

BORN:
July 13, 1972, Minneapolis, Minnesota

HEIGHT:
6' 2"

WEIGHT:
212 pounds

PROFESSIONAL DEBUT:
1990

PROFESSIONAL AFFILIATIONS:
New World Order, Degeneration X

FINISHING MOVE:
the buzzkiller, the facebuster

TITLES HELD:

PWA **Light Heavyweight title**
Won: April 12, 1990, over Matt Derringer
Lost: May 6, 1990, to Matt Derringer
Regained: April 8, 1991, over Jerry Lynn
Lost: December 22, 1991, to Ricky Rice

GWF **Light Heavyweight title**
Won: July 13, 1991 (tournament win)
Lost: September 13, 1991, to Chaz
Regained: September 15, 1991, over Chaz
Lost: December 27, 1991, to Jerry Lynn

PWA **Tag-Team title**
(with Jerry Lynn)
Won: March 2, 1993, over Tony Denucci
and Tommy Ferrera
Titles later declared vacant

WWF **Tag-Team title**
(with Marty Jannetty)
Won: January 10, 1994, over The
Quebecers
Lost: January 17, 1994, to The Quebecers

(with Bob Holly)
Won: January 22, 1995, over Tatanka and
Bam Bam Bigelow (tournament win)
Lost: January 23, 1995, to The Smoking
Gunns

(with Kane)
Won: March 30, 1999, over Jeff Jarrett
and Owen Hart

WCW **Cruiserweight title**
Won: February 23, 1997, over Dean
Malenko
Lost: June 28, 1997, to Chris Jericho

WWF **European title**
Won: September 21, 1998, over D-Lo
Brown
Lost: October 5, 1998, to D-Lo Brown
Regained: October 18, 1998, over D-Lo
Brown
Lost: February 15, 1999, to Shane
McMahon

Sean Waltman ran away from home when he was 15 years old. Three years later, he made his professional wrestling debut, still looking 15. The slight, babyfaced Waltman looked like he belonged in study hall, not WrestleMania, and the promoters packaged him accordingly. His early characters came with such youth-inspired handles as The Lightning Kid, The Cannonball Kid, The Kamikaze Kid, and The 1–2–3 Kid.

Waltman was trained in the finer points of the sport by Boris Malenko and his sons Joe and Dean. He debuted in the independent PWA promotion as The Lightning Kid, a snot-nosed heel who reigned twice as Light Heavyweight champion. He jumped to the new Global Wrestling Federation in 1991 and received his first national exposure when ESPN began broadcasting GWF matches.

But by 1992 Waltman was already contemplating retirement. Despite winning gold in both the PWA and the GWF and gaining a cult following during a PWA tour of Japan, he was unable to convince bookers at the top federations to give him a chance. He had the necessary grappling and martial-arts skills, but he was too young and too thin for anyone to take seriously.

In 1993, Waltman was signed by the WWF: his modest contract may as well have read "will job for money." In three consecutive *Raw* broadcasts, he was introduced by three different names — The Lightning Kid, The Kamikaze Kid, and then The Cannonball Kid. Each time, he ended up pinned to the canvas. But Vince McMahon and the federation's bookers had noticed his work ethic, and they decided to take a chance by inserting Waltman into one of the most audacious storylines ever introduced.

On May 17, 1993, Waltman faced Razor Ramon, "The Bad Guy," in an early match on a regular Monday-night telecast. It looked like another slam dunk for Ramon (Scott Hall), whose star was on the rise, especially since he outweighed his opponent by more than 100 pounds. But The Kid, as Waltman was now called, absorbed everything Ramon dished out and scored what seemed to be a miracle pin. The moment was sold so well by Razor and The Kid that fans who should have known better actually believed the outcome was not premeditated.

Waltman became an instant star and was rechristened The 1–2–3 Kid in honor of his win over Razor Ramon. Razor, of course, demanded a rematch, even going so far as to offer Waltman money to sign the rematch contract. After four weeks, when Razor's bid had reached $10,000, The Kid took the challenge and beat The Bad Guy again. He won by count-out then ran out of the arena and jumped into a waiting car while his vanquished opponent gave chase.

Give Scott Hall credit here as well: not yet a superstar, he played a part that could have derailed a career full of promise. Turns out, however, that the story proved beneficial to everyone; Hall became a face after being taunted by Ted DiBiase, and then helping The Kid to beat DiBiase by providing a convenient outside distraction.

In his first pay-per-view appearance, Waltman lost to DiBiase's Money,

Inc. tag partner, Irwin R. Schyster (Mike Rotundo). But The Kid was famous now and had erased all doubts about his ability to compete with the big boys. His martial-arts moves had become the cornerstone of an effective offense, and opponents liked the way he used his phenomenal speed to sell their strength. When The Kid was Irish-whipped into a corner, he would accelerate and then hit with such impact that his whole body would snap with whiplash ferocity.

Though he'd occasionally team with new buddy Razor Ramon for tag matches, The Kid found greater success with Marty Jannetty: the duo took the Tag belts from The Quebecers in January of 1994. It was a brief title reign, but it would not be Waltman's last. In 1995, The Kid teamed with Bob "Spark Plug" Holly to defeat Tatanka and Bam Bam Bigelow in a tournament final and reclaim the gold. The following night, however, they lost the belts to The Smoking Gunns.

Two years after his shocking pin of Razor Ramon some of the heat around Waltman had dissipated, and he was relegated to a supporting role, jobbing for the likes of Hakushi and The Roadie. For his second WWF push he turned heel by attacking tag partner Razor Ramon after an October 1995 loss to The Smoking Gunns. He allied himself with Ted DiBiase's Million Dollar Corporation and competed alongside Sycho Sid. They were billed as "Sid and The Kid," which sounded like the name of a bad situation comedy — the idea was quickly dropped.

Waltman then embarked on a second feud with Razor Ramon, which brought better results, albeit briefly. The Kid lost a "crybaby" match and was forced to don a diaper and endure public humiliation. But there would be no revenge match this time: Waltman's battle with drug abuse landed him twice in rehab and led to his dismissal by the WWF in early 1996.

Waltman was out of work when Ted Turner went on his WWF buying spree, and so he joined Scott Hall, Kevin Nash, and Hulk Hogan in WCW's outlaw organization New World Order. As Syxx (so named because he was NWO's sixth member), Waltman feuded with Eddie Guerrero and defeated Dean Malenko for the Cruiserweight title.

Still looking kidlike, Syxx was pitted against wrestling's grand old man, Ric Flair. His merciless verbal attacks on Flair's advancing age and diminishing skills did much to advance the NWO's reputation as the enemy of wrestling tradition. During one memorable skit, in which the NWO did a *Saturday Night Live*-style parody of The Four Horsemen, Waltman unveiled a hilarious imitation of Flair, turning himself into a credible heel and microphone worker.

Syxx frequently faced Malenko and Chris Jericho but avoided the *luchadores*, which seems odd considering his aerial-maneuver expertise. But Waltman preferred taking on bigger opponents and humiliating them, usually by straddling his prone victim in the corner and riding him like a rodeo cowboy. It was a dumb move, really, but it looked good.

In 1997, after losing the Cruiserweight title to Jericho, Waltman suffered a career-threatening neck injury and was sidelined for almost a year. He made occasional nonwrestling appearances on *Monday Nitro*, but that was not enough for Eric Bischoff, who had grown tired of the locker-room antics of Waltman and his two best friends in NWO Wolfpack, Scott Hall and Kevin Nash. Waltman was fired via a Federal Express letter in March of 1998. "I did take a lot of heat for shit that they thought they couldn't get on Kevin and Scott, so they dumped it all on me," he claimed shortly thereafter.

Just weeks later, on a March 30 *Monday Night Raw*, Sean Waltman returned to the WWF as X-Pac, the newest member of Degeneration X. He verbally blasted both Bischoff and Hulk Hogan, immediately endearing himself to the partisan crowd. Still recovering from his neck injury, he participated in several uproarious DX comic routines, including a military takeover of WCW on an army tank.

When Waltman did return to action, it was with a surprising lack of ring rust. If anything, his spinning heel kicks looked more polished than ever as he took on everyone from D-lo Brown to Jeff Jarrett. If the WWF ever gets serious about its Light Heavyweight division, X-Pac will finally have a title to go with his DX membership privileges.

The 10 Best Wrestling Matches Of All Time

1. AMERICAN HEAVYWEIGHT TITLE MATCH
FRANK GOTCH VS. TOM JENKINS
MADISON SQUARE GARDEN; NEW YORK CITY, NEW YORK
MAY 19, 1905

The two most dominant wrestlers in the first decade of the twentieth century were Frank Gotch and Tom Jenkins. They clashed several times over the American Heavyweight championship, exchanging the title four times between 1903 and 1906. In their most famous confrontation, a best-of-three-falls match described in the press as the most epic of the decade, Jenkins defeated Gotch by taking the first fall at 1:27:57, losing the second at 36:27, and taking the third at 11:10. The victory was all the more impressive considering that Jenkins had been defeated just two weeks earlier in a grueling match against George Hackenschmidt. Gotch, after battling Jenkins for more than two hours, had to be carried from the ring by his seconds.

2. WWF INTERCONTINENTAL TITLE MATCH
RANDY SAVAGE VS. RICKY STEAMBOAT
WRESTLEMANIA III
PONTIAC SILVERDOME; DETROIT, MICHIGAN
MARCH 29, 1987

The running time for this match was 14:35, but when I first watched it I was sure it had lasted for at least an hour. With all the near-falls and momentum changes, it certainly seemed that way.

Randy Savage had been the Intercontinental champ for more than a year when he faced Ricky "The Dragon" Steamboat in what was billed as a revenge match; at one point during the weeks leading up to WrestleMania III, Savage had dropped Steamboat on his throat across a steel safety rail, damaging his larynx. This match would be The Dragon's first since returning from his recuperation break.

At the bell, Savage resumed his attack on Steamboat's throat while The Dragon responded with some vicious arm drags. In the early moments, Savage nailed Steamboat with a flying knee to the back, sending him over the safety rail and into the crowd. The match could have ended then with a count-out or a disqualification, but Steamboat was helped back into the ring by George "The Animal" Steele. The human hairball's distracting presence at ringside could have ruined a splendid battle, but fortunately his "Beauty and the Beast" pursuit of Savage's manager, Miss Elizabeth, did not play a significant role in the outcome of the contest.

Savage owned the middle third of the match. Though Steamboat had the edge when it came to speed, The Macho Man proved he could move just as quickly by planting Steamboat's throat on the top rope and allowing his momentum to carry him over the top and out of the ring. Within seconds of Steamboat's crash landing, Savage had scrambled back into the ring for a pin attempt. Later, an Irish whip Savage was attempting on Steamboat "accidently" caught referee Dave Hebner in the corner; while Hebner was stunned, Savage was denied a cover that would have given him the victory.

Steamboat used his martial-arts skills to get back into the match, and the near-falls came fast and furious in the final five minutes. There was a total of 19 two-counts in the match: 11 from Steamboat; 8 from Savage. After Steele prevented Savage from using the bell as a weapon, Steamboat, who had already recovered from Savage's famous flying-elbow finisher, rallied to get the pin.

3. WWF HEAVYWEIGHT TITLE MATCH
HULK HOGAN VS. ANDRE THE GIANT
WRESTLEMANIA III
PONTIAC SILVERDOME; DETROIT, MICHIGAN
MARCH 29, 1987

Hulk Hogan and Andre the Giant had always been characterized as the best of friends. In 1987, they were also the two most successful and celebrated wrestlers in the world, and both were considered unbeatable. Angles don't come easier than that.

A feud was awkwardly set in motion as Andre, guided by Bobby "The Brain" Heenan, became Hogan's jealous rival for the preeminent place in wrestling history. Once the match was set, however, all the buildup was forgotten. Hulk vs. Andre instantly became the most talked-about main event since the early decades of the century. When the 90,000-seat Pontiac Silverdome sold out for WrestleMania III (still an American attendance record), even the mainstream press had to take notice.

Andre was pelted with garbage on the way to the ring. It was an inappropriate denouement for a proud man nearing the end of his career. Hogan received a thunderous ovation as he performed his familiar medley of applause-baiting antics.

The match opened with a long staredown. Hogan broke the standoff with a failed body-slam. He seemed to have injured his back in the attempt, and Andre fell on top of him for what at first appeared to be a three-count. After the referee confirmed that Hogan did raise his shoulder in time, Andre continued to work on Hogan's back with forearm shots. Hogan remained on the defensive until Andre missed a head butt and collided with the ringpost. Hogan used the opportunity to "Hulk up" and change the momentum. In his second attempt, Hogan successfully body-slammed his 450-pound opponent and scored the pin at 12:01.

Thousands of matches have been wrestled better, but as a wrestling "event," Hulk Hogan vs. Andre the Giant remains unrivaled to this day. Andre, who agreed to lose but who could have changed his mind (he had done so on previous occasions), respectfully passed the torch to his younger, more charismatic successor, and Hogan went on to transform wrestling into a pop-culture phenomenon.

4. WWF HEAVYWEIGHT TITLE MATCH
HULK HOGAN VS. THE ULTIMATE WARRIOR
WRESTLEMANIA VI
SKYDOME; TORONTO, ONTARIO, CANADA
APRIL 1, 1990

Only the marks didn't know that Hulk Hogan would beat Andre the Giant at WrestleMania III, but this title match was different. The WWF's two most popular wrestlers, in the prime of their careers, squared off in a champion-vs.-champion main event (Hogan was the Heavyweight champ; The Ultimate Warrior held the Intercontinental belt). Each had been a face since his federation debut, and neither was showing any signs of turning heel.

It was the kind of match that had "no decision" written all over it. Something was bound to happen — outside interference, a time-limit draw, a double count-out — because jobbing either of these superstars seemed out of the question. Or did it?

Both combatants entered to huge ovations and then traded some basic moves — scoop-slams, shoulder blocks, clotheslines — with little or no effect. Hogan actually expanded his arsenal, applying a reverse chin-lock and going for a small-package pin at one point, but it was The Warrior who gained the upper hand, when Hogan appeared to injure his knee after tumbling out of the ring. A series of quick two-counts and kick-outs followed. Hogan regained the momentum while referee Dave Hebner was knocked out and scored what should have been a victory.

The Warrior, having avoided defeat thanks to an incapacitated ref, executed both of his finishing moves, the gorilla press and the Warrior splash. Hebner regained his senses to make the count, but Hogan kicked out at two and waved his finger in The Warrior's face. Fans now figured they knew what was coming. Hogan began his standard finishing routine, but there were gasps in the SkyDome when The Warrior dodged Hogan's leg drop and nailed the Heavyweight champ with a second Warrior splash to get the pin at 22:51.

The Warrior's win was the most unlikely of all possible conclusions, and the WWF deserves credit for crafting a payoff that was a genuine surprise to most of the fans. Gracious in defeat, Hogan handed The Warrior his title belt and raised his opponent's hand in victory, but no torches were passed as in the Hulk Hogan-Andre the Giant match of 1987. Ten years after WrestleMania VI, Hogan remained the sport's top draw, and in 1998 he was finally able to avenge his loss to The Warrior, albeit under radically different circumstances.

5. THE LADDER MATCHES
WWF INTERCONTINENTAL TITLE
SHAWN MICHAELS VS. RAZOR RAMON
• WRESTLEMANIA X
MARCH 20, 1994
MADISON SQUARE GARDEN; NEW YORK CITY, NEW YORK
• SUMMERSLAM 1995
AUGUST 27, 1995
CIVIC ARENA; PITTSBURGH, PENNSYLVANIA

Too close to call: these were two incredible matches, and both deserve inclusion in any top-10 list of classic battles. During each, the Intercontinental belt was suspended above the ring and an eight-foot ladder was placed outside. The first wrestler to bring the ladder into the ring, climb it, and retrieve the belt would win the title.

Razor Ramon was the crowd favorite in the first match, as Shawn Michaels was still in the runaway-ego phase of his career. Diesel (Kevin Nash) accompanied Michaels to the ring and interfered in the first two minutes, prompting the referee to order him back to the locker room. Michaels took several of his famous circuslike falls out of the ring. At one point, Razor ripped the mat away from the floor, but he was caught in his own trap when Michaels flipped him out of the ring and onto the concrete.

Nearly five minutes passed before either wrestler could get to the ladder, which according to the rules could be used by either combatant as a weapon. Michaels gained the upper hand by laying the ladder on the apron while Razor was disoriented outside the ring. He then executed a running baseball slide into the ladder, driving it into Razor's ribcage. Michaels's first attempt to climb, however, was interrupted by Razor, who pulled him off by the tights, in the process revealing a full-moon view of The Heartbreak Kid.

At the nine-minute mark, Michaels was back up. He managed to brush the belt with his hand but toppled back onto the canvas when Razor dived into the ladder. Razor did not attempt to secure the belt until 13 minutes into the match. Michaels was on the floor and out of the picture. With an amazing burst of speed, Michaels jumped up and scrambled to the top turnbuckle. He dived towards Razor and made just enough contact to knock him off the ladder. After many more close calls that ended with both men taking severe bumps, Michaels became tangled in the ring ropes, allowing Razor just enough time to grab the gold.

The rematch was scheduled to take place 17 months later. It turned out to be one of those sequels that compare favorably to the original. The second match ran longer (25:01 as opposed to 18:45), but the first was more balanced. Michaels, now the people's choice, absorbed most of the punishment, including an awkward landing coming out of a Razor Ramon suplex and a fall from the ladder, in the course of which his leg got caught between the rungs; he appeared to wrench his knee.

Razor was in control for most of the match, and clearly hoped to secure a victory that would bring him the Intercontinental title for an unprecedented fourth time. Michaels, however, just kept going and going like the Energizer bunny, absorbing every bump and bouncing right back. He executed both a moonsault and a swan dive off the top of the ladder and was able to withstand his opponent's finisher, the Razor's edge.

A second ladder was introduced during the match, but it was not utilized as much as it could have been. When Razor finally seemed incapacitated, a severely fatigued Michaels made two unhindered climbs towards victory but missed the belt both times. His third attempt was successful, and it was followed by a handshake from the defeated Razor Ramon, who acknowledged that the better man had won that day. Rarely have Michaels's speed and resilience been better displayed.

6. THE IRON-MAN MATCH
WWF HEAVYWEIGHT TITLE
BRET HART VS. SHAWN MICHAELS
WRESTLEMANIA XII
ARROWHEAD POND; ANAHEIM, CALIFORNIA
MARCH 31, 1996

From the 1900s to the 1930s, wrestling title matches would routinely last one hour or more. As the sport shifted away from mat wrestling and gravitated towards acrobatic and aerial assaults, most matches shortened to approximately 15 minutes.

The WWF turned back the clock in 1996: it pitted two of its most technically proficient competitors — Heavyweight champion Bret Hart and Shawn Michaels — against each other in an iron-man match, a 60-minute contest that would test not only their skills but also their endurance. There was a genuine heat between The Hit Man and The Heartbreak Kid, dating back to their tag-team battles as members of The Hart Foundation and The Rockers. While a shoot match was too much to hope for, discerning fans thought that a few genuine exchanges were possible.

The opening was predictably slow as both combatants paced themselves for the long match to come. The Hit Man applied an early standing side head-lock for more than two minutes, setting a pattern of long holds followed by reversals, quick flurries of exchanged moves, and then a return to another basic hold.

Hart's methodical approach and reliance on arm bars, front face-locks, and other traditional tactics gave him an early advantage. He was considered the favorite due to his experience and superior technical skills. As long as the match stayed on the mat, Hart was likely to stay in control.

But the ever-resilient Michaels proved surprisingly adept at the amateur style and was able to frustrate Hart with escapes and reversals. At the 15-minute mark, he attempted to nail Hart with his "sweet chin music" outside the ring, but Hart ducked and Michaels caught the timekeeper instead. It may have been a work, but the impact of the kick was rock solid.

At the 30-minute mark, Michaels was able to kick out of a weak cover following a piledriver, and Hart responded by escaping a perfectly applied bridge suplex. He followed up with a suplex off the top rope — but to no avail. Enraged, Hart attacked Michaels outside the ring and whipped Michaels into his trainer, Mexican wrestling legend Jose Lothario. The boos cascaded from the sold-out crowd as The Hit Man's subtle heel turn accelerated.

As the 60-minute mark approached, neither wrestler had scored a pin. During the final three minutes, Michaels unleashed a series of aerial attacks — so far in the match, neither man had done much work above the ropes. The moves were striking proof of Michaels's cardiovascular training, but they couldn't get the job done. Hart applied the sharpshooter; Michaels refused to tap out and was saved by the bell.

Hart, believing the draw allowed him to keep the belt, began walking back to the locker room. He was ordered back to the ring, however, and told he had to continue the match until a winner could be declared. At the 61:52 mark, Michaels caught Hart with his lethal standing side kick and scored the pin.

7. KING OF THE DEATH MATCH TITLE
AWA TOURNAMENT FINAL
CACTUS JACK VS. TERRY FUNK
KAWASAKI STADIUM; TOKYO, JAPAN
AUGUST 20, 1995

The legend of Cactus Jack was born not in the United States with WCW but in Japan, in the kind of anything-goes hardcore matches that must be seen to be believed. Cactus Jack (Mick Foley), Terry Funk, and other veterans of these savage contests gathered in Tokyo in 1995 for a tournament that had been organized to crown the King of the Death Match.

From the opening rounds, it was apparent that this would be a hardcore gauntlet not for the faint of heart. To reach the finals, Foley beat Terry Gordy with a baseball bat in a ring bristling with 10,000 thumbtacks. He then bested Shoji Nakamaki in a match involving a bed of nails and barbed-wire-wrapped boards. Meanwhile, Terry Funk defeated Leatherface in a barbed-wire chain match and then pinned Tiger Jeet Singh after hurling him through a pane of glass.

The carnage of the early matches had left its mark on Foley and Funk; they limped into the ring for the tournament final. Both were heavily bandaged, and blood was flowing before the opening bell. Barbed wire surrounded the ring, and barbed-wire-wrapped boards laced with C-4 explosives were strategically placed inside it. Funk felt the blast first after being knocked backward into one of the boards.

Despite a deep gash that had opened above his right eye, Funk sent Cactus Jack reeling into the next two exploding boards, one of them face first. Undaunted, Cactus placed a board over Funk's prone body and broke it on top of him.

Both men tasted the barbed wire around the ring; after one ugly collision, Foley had to pull his arm out of the wire, tearing his flesh. At the 10-minute mark, the fans began a 10-second countdown to the detonation of some other, preset explosives. Cactus Jack managed to roll out of the ring, but Funk could not rally to escape in time, and he absorbed the impact of the blast.

Amazingly, Funk was able to mount one last attack on Cactus Jack, whose face was by now caked in drying blood. But Cactus brought a ladder into the ring and landed a flying elbow from near the top rung. He tried to repeat the maneuver, but Funk was able to upset the ladder enough to send Cactus crashing back onto the canvas. Funk was too badly injured to follow up on the move, however, and Cactus Jack rolled over on top of his prone adversary at 13:21 to score his first win ever over his hardcore idol.

"This was the longest day of my life," said Mick Foley, who ended up with 7 stitches in his right hand, 7 over his right eyebrow, 14 behind his left ear, and 21 in his forehead, as well as second-degree burns from his wrist to his shoulder. "But I won," he asserted proudly. "I became the King of the Death Matches."

8. HELL IN THE CELL
SHAWN MICHAELS VS. THE UNDERTAKER
WWF IN YOUR HOUSE
KIEL CENTER; ST. LOUIS, MISSOURI
OCTOBER 5, 1997

"Badd Blood" was the moniker assigned to this WWF pay-per-view — an appropriate description of the conflict between Shawn Michaels and The Undertaker. Months earlier, at the 1997 SummerSlam, Michaels had served as special referee for a Heavyweight title match between The Undertaker and Bret Hart. He'd attempted a chair shot on Hart, but he'd nailed The Undertaker instead, costing him the match. The Undertaker demanded revenge.

A 16-foot, roofed-in steel cage was the setting for Hell in the Cell, and, as expected, it was The Undertaker who thrived in that hellish environment. The Heartbreak Kid is in a class by himself when it comes to selling bumps, and he had plenty of opportunity to do so in the early going. The Undertaker threw him all over the ring and around the cage, producing some spectacularly athletic flops.

Michaels tried to mount an offense using the steps outside the ring as a weapon and making offensive use of a steel chair that was conveniently left inside. But even the vaunted HBK "sweet chin music" was not enough to slow down The Undertaker.

When a cameraman was injured in the melee, the door of the cell was opened so that he could be assisted out. Michaels took advantage of this and made a run for it. He was caught from behind by The Undertaker and driven face first into the side of the cell; his face was busted wide open. Michaels tried to escape by climbing the side of the cage, but The Undertaker followed and the battle continued on top of the cell. As Michaels made his way back down the side, he was knocked off the cage and into the Spanish announcers' table, thus inaugurating a tradition of destroying that particular piece of furniture.

Once both men touched ground, they headed back into the cell, and the fight continued. Victory seemed to be The Undertaker's at last after he leveled Michaels with a ringing chair shot. He did not get the pin, however, due to the unexpected arrival of Kane, in his first WWF appearance. Kane tombstoned The Undertaker, and Michaels was declared the victor since the match was of the no-disqualification variety. But, as he was carried back to the locker room by Hunter Hearst Helmsley and Chyna, his face a bloody mess, Michaels hardly looked like a winner. Despite its screwjob ending, Hell in the Cell I remains the best cage match of all time.

9. SUPER J TOURNAMENT FINAL
WILD PEGASUS VS. THE GREAT SASUKE
SUMO HALL; TOKYO, JAPAN
APRIL 16, 1994

In America, he is Chris Benoit, one of the most respected wrestlers in WCW; yet the bookers believe he is not flamboyant enough to hold a belt. In Japan, where wrestlers are judged more by what they do in the ring than what they say outside it, he is Wild Pegasus, one of New Japan's most fearsome and popular competitors and the holder of several prominent titles.

On April 16, 1994, New Japan's Super J tournament attracted 14 entrants, among them Dean Malenko, Eddie Guerrero, and Jushin Liger. At the end of the evening, all of the vanquished competitors gathered around the ring to watch the final match: Wild Pegasus vs. The Great Sasuke. It was to be a contest of power, grace, and athleticism with few equals.

The pace was primarily methodical but, at regular intervals, furious flurries of holds and counterholds would suddenly erupt. Early on, Benoit attempted a swinging neck-breaker out of which Sasuke was able to contort his body and land on his feet — an astonishing display of agility. Sasuke pressed his advantage after that, employing martial-arts maneuvers and then avoiding a Benoit gut kick with a high dive and roll that would have earned 10 points from Olympic judges.

Benoit's never-say-die attitude, familiar to wcw viewers, allowed him to withstand the assault. He reversed the momentum again with snap suplexes (no one has ever done them better), clotheslines, and a tilt-a-whirl back-breaker, followed by his famous flying head butt. Every move was executed with textbook precision, but the tenacious Sasuke kicked out of the pin attempt and reverted to gymnastics. He nailed Benoit with a flying crossbody out of a cartwheel that sent both men to the floor.

Back in the ring, Benoit sidestepped a missile dropkick and regained the edge. He caught Sasuke going up to the top rope for an aerial assault and suplexed him almost into the center of the ring, scoring the pin at 18:45.

10. HELL IN THE CELL II
THE UNDERTAKER VS. MANKIND
WWF KING OF THE RING
THE IGLOO; PITTSBURGH, PENNSYLVANIA
JUNE 28, 1998

Truth be told, there wasn't much actual wrestling in this match. However, it did contain what is, indisputably, the most insane, unbelievable bump in any American wrestling match. It was Mick Foley who took the dreadful fall, which should surprise no one who's watched him wrestle in Japan as Cactus Jack.

Foley, as Mankind, was introduced first and immediately climbed to the top of the cell carrying a steel chair. The Undertaker joined him high above the crowd and was greeted with two chair shots. The Undertaker fought back — and how — by hurling Foley off the cage, a drop of 16 feet. Foley crashed into the Spanish announcers' table (of course) and lay almost motionless for three minutes. "Oh my God, he killed him!" yelled announcer Jim Ross. "He's broken in half!" Though overstatement is a constant in wrestling commentary, it seemed possible that this time Ross was right.

While The Undertaker looked on from the top of the cell, Foley was attended by doctors and trainers. Terry Funk and Vince McMahon also appeared and checked his condition. A stretcher was brought in, and as Foley was wheeled off it seemed that the match was over. But then, incredibly, Foley got up from the stretcher and began climbing the cage again!

The astonished crowd roared as The Undertaker met Foley at the edge of the cage, picked him up, and choke-slammed him through the roof. Foley once more fell 16 feet with a sickening thud. This bump, unlike his previous fall, was not planned. He landed flat on his back in the center of the ring and was unable to cushion the fall or roll with the impact. "Will somebody stop the damn match!" Ross pleaded. "Enough is enough!"

By now, even the most jaded wrestling fans were marking out to Foley's efforts. Sure, he had padding under his costume to help absorb the impact, but twice in one match far exceeded anyone's expectations and ran the very real risk of causing permanent injury.

Funk returned to the ring to buy Foley some recovery time only to be choke-slammed for his efforts. Somehow, Mankind did, indeed, get back on his feet and even managed to mount a brief offense, which culminated with a piledriver that propelled The Undertaker onto a steel chair and earned a two-count.

Just when it seemed the match couldn't get more violent, Foley rolled out to the floor and retrieved a bag of thumbtacks, which he sprinkled all over the ring. But by this time, he was clearly suffering from a multitude of injuries and was unable to spring his trap. Instead, he was dropped twice onto his own tacks by The Undertaker, who then followed up with his tombstone finisher to get the pin at 17:01.

The stretcher was brought back to the ring, but Foley managed to walk out of the cage to a standing ovation. After the match, it was reported that he had blacked out twice — once after each fall. He had also suffered broken ribs, a broken ankle, and a dislocated jaw.

The Top 10 Wrestling Events
(By Attendance)

1. **PYONGYANG INTERNATIONAL SPORTS AND CULTURE FESTIVAL FOR PEACE**
   MAYDAY STADIUM; PYONGYANG, NORTH KOREA
   APRIL 29, 1995
   ATTENDANCE: 190,000

In the final day of this three-day festival, Ric Flair and Antonio Inoki met for the first time. Flair was pinned in just under 15 minutes, to the delight of the crowd.

2. **PYONGYANG INTERNATIONAL SPORTS AND CULTURE FESTIVAL FOR PEACE**
   MAYDAY STADIUM; PYONGYANG, NORTH KOREA
   APRIL 28, 1995
   ATTENDANCE: 150,000

Day two of this three-day event saw IWGP champion Shinya Hashimoto battle to a 20-minute draw against American Scott Norton.

3. WRESTLEMANIA III
PONTIAC SILVERDOME; PONTIAC, MICHIGAN
MARCH 29, 1987
ATTENDANCE: 93,173

The WWF Heavyweight title match between Hulk Hogan and Andre the Giant was the most talked-about wrestling event since the end of World War II. Hogan won the match and penned a new chapter in his legend, but the contest was nearly overshadowed by Ricky Steamboat's dramatic victory over Randy Savage for the Intercontinental belt.

4. SUMMERSLAM 1992
WEMBLEY STADIUM; LONDON, ENGLAND
AUGUST 29, 1992
ATTENDANCE: 80,355

Local favorite The British Bulldog upset brother-in-law Bret "The Hit Man" Hart to win the WWF Intercontinental title. Also on the card, The Ultimate Warrior beat Randy Savage by count-out, and The Undertaker won a decision over Kamala the Ugandan Headhunter as a result of outside interference.

5. WWF HOUSE SHOW
EXHIBITION STADIUM; TORONTO, ONTARIO, CANADA
AUGUST 28, 1986
ATTENDANCE: 74,080

At the dizzying height of Hulkamania, the WWF brought its touring show to Canada, and nearly 75,000 fans turned out to watch the Hulkster successfully defend his title against Paul "Mr. Wonderful" Orndorff.

6. WRESTLEMANIA VI
SKYDOME; TORONTO, ONTARIO, CANADA
APRIL 1, 1990
ATTENDANCE: 67,678

World Wrestling Federation history was made when The Ultimate Warrior scored a clean pin over Hulk Hogan and was presented with the Heavyweight title belt by the defeated Hulkster. This unique WrestleMania card also featured the WWF's first mixed tag-team match: Dusty Rhodes and

Sapphire beat Randy Savage and Sensational Sherri Martel. Also, in one of the briefest matches on record — it lasted 19 seconds — The Hart Foundation defeated The Bolsheviks.

7. NEW JAPAN VS. UWFI
TOKYO DOME; TOKYO, JAPAN
APRIL 29, 1996
ATTENDANCE: 65,000

Two of the Far East's most successful promotions, New Japan and UWFI, came together for a series of matches that settled old feuds and created new ones. The main event featured New Japan's Shinya Hashimoto, who defeated UWFI's Nobuhiko Takada to earn the IWGP Heavyweight title.

8. TOKYO DOME EVENT
TOKYO DOME; TOKYO, JAPAN
MARCH 21, 1991
ATTENDANCE: 64,500

In the 1980s and 1990s, wrestling cards at the Tokyo Dome would routinely draw more than 50,000 fans, and that number always increased when The Nature Boy was in town. Ric Flair, then WCW Heavyweight champion, squared off against Tatsumi Fujinami and battled more than 30 minutes to a no-contest decision.

9. NEW JAPAN VS. UWFI
TOKYO DOME; TOKYO, JAPAN
JANUARY 4, 1996
ATTENDANCE: 64,000

The second match in an epic feud between New Japan's Keiji Muto and UWFI's Nobuhiko Takada drew an even bigger crowd than the first. Takada got the pin with a cross-arm-breaker.

10. TOKYO DOME EVENT
TOKYO DOME; TOKYO, JAPAN
FEBRUARY 10, 1990
ATTENDANCE: 63,900

Shinya Hashimoto and Masa Chono, top names in Japanese wrestling, were defeated by Antonio Inoki and Seiji Sakaguchi, two of the sport's all-time great grapplers, who came out of retirement for this special event.

The Top 10 Wrestling Events in the United States
(By Attendance)

1. WWF **WRESTLEMANIA III**
   PONTIAC SILVERDOME; PONTIAC, MICHIGAN
   MARCH 29, 1987
   ATTENDANCE: 93,173
   FEATURED MATCH: HULK HOGAN VS. ANDRE THE GIANT.

2. WWF **WRESTLEMANIA VIII**
   HOOSIER DOME; INDIANAPOLIS, INDIANA
   APRIL 5, 1992
   ATTENDANCE: 62,167
   FEATURED MATCH: RIC FLAIR VS. RANDY SAVAGE.

3. WWF **ROYAL RUMBLE 1997**
   ALAMODOME; SAN ANTONIO, TEXAS
   JANUARY 19, 1997
   ATTENDANCE: 60,525
   FEATURED MATCH: SHAWN MICHAELS VS. SID VICIOUS.

4. NWA **EVENT**
   TEXAS STADIUM; IRVING, TEXAS
   MAY 6, 1984
   ATTENDANCE: 43,517
   FEATURED MATCH: RIC FLAIR VS. KERRY VON ERICH.

5. WWF **SUPERCARD**
   SHEA STADIUM; NEW YORK, NEW YORK
   JUNE 25, 1976
   ATTENDANCE: 42,000
   FEATURED MATCH: BRUNO SAMMARTINO VS. STAN HANSEN.

6. WCW **MONDAY NITRO**
   GEORGIA DOME; ATLANTA, GEORGIA
   JANUARY 4, 1999
   ATTENDANCE: 41,000 (APPROXIMATE)
   FEATURED MATCH: HULK HOGAN VS. KEVIN NASH.

7. WWF **SUPERCARD**
   SHEA STADIUM; NEW YORK, NEW YORK
   AUGUST 9, 1980
   ATTENDANCE: 40,671
   FEATURED MATCH: BRUNO SAMMARTINO VS. LARRY ZBYSZKO.

8. WCW **MONDAY NITRO**
   GEORGIA DOME; ATLANTA, GEORGIA
   ATTENDANCE: 39,800
   FEATURED MATCH: HULK HOGAN VS. BILL GOLDBERG.

9. NWA **EVENT**
   COMISKEY PARK; CHICAGO, ILLINOIS
   JUNE 30, 1961
   ATTENDANCE: 38,622
   FEATURED MATCH: BUDDY ROGERS VS. PAT O'CONNOR.

10. NWA **EVENT**
    WRIGLEY FIELD; CHICAGO, ILLINOIS
    SEPTEMBER 20, 1934
    ATTENDANCE: 35,265
    FEATURED MATCH: JIM LONDOS VS. ED "STRANGLER" LEWIS.

The 10 Most Embarrassing Wrestling Matches/ Gimmicks

1. THE KING AND HIS COURT VS. DOINK AND THE DINKS

World Wrestling Federation fans still cringe when they recall Doink the Clown (Matt Osborne), a wrestler who would torment his opponents with squirting flowers and other novelty items from the Johnson-Smith catalog. Doink was a bad joke, especially when Dink, an identically dressed clown midget, would accompany him to the ring. A feud between Doink and Jerry "The King" Lawler culminated in a special match at the 1994 Survivor Series (November 23); Lawler, joined by three crown-wearing midgets named Sleazy, Queasy, and Cheesy, wrestled Doink and his three midget partners, Dink, Pink, and Wink. The result was a ridiculous spectacle worthy of neither wrestling nor the Ringling Brothers.

2. THE HUMILIATION OF DUSTIN RUNNELS

Once upon a time, Dustin Runnels was a promising wrestler with an impressive pedigree (his father is American Dream Dusty Rhodes). But after years stranded in the middle of WWF and WCW cards, Dustin donned a long, blond wig, a gold lamé costume, and feminine face paint to become Goldust. A cross between Adrian Adonis and Dr. Frank N. Furter from *The Rocky Horror Picture Show*, the androgynous Goldust ignited a feud with Razor Ramon by attempting to kiss him in the ring. The character was Runnels's ticket to featured matches, but the price of such fame was profound embarrassment. When he abandoned the persona, things got even worse. Runnels paraded through WWF events in a series of degrading outfits: he appeared as Marilyn Manson and then as Sable. On *Monday Night Raw*, he donned a giant diaper to play the New Year baby and got shoved into an outhouse by Stone Cold Steve Austin. He wore leather bondage outfits and dog collars and swapped icky tongue kisses with Luna Vachon. In June of 1998, Runnels burned his Goldust costume on a *Raw* telecast and vowed that his days of being anyone other than himself were over. Six months later, he was wearing those duds again.

(Photo Credit: Marko Shark)

"Goldust"

3. THE GLOW FEDERATION

The Gorgeous Ladies of Wrestling (GLOW) was a mid-1980s federation based at the Riviera Hotel in Las Vegas. The idea was to take beautiful women, teach them a few basic holds, and put them in costumes so sexy that no one would care about anything else. In each 30-minute show, third-rate wrestling was mixed with lame comic skits and cheesecake music videos. Among the regulars: Madame Ninotchka, a white-haired Russian villain; a red-white-and-blue-garbed cheerleader named Americana; a beach blonde called the California Doll; and the federation's "heavy" (literally and figuratively), the 300-pound Matilda the Hun.

4. THE NATURE GIRL

In the course of a legendary 27-year career, Ric Flair has done it all. But at WCW Uncensored 1995 (March 19), he did something that he probably wishes he hadn't. Earlier that year, Flair had lost a retirement match to Hulk Hogan, but that didn't stop him from renewing a feud with Randy Savage that began when both were in the WWF. At Uncensored, during Savage's match with Earthquake, Flair emerged from the audience in drag and began pounding on Savage (but not with his purse). The sight of The Nature Boy dressed in a black silk blouse, a long brown skirt, nylons, heels, and a Jaclyn Smith brunette wig, is one that wrestling fans could not soon forget, no matter how hard they tried.

5. THE SISTERS OF MERCY

Glen Ruth and Chaz Warrington are now better known as Mosh and Thrasher of the WWF's Headbangers team. But they didn't have their first professional experience wearing skirts while playing their current grunge-rock characters. When WWF's *Shotgun Saturday Night* debuted on January 4, 1997, Ruth and Warrington made their one-and-only television appearance as wrestling nuns — they were billed as The Sisters of Mercy. Mother Smucker (Ruth) and Sister Angelica (Warrington) walked to the ring (these were not flying nuns, unfortunately) to be met with reactions ranging from stunned silence to uncontrollable laughter. I'm surprised Vince McMahon didn't give them a manager dressed as the pope.

6. IRWIN R. SCHYSTER

In theory it wasn't a bad idea: a wrestling Internal Revenue Service agent. Who wouldn't want to watch this guy get smacked around? Assuming the role was veteran Mike Rotundo, a former NWA titleholder. In 1992, he began to appear alongside The Million Dollar Man, Ted DiBiase and, as Money Inc., the two actually enjoyed a short reign as WWF Tag champions. But really, who could take seriously a wrestler who performed in glasses, a white shirt, tie, suspenders, and dress pants? Why didn't more opponents just grab him by the tie and flip him across the ring?

7. THE MANY FACES OF GLENN JACOBS

Most wrestlers make several attempts to find a successful gimmick, but no wrestler ever had to endure as many silly characters as Glenn Jacobs. In the early 1990s, the 6' 7" Jacobs wrestled as "The Christmas Creature," Santa's biggest elf. In 1994, he entered Smoky Mountain Wrestling as "Unabom" — nothing like modeling a character after a deranged mass murderer. In 1995, he appeared in the WWF as Jerry Lawler's dentist, "Isaac Yankem, DDS." Sporting yellow, crooked teeth that matched his yellow, crooked hairstyle, "Yankem" lost a title shot against Bret Hart, but Jacobs was soon to return as "The New Diesel," a bad carbon copy of the Kevin Nash character (Nash had left the WWF for WCW). He now appears as "Kane," The Undertaker's fire-obsessed younger brother, but he's still not immune to embarrassment — how would you feel if you had to pretend that Paul Bearer was your father?

8. THE DISCO INFERNO

Maybe it's the whole 1970s revival, but lately fans have started cheering for The Disco Inferno. Since his debut in 1991, Disco (Glen Giburnetti) has been used primarily as a comic-relief jobber whose losses don't do much to enhance his opponents' reputations because he isn't considered a serious threat in the first place. To the strains of watered-down Chic, Disco struts to the ring in silk shirt, tight pants, and gold chains. Inside the squared circle, he strikes *Saturday Night Fever* poses until his fed-up opponent starts knocking him into the 1990s. But, win or lose, no matter how difficult the match, The Disco Inferno's Tony Manero hairstyle always remains perfect.

9. JAY LENO WRESTLES

If you can call it wrestling. In 1998, wcw had a wealth of wrestling talent, yet Eric Bischoff still thought it necessary to feature guest performers to sell his pay-per-views. Undaunted by the Karl Malone debacle at that year's Bash at the Beach, Bischoff ignited a feud with *Tonight Show* host Jay Leno by hosting a talk-show parody on *Nitro*. Leno signed to appear at Road Wild (August 8) alongside Diamond Dallas Page and square off against Bischoff and Hulk Hogan. Leno, whose schedule apparently allowed little time for training, could not even sell a fight with the diminutive Bischoff. He could not execute even the most basic hold, and to say he punched like a girl is an insult to girls everywhere. But announcer Tony Schiavone, in his typical bombastic fashion, thought he was witnessing the second coming of Lou Thesz: "I'm impressed! Leno's really showing us something!" he declared. What was shown was that wcw should leave the wrestling to wrestlers.

10. THE GOBBLEDYGOOKER

Hector Guerrero in a chicken suit. 'Nuff said.

The Women of Wrestling

Sixteen-year-old wrestler Sue Marshall gets slammed by an opponent

Female wrestlers have appeared off and on for decades in the major federations, including WCW and the WWF, but they have never achieved the same prominence as their male counterparts. Only a handful of champions — the Fabulous Moolah, Wendy Richter, Madusa, Luna Vachon, Akira Hokuto — have ever really gotten over with the fans. Considering the limited appeal of the women's ranks, it's ironic that *All the Marbles*, a 1981 film starring Peter Falk as the manager of a female tag team called The California Dolls (Vicki Frederick and Laurene Landon), is the best movie about wrestling ever made.

Women's wrestling found its most notorious niche when bikini-clad combatants wrestled in such slippery substances as mud, Jello, and baby oil at adult nightclubs like the Hollywood Tropicana in Los Angeles. The attraction of these events had little to do with wrestling. Short-lived federations such as GLOW (The Gorgeous Ladies of Wrestling) also traded more on sex appeal than athletic ability.

Though the WWF revived its Women's title in 1998, the most popular ladies in the sport's recent history have been valets, assistants, or managers. Whatever the title, their job consists mainly of wearing revealing outfits and distracting their man's opponent by any means necessary.

CHYNA

Talk about your strong, silent type. Chyna, "the ninth wonder of the world," could score a pin on most male wrestlers. Her character is that of a body-guard: first she served Hunter Hearst Helmsley; currently, she watches over all the members of Degeneration X.

Born Joanie Laurer in Rochester, New York, the woman who now intimidates the WWF's most fearsome wrestlers discovered weightlifting at the age of 16, and it wasn't long before she was powerlifting with the guys. She traveled through Europe on her own between the ages of 16 and 18 (Chyna may not talk much, but Joanie is fluent in three languages) and then enrolled in the University of Tampa. She joined the Peace Corps in 1992 and considered a career as a diplomat or as a member of the US Secret Service.

After leaving the Peace Corps, Laurer was led by her passion for body-building to Killer Kowalski's wrestling school. She wrestled in small women's circuits for awhile and competed in women's boxing matches before the sport had gained any mainstream exposure. Joanie joined the WWF in February of 1997 at the urging of Hunter Hearst Helmsley, whom she had met during her time with Kowalski.

At first, the "female bodyguard" angle didn't make much sense to Vince McMahon; he saw the drop-dead gorgeous Sable soar in popularity when she accompanied Helmsley to the ring and wanted to team Helmsley with another dreamgirl. But the angle was too unique to resist, and Chyna made an unforgettable first impression at a February 1997 pay-per-view during an Intercontinental match between Helmsley and Rocky Maivia. The interference of Goldust and Marlena cost Helmsley the match, but the two meddlers did not come out of it unscathed. Unannounced and unexpected, Chyna rose from a ringside seat, picked up Goldust's diminutive director, and shook her violently, as if she were mixing a cocktail.

Attacking one of the WWF's glamour girls was an express route to heel status, so when Chyna accompanied Helmsley to the ring the following week her reputation had already been established as a lantern-jawed bully. A brief feud with Marlena gave way to a period of playing the WWF's new mystery woman — the biggest mystery being whether she actually *was* a woman. "Chyna is a man!" signs became commonplace at the arenas.

When Helmsley joined DX, he brought Chyna along. As the popularity of that comically crude outlaw band has soared, so has that of Chyna, who now plays many roles, most notably that of a Margaret Dumont type coping with the Marx Brothers-like antics of Helmsley, Sean Waltman, and The New Age Outlaws. She still doesn't talk very often, but her voice has been heard on occasion. Chyna's first words in the WWF, spoken at the 1997 King of the Ring tournament, were "Kiss my ass!" — a sentiment directed at Mankind.

Her body is still hard, but her appearance has gradually softened with the help of makeup, a more flattering hairstyle, and plastic surgery (her enhanced breasts were introduced by Shawn Michaels in December of 1997 as "the two newest members of DX"). She even had a love interest for a while, in weightlifter-turned-wrestler Mark Henry.

ELIZABETH

There are fans who probably think that her last name is Elizabeth, and her first name is "Miss," or "The Lovely," because that's how she's been introduced since 1986. Born Elizabeth Heulette in Frankfort, Kentucky, Elizabeth became the first lady of wrestling when she began accompanying her real-life husband, Randy "The Macho Man" Savage, to the ring during the WWF's mid-1980s heyday. She was, in fact, the cause of one of Savage's first WWF feuds, after George "The Animal" Steele developed a crush on her.

When The Macho Man was triple-teamed by The Hart Foundation and The Honky Tonk Man in 1987, it was Elizabeth who dashed backstage and returned with Hulk Hogan, resulting in the formation of The Megapowers tag team. Savage won both the Intercontinental and, in 1988, the Heavyweight title with Elizabeth by his side. She was as well known to fans as any wrestler, despite the fact that she did little more than walk to and from the ring.

Demure and soft-spoken, Elizabeth never seemed comfortable with interviews; she rarely did any talking at all. She was not strong or aggressive enough to serve as anything more than a visual distraction, though she made the most of her qualifications in that capacity. Her most memorable moment of outside interference came during the main event of the 1988 SummerSlam. During the match, which pitted The Megapowers (Savage and Hogan) against Andre the Giant and Ted DiBiase, Elizabeth jumped to the ring apron and removed her skirt. A mesmerized DiBiase froze, allowing Savage to roll him up for the pin.

Savage became jealous when Elizabeth started managing Hogan during his singles matches, prompting a feud that was settled at WrestleMania V, when Hogan regained his Heavyweight title over The Macho Man. Elizabeth remained with Hogan then disappeared from the scene for awhile; Savage, not used to working alone, hired a new female manager: Sherri Martel. Returning in 1990, Elizabeth was eventually reunited with Savage. At SummerSlam 1991 they were married (though in real life they were already man and wife).

Elizabeth's last major WWF storyline developed from Ric Flair's assertion that she had been unfaithful to Savage with him, and that he had the pictures to prove it. The allegation turned out to be false, and Savage beat Flair to win the Heavyweight title at WrestleMania VIII in 1992. Elizabeth vanished soon after, and Savage went into semiretirement; he then jumped to WCW.

In 1996, after Hogan and Savage were reunited as a tag team in a new federation, Elizabeth returned to manage them. A few weeks later, however, she betrayed them to become a member of The Four Horsemen's entourage. For the first time, she was cast as a heel, but Elizabeth seemed too sweet to be evil, and even her membership in the New World Order couldn't sell the turnabout.

In her current role as Eric Bischoff's assistant, Elizabeth still holds her NWO membership. Her profile in WCW seemed to be dwindling, but in January of 1999 she was instrumental in forcing Goldberg to miss a Heavyweight title defense against Kevin Nash.

MARLENA

How does a former makeup artist for *The Larry King Show* wind up playing bondage games with a man called Sexual Chocolate on national television? For Terri Ann Boatwright, that long, strange journey began when she married Dustin Rhodes, a WCW wrestler. Her exotic beauty inspired promoters to send her into the spotlight, but not alongside her husband. As a bespectacled redhead named Alexandra York, the laptop-carrying "accountant" for Mike Rotunda, Terri debuted in 1990.

After Rotunda left for the WWF where he would create a similar character — Irwin R. Schyster — "Alexandra" started The York Foundation, a team of six-man-tag specialists comprised of Terry Taylor, Rick Morton, and Tommy Rich. These wrestlers towered over the diminutive Terri (who is just 5' tall and weighs 100 pounds), but even dressed in a business suit she had no trouble standing out in the crowd. Her husband, Dustin, was often on the receiving end of York Foundation attacks; it was only after he jumped to the WWF that Terri and Dusty began working together.

As the bizarre Goldust, Rhodes (a.k.a. Dustin Runnels) tried to kiss his opponents in the ring and claimed to have a crush on Razor Ramon. Fans who wondered if they were witnessing the emergence of the first openly gay wrestler in WWF history became further confused when Terri accompanied him to the ring. She was called Marlena, Goldust's "personal director." She wore a tight gold-lamé dress, and she smoked a cigar as if to echo the gender-switching attributes of her "star."

Marlena did not involve herself in Goldust's matches very often, though she was attacked repeatedly by Chyna in the early days of Degeneration X, prompting a feud between Goldust and Hunter Hearst Helmsley. Her most famous act of outside interference, however, took place at the WWF's Shotgun Saturday Night series; during a match with The Sultan, Marlena jumped to the ring apron and dropped her dress to the waist, distracting The Sultan and allowing Goldust to get the pin.

In May of 1997, the WWF revealed the man beneath the Goldust makeup in a series of interviews and introduced Marlena as his wife, Terri. When the heat around Goldust began to dissipate, the WWF enlarged Marlena's role in his storylines. She became the stakes in a series of Goldust-Brian Pillman matches, which took place shortly before Pillman's death. Marlena was cast as the victim of Goldust's betrayal with Luna Vachon, all part of an attempt to reignite Goldust's career as a heel. After the couple separated (as part of the angle), Marlena disappeared for several months.

Dustin Runnels abandoned his Goldust persona in 1998 to take on a series of humiliating characters. During Runnels's stint as an obnoxious religious zealot, Marlena returned: she turned up in the bed of porn star Val Venis! The feud that ensued returned Runnels to prominence (once again as Goldust), and depended on Terri (as she was now called) portraying herself an unfaithful wife. With Miss Jacqueline, Terri has become a partner in PMS (Pretty Mean Sisters), a duo that delights in tormenting wrestlers such as Val Venis and Mark Henry. A storyline in which Terri became pregnant, supposedly by Val Venis, and then lost her baby while interfering in a match was in very poor taste and quickly forgotten.

DEBRA MCMICHAEL

As did Elizabeth and Marlena, Debra McMichael entered wrestling by accompanying her husband to the ring. Former Chicago Bear Steve "Mongo" McMichael joined the elite Four Horsemen group of the WCW, and Debra, wearing a sash and a tiara to symbolize her 1996 Mrs. America pageant win, joined The Horsemen entourage along with Elizabeth and Woman (Nancy Sullivan).

She became the focal point in a feud between Mongo and Jeff Jarrett and ultimately switched sides. The McMichaels separated, but this split was not just part of a storyline: their marriage really was in the process of ending. Both took some time off, but when Mongo returned Debra did not.

By the fall of 1998, Jeff Jarrett had resumed his Double J character in the WWF, and Debra was once again by his side. Jarrett has struggled his entire career to find the persona that will get him over; Vince McMahon finally took the easy way out by having Debra strip to distract Jarrett's opponents. It may have been the only way to generate excitement over Jarrett's matches, and it certainly worked.

THE NITRO GIRLS

Kimberly Page spent years as the valet of husband Diamond Dallas Page, and she became well known to WCW fans as both The Diamond Doll and, later, The Booty Babe. In 1997, at the suggestion of Eric Bischoff, the former *Playboy* model with a master's degree in advertising became the leader of a dance troupe called The Nitro Girls.

Kim held auditions and eventually hired six girls. First came Chae, a former Atlanta Falcons cheerleader; Fyre (Teri Byrne), a fitness instructor; and Spice (Melissa Bellin), a trained chiropractor. Tayo and A.C. completed the line-up. New girls Whisper and Storm joined in 1998.

After just two weeks of rehearsal, The Nitro Girls debuted on *Monday Nitro*. In their first few appearances, the dance routines were so out of sync that you'd have thought they were all wearing Walkmans tuned to different radio stations. But after a few months they developed into a tight, energetic troupe and became WCW's most visible touring ambassadors. Whisper married wrestler Shawn Michaels in 1999.

SABLE

Rena Mero, a former Guess Jeans model, married Marc Mero while he was still a WCW wrestler named Johnny B. Badd. When Mero joined the WWF, Rena was invited into the federation as well. At WrestleMania XII, she was introduced as Hunter Hearst Helmsley's ring girl, Sable. Mero first got over with the fans for rescuing Sable from a Helmsley tirade following a loss. She became his manager, and Mero became the WWF Intercontinental champion in September of 1996. At that year's Slammy Awards, Sable appeared in a barely there bathing suit that had jaws dropping across the country.

A knee injury sidelined Mero for several months, but Sable continued to appear on *Monday Night Raw* almost every week. The elegant black evening gowns she wore for her early appearances were replaced with tight, black, wet-leather catsuits cut to reveal her every curve and her abundant cleavage. She modeled various wrestlers' T-shirts and sold inflatable WWF chairs until Mero returned and started dragging her out of the arena.

Mero had become jealous of Sable's popularity, and when he resumed action in October of 1997 as "Marvelous" Marc Mero, he tried to limit Sable's exposure, eventually barring her from ringside. "Sable" chants echoed throughout Mero's matches and only grew louder when Mero tried to humiliate Sable by dressing Goldust in one of her catsuits. Mero turned against Goldust when he tried to protect Sable from Luna Vachon. Threats and challenges were exchanged, culminating in a mixed-tag match in which Mero and Sable faced off against Goldust and Luna. Fans were shocked to see that Sable could perform polished wrestling maneuvers. She executed a powerbomb (or "Sablebomb") on Vachon and she pulled off one of Mero's TKO finishers to get the pin.

The WWF revived the Women's title just to give Sable more to do, but good competition has been hard to find. Between matches, Sable still makes regular appearances, wearing less and less clothing each time. In the summer of 1998, she won a bikini contest over Miss Jacqueline by going topless, though her breasts were obscured by painted-on black handprints. A 1999 *Playboy* pictorial left nothing to the imagination.

SUNNY

One million times. That's how often pictures of Sunny (a.k.a. Tammy Sytch) were downloaded from the WWF America Online site. No other celebrity from the worlds of film, television, or music has been downloaded more often. The bodacious blonde with the sexy smile hasn't done much *but* pose for pictures since her stint as manager of the tag-team champions The Bodydonnas. But when she would burst through the curtain with a confident, bouncing stride, to the musical strains of "I Know You Want Me," no one was thinking about her résumé.

Tamara Murphy Sytch was born and raised in New Jersey, the youngest of four children. It should surprise no one that she was a cheerleader in high school, but that's where the blond stereotype ends: Tammy also made the National Honor Society and earned a full academic scholarship to the University of Miami.

Though she had hoped to major in biology and become an orthopedic surgeon, Tammy changed her plans when, at the age of 17, she met Chris Candido, a boy whose goal was to be a professional wrestler. In 1993, Chris joined the Smoky Mountain circuit, and Tammy took classes at the University of Tennessee at Knoxville. It was Jim Cornette who first suggested to Chris that Tammy accompany him to the ring; she agreed to try it for six months.

As Tammy Sytch, she was Candido's valet and almost immediately became embroiled in a head-

(Photo Credit: Seth Poppel Yearbook Archives)

Tamara Sytch (Sunny), far right, when she was co-captain of her senior varsity cheerleading team

line-grabbing angle — she threatened to sue the promotion for sexual discrimination. She then broke up partners Brian Lee and Tracy Smothers, and, acting as a manager for the first time, she took Lee to the Heavyweight title. In February of 1994, Tammy was hired to manage her boyfriend. Just two months later, Candido and Brian Lee won the Tag belts from The Rock and Roll Express. Tammy was already a good-luck charm.

In November, Candido won the NWA World Heavyweight title. The following month, Tammy suffered a broken arm after being knocked off the ring apron during a match. Who said managing is easy?

In 1995, after Candido lost the title to Dan Severn, Tammy and Chris brought their act to the WWF. Starting out in the federation, Tammy played news correspondent "Tamara Murphy," but she was soon back at ringside. The young couple was initially billed as Chris and Tammy Spirit, but by the time their first TV match had aired they'd changed their names to Skip and Sunny, The Bodydonnas.

Sprinting to the ring in matching aerobics outfits, Skip and Sunny played annoying fitness gurus who chastised the crowd for being fat, lazy slobs. The fans booed right on cue, but who could stay mad at Sunny? While Skip was jobbing for the likes of Barry Horowitz, the crowd would chant, "Sun-ny! Sun-ny!" Her character wasn't supposed to like it, but Tammy couldn't help smiling.

Skip found a lookalike tag partner in "Zip" (Tom Pritchard), and The Bodydonnas went on to win the WWF Tag belts over The Godwinns in March of 1996. Sunny's role in the push that elevated this obscure team cannot be underestimated: no one in the stands could tell Skip from Zip, but everybody knew their curvaceous manager.

Sunny remained a heel for the rest of the year, first by dumping The Bodydonnas for The Godwinns and then by switching her allegiance to The Smoking Gunns. Each of her teams claimed the belts while she, with audacity, played the role of the fickle gold digger. The Bodydonnas exacted some revenge by hiring as their new manager a cross-dressing fat man named Cloudy. Meanwhile, Sunny introduced Farooq to the WWF.

Chris Candido joined ECW, but Sunny was too hot a commodity for the WWF to lose. She remained with the federation as a guest ring announcer and spokesmodel but was allowed to make occasional visits to ECW in order to manage her husband under a contract provision that no wrestler would have been granted.

A family tragedy — the death of her niece in an automobile accident — kept Tammy away from the ring throughout the summer of 1997, but she returned to the WWF and to managing in 1998. She hooked up with The Legion of Doom, which had been rechristened LOD 2000, but for the first time her magic touch did not bring gold. Shortly thereafter, she left to join her husband in ECW on a full-time basis.

Wrestling in Japan and Mexico
by Dorran Jack Epstein

Professional wrestling has fans around the world, from Europe to Australia. But the sport has attracted a particularly enthusiastic following in Japan and Mexico, where national federations and athletes have developed their own unique traditions, many of which have since been incorporated into the American wrestling scene.

JAPAN

Wrestling isn't known as "sports entertainment" in Japan; rather, it is taken seriously as a spectator sport, called *puroresu*, which dates back to 1883. That year, Shokichi Hamada, a former sumo wrestler, came to the United States to tour as the first Japanese professional wrestler. In 1887, Hamada brought 20 American wrestlers to Japan for a series of shows. The shows were a success, but they failed to spark any interest in the sport, and subsequent shows were complete duds. Over the next 60 years, there were many attempts to revive professional wrestling in Japan, all of which proved unsuccessful.

All that changed with the arrival of the powerful, charismatic Rikidozan, a former sumo wrestler who became the top draw in Japanese wrestling after he made his professional debut in 1951. In 1957, he wrestled Lou Thesz in Tokyo, in the first NWA World title match ever held in Japan. The match ended in a 60-minute time-limit draw. One year later, at a rematch in Los Angeles, Rikidozan defeated Thesz to win the NWA International title, which remains a part of All-Japan's Triple Crown.

In 1962, Rikidozan became the first Japanese wrestler to hold a major US title when he defeated Freddie Blassie for the WWA Heavyweight belt. But one year later, the Japanese wrestling world was shocked when Rikidozan was defeated by The Destroyer, who achieved instant celebrity status. The match is still remembered as one of the greatest in Japanese history. Rikidozan's life and career came to a tragic end in December of 1963, when he was stabbed to death in Osaka. He is still celebrated as the father of Japanese wrestling and the creator of the Japan Wrestling Alliance (JWA).

Kanji Inoki, later billed as Antonio Inoki, was recruited by Rikidozan in 1960 to wrestle for the JWA. In 1966, Inoki, who'd always had big dreams of starting his own federation, formed Tokyo Pro Wrestling, but his federation folded one year later, and he rejoined the JWA. Inoki was kicked out of the JWA in 1971 after it was discovered that he was planning a coup to take over the promotion. In 1972, Inoki's long-cherished dream came true as New Japan Pro Wrestling (NJPW) ran its inaugural card. The federation is currently the biggest in the world outside of North America.

Though he never became well known in the United States, Inoki did pin Bob Backlund in November of 1979 to win the WWF World Heavyweight title. The victory was never officially recognized, and Backlund won a rematch one week later. Inoki also scored a submission victory over Andre the Giant in 1986, and he pinned boxer Leon Spinks in a boxer-vs.-wrestler bout held in Tokyo.

In 1983, New Japan created the International Grand Prix titles for each of its divisions. These included the IWGP Heavyweight title, Junior Heavyweight title, and Tag-Team titles. Among the elite in the Heavyweight division are The Great Muta (also known — without the face paint — as Keiji Mutoh, Tatsumi Fujinami, and Shin'ya Hashimoto. Three Americans have held the IWGP Heavyweight belt as well: Hulk Hogan, Big Van Vader, and, most recently, Scott Norton.

Tag-team wrestling in NJPW has taken a backseat to the wrestling within the incredible Junior Heavyweight division. New Japan Pro Wrestling has provided fans with many memorable tournaments, such as the J Crown and the Super J Cup. Wrestlers like Jushin "Thunder" Liger, Chris Benoit, Shinjiro Ohtani, and Koji Kanemoto have dazzled crowds with their unique wrestling abilities. Liger holds the distinction of being the only wrestler in New Japan to have held the IWGP Junior Heavyweight title nine times.

New Japan holds the record for drawing some of the largest wrestling crowds ever. In 1995, in back-to-back shows mounted at the Mayday Stadium in Pyongyang, North Korea, the federation drew over 340,000 fans to two shows. Many NJPW shows in the Tokyo Dome draw more than 60,000 fans.

A new boom in Japanese wrestling took place in the early 1990's when groups like Frontier Martial Arts Wrestling (FMW), Wrestle and Romance (WAR), Michinoku Pro (Northeastern Wrestling), IWA (International Wrestling Alliance), and Big Japan sprouted up. In 1994, there were over 30 wrestling organizations operating in Tokyo alone. Michinoku Pro was started by The Great Sasuke in 1993, and it features some of the most talented junior heavyweights in the world. Most wrestlers in Michinoku Pro use the *lucha libre* style usually associated with Mexico. In fact, most of the group's membership has wrestled in masks.

Another prominent organization, All Japan Pro Wrestling, was formed in 1972 by Shohei Baba, a former baseball player and JWA star. All Japan is currently the second-largest wrestling promotion in Japan. The main titles in AJPW include the Triple Crown (unified United National, International, and PWF Heavyweight titles), the World Tag-Team title, the World Junior Heavyweight title, and the Asian Tag-Team title. All Japan has ties to the WWF, and Shohei Baba has met with Vince McMahon to discuss future dealings. The federation also boasts a roster of impressive heavyweight wrestlers, including Mitsuharu Misawa, Kenta Kobashi, Big Van Vader, Toshiaki Kawada, and Stan Hansen. Misawa and Kobashi are considered two of the best and most talented performers in the world.

All Japan isn't known for its Junior Heavyweight division, but credit certainly goes to Masanobu Fuch, who has held the Junior Heavyweight title an unprecedented five times. The federation has also built an incredible Tag division that has put on some of the greatest matches ever. Teams like Dan Kroffat and Doug Furnas, Terry Gordy and Steve Williams, and Toshiaki Kawada and Akira Taue have dominated the scene for years. For its major shows, AJPW usually draws respectable crowds (16,000 plus). All Japan also features some of the greatest women's wrestling in the world. The Women's division was actually formed in 1968, two years before the Men's division. To avoid confusion, it is referred to as AJWPW.

In addition to presenting the standard wrestling matches familiar to American audiences, federations like IWA Japan, Big Japan, W*ING, and FMW also put on some of the most bizarre and disturbing matches ever conceived: IWA hosted the King of the Death Match tournament in 1995, which featured a bizarre series of matches involving barbed wire, explosives, broken glass, chains, ladders, thumbtacks, baseball bats, tables, beds of nails, and many more gruesome objects; Big Japan hosted the 1998 version of the tournament, which was nothing short of a bloodbath.

Famous for its mix of stiff, garbage, high-flying, and women's wrestling, FMW was founded by Astushi Onita, the inventor of the exploding-ring death match. The federation's wrestlers usually end up with broken bones, bad burns, and skin ripped to shreds on the barbed wire engulfing the ring. And if you think that is disturbing, consider this: these bizarre matches are aired regularly on national television.

Over time, Japan has developed all the aspects of wrestling that we've come to love — and then some. In America, wrestlers like TAKA Michinoku, Dick Togo, and The Great Muta can't get over with the fans, but in Japan they would headline any main event. Japanese fans seem more appreciative of the performances that wrestlers give. They don't walk out in the middle of a match, they don't chant "Bor-ing," and they don't hold up derogatory signs. Instead, they cheer, they applaud, they throw streamers into the ring, and they have a good time. Also, Japanese wrestling fans aren't ridiculed by the population at large as their American counterparts are; in fact, wrestling is as mainstream in Japan as any other sport. Match results are reported in the newspaper sports pages.

MEXICO

Mexican wrestling has become more mainstream in the last few years with the arrival in the American federations of Rey Misterio Jr., Eddie Guerrero, and others. In fact, Mexican wrestling, or *lucha libre*, is now the most emulated style among up-and-coming wrestlers. *Lucha libre* describes the high-flying, acrobatic style of wrestling found in Mexico and Puerto Rico. A loose translation of *lucha libre* would be "the free fight." Its performers are called *luchadores*. The oldest federation in Mexico is the Consejo Mundial de Lucha Libre (CMLL); it put on its first show on September 21, 1933.

The masked wrestler, El Santo, was born within the CMLL. A national hero in Mexico, Santo held numerous titles in the course of his 40-year career, beginning in 1946 with the NWA World Welterweight title. He also starred in several movies, including *Santo vs. the Martian Invasion* (1966) and *Santo vs. Frankenstein's Daughter* (1971). Several wrestlers played the role of the masked El Santo, but sharp-eyed fans can tell the original from his many stand-ins. Santo died in 1985 and was buried with his mask on. El Hijo del Santo (The Son of Santo) was a megaface in CMLL; when he turned heel it incited a riot in the arena that spread out into the streets.

Another revered Mexican wrestler was Gory Guerrero, who pinned Tarzan Lopez in 1946 to win the NWA World Middleweight title. Guerrero's four sons — Chavo, Mondo, Hector, and Eddy — would all go on to win the NWA World titles in the Welterweight and Light Heavyweight divisions. Eddy and his nephew, Chavo Guerrero Jr., now wrestle for WCW.

The *luchador's* mask is a revered tradition with an interesting history behind it. It isn't just there to conceal the identity of a wrestler; instead, it is

(Photo Credit: American Stock Photos)

Mil Mascaras

the most important thing a *luchador* possesses. The wearing of it was inspired by the ancient Aztec tradition of masked warriors. Losing a mask is considered the ultimate humiliation a wrestler can endure. Only a few have ever finished their careers without at some point losing their masks, however: mask-vs.-mask matches are very popular in Mexico. Many wrestlers of other nationalities, like Jushin Liger and Sasuke, wear masks to pay tribute to the style they emulate.

In 1972, Mil Mascaras became the first masked wrestler to compete in New York's Madison Square Garden. Ironically, he defeated The Spoiler, a wrestler who had previously been denied the right to compete with a mask in New York.

Other federations in Mexico include Antonio Pena's AAA, which broadcast a national pay-per-view back in 1993 entitled When World's Collide, and Konnan's Pro Azteca. In 1993, the AAA brought a card to the Los Angeles Sports Arena that drew a sold-out crowd of more than 16,000; 8,000 more fans were turned away at the door. In the main event, Konnan defeated Cien Caras and Jake Roberts in a triangle match.

The rules of *lucha libre* wrestling vary somewhat from those that regulate American wrestling. There are unusually large numbers of six-man-tag and two-out-of-three-falls matches; and in tag competition, going outside of the ring is the same as tagging in one of your partners. It's done this way to keep the action fast-paced and the viewers interested. Most matches also involve a series of comedic moments (that is, all six wrestlers will mess up some of their spots).

Midgets are an essential part of Mexican wrestling. However, they are not considered to be comic relief, as they are in American wrestling; instead, they are taken as seriously as their larger peers. They work an intense *lucha libre* style and usually adopt the gimmick of their favorite *luchador* (for example, "Mini" Mascarita Sagrada emulates the style and look of Mascara Sagrada). Any wrestler under 5' tall is usually considered to be a midget.

Mexican wrestlers are generally divided into two classes: *technicos* and *rudos*. A *technico* is a face, or good guy; a *rudo* is a heel, or bad guy. The most emulated wrestling move is the *hurancurana*, first made famous by Hurricane Ramirez and his descendants. The same move has been called a "frankensteiner" in America, where it is used by The Steiner Brothers.

Lucha libre is, in my opinion, the most electrifying form of wrestling out there. At *lucha libre* matches you won't find beer-bellied brawlers screaming into a microphone; rather, you will witness a beautiful display of athleticism and showmanship. After more than 60 years, the style is finally finding its way into the American federations. Let's hope the trend continues.

Title Histories

The following is a list of all titleholders in the most significant wrestling associations, past and present. Numbers following some names indicate the number of times a wrestler or tag team has held the title.

American Wrestling Association (AWA)
World Heavyweight title

Champion	Won
Verne Gagne	August 16, 1960
Gene Kiniski	July 11, 1961
Verne Gagne (2)	August 8, 1961
Mr. M	January 8, 1962
Verne Gagne (3)	August 21, 1962
The Crusher	July 9, 1963
Verne Gagne (4)	July 20, 1963
Fritz Von Erich	July 27, 1963
Verne Gagne (5)	August 8, 1963
The Crusher (2)	November 28, 1963
Verne Gagne (6)	December 14, 1963
Mad Dog Vachon	October 20, 1964
The Crusher (3)	August 21, 1965
Mad Dog Vachon (2)	November 11, 1965

Champion	Won
Verne Gagne (7)	February 26, 1967
Dr. X	August 17, 1968
Verne Gagne (8)	August 31, 1968
Nick Bockwinkel	November 8, 1975
Verne Gagne (9)	July 18, 1980
Nick Bockwinkel (2)	May 19, 1981
Otto Wanz	August 29, 1982
Nick Bockwinkel (3)	October 9, 1982
Jumbo Tsuruta	February 22, 1984
Rick Martel	May 13, 1984
Stan Hansen	December 29, 1985
Nick Bockwinkel (4)	June 29, 1986
Curt Hennig	May 2, 1987
Jerry Lawler	May 9, 1988
Larry Zbyszko	February 7, 1989
Mr. Saito	February 10, 1990
Larry Zbyszko (2)	April 8, 1990

AWA World Tag-Team title

Champion	Won
Hardboiled Haggerty, Len Montana	October 4, 1960
Wilbur Synder, Leo Nomellini	May 23, 1961
Hardboiled Haggerty, Gene Kiniski	July 19, 1961
Dale Lewis, Pat Kennedy	November 16, 1961
Bob Geigel, Otto Von Krupp	November 23, 1961
Larry Hennig, Duke Hoffman	January 15, 1962
Bob Geigel, Stan Kowalski	February 13, 1962
Art and Stan Neilson	April 4, 1962
Doug Gilbert, Dick Steinborn	December 16, 1962
Ivan and Karol Kalmikoff	January 1, 1963
The Crusher, Dick the Bruiser	August 20, 1963
Verne Gagne, Moose Evans	February 9, 1964
The Crusher, Dick the Bruiser (2)	February 23, 1964
Larry Hennig, Harley Race	January 30, 1965
The Crusher, Verne Gagne	July 24, 1965
Larry Hennig, Harley Race (2)	August 7, 1965
The Crusher, Dick the Bruiser (3)	May 28, 1966
Larry Hennig, Harley Race (3)	January 6, 1967
Pat O'Connor, Wilbur Snyder	November 10, 1967

Champion	Won
Mitsu Arakawa, Dr. Moto	December 2, 1967
The Crusher, Dick the Bruiser (4)	December 28, 1968
Mad Dog and Butcher Vachon	August 30, 1969
Red Bastien, Hercules Cortez	May 15, 1971
Nick Bockwinkel, Ray Stevens	January 20, 1972
Verne Gagne, Billy Robinson	December 30, 1972
Nick Bockwinkel, Ray Stevens (2)	January 6, 1973
The Crusher, Billy Robinson	July 21, 1974
Nick Bockwinkel, Ray Stevens (3)	October 24, 1974
The Crusher, Dick the Bruiser (5)	August 16, 1975
Blackjack Lanza, Bobby Duncan	July 23, 1976
Greg Gagne, Jim Brunzell	July 7, 1977
Pat Patterson, Ray Stevens	September 22, 1978
Verne Gagne, Mad Dog Vachon	June 6, 1979
Adrian Adonis, Jesse Ventura	July 20, 1980
Greg Gagne, Jim Brunzell	June 14, 1981
Crusher Blackwell, Ken Patera	June 26, 1983
The Crusher, Baron Von Raschke	May 6, 1984
The Road Warriors	August 25, 1984
Jim Garvin, Steve Regal	September 29, 1985
Scott Hall, Curt Hennig	January 18, 1986
Buddy Rose, Doug Somers	May 17, 1986
Shawn Michaels, Marty Jannetty	January 27, 1987
Soldat Ustinov, Boris Zhukov	May 25, 1987
Bill Dundee, Jerry Lawler	October 11, 1987
Dr. D, Hector Guerrero	October 19, 1987
Bill Dundee, Jerry Lawler (2)	October 26, 1987
Dennis Condrey, Randy Rose	October 30, 1987
Shawn Michaels, Marty Jannetty (2)	December 27, 1987
Paul Diamond, Pat Tanaka	March 19, 1988
Ken Patera, Brad Rheingans	March 25, 1989
Wayne Bloom, Mike Enos	October 1, 1989
D.J. Peterson, The Trooper	August 11, 1990

Eastern Championship Wrestling/Extreme
Championship Wrestling (ECW) Heavyweight title

Champion	Won
Jimmy Snuka	April 25, 1992
Johnny Hot Body	April 26, 1992

Champion	Won
Jimmy Snuka (2)	July 12, 1992
Don Muraco	October 24, 1992
The Sandman	November 16, 1992
Don Muraco (2)	April 3, 1993
Tito Santana	August 8, 1993
Shane Douglas	September 9, 1993
Sabu	October 2, 1993
Terry Funk	December 26, 1993
Shane Douglas (2)	March 26, 1994
The Sandman (2)	April 15, 1995
Mikey Whipwreck	October 28, 1995
The Sandman (3)	December 9, 1995
Raven	January 27, 1996
The Sandman (4)	October 5, 1996
Raven (2)	December 7, 1996
Terry Funk (2)	April 13, 1997
Sabu (2)	August 9, 1997
Shane Douglas (3)	August 17, 1997
Bam Bam Bigelow	October 16, 1997
Shane Douglas (4)	November 30, 1997
Tasmaniac	January 10, 1999

ECW Tag-Team title

Champion	Won
The Super Destroyers	June 23, 1992
Tony Stetson, Larry Winters	April 2, 1993
The Suicide Blonds	April 3, 1993
The Super Destroyers (2)	May 15, 1993
The Suicide Blonds (2)	May 15, 1993
Eddie Gilbert, The Dark Patriot	August 7, 1993
Tony Stetson, Johnny Hot Body	September 18, 1993
Tommy Dreamer, Johnny Gunn	November 13, 1993
Kevin Sullivan, Tasmaniac	December 4, 1993
Public Enemy	March 6, 1994
Cactus Jack, Mikey Whipwreck	August 27, 1994
Public Enemy (2)	November 5, 1994
Sabu, Tasmaniac	February 4, 1995
Chris Benoit, Dean Malenko	February 25, 1995
Public Enemy (3)	April 8, 1995

Champion	Won
Raven, Stevie Richards	June 20, 1995
The Pit Bulls	September 16, 1995
Raven, Stevie Richards (2)	October 7, 1995
Public Enemy (4)	October 7, 1995
Sandman, 2 Cold Scorpio	October 28, 1995
Cactus Jack, Mikey Whipwreck (2)	December 29, 1995
The Eliminators	February 3, 1996
The Gangstas	August 3, 1996
The Eliminators (2)	December 20, 1996
Buh Buh Ray, D-Von Dudley	March 15, 1997
The Eliminators (3)	April 13, 1997
Buh Buh Ray, D-Von Dudley (2)	June 20, 1997
The Gangstas (2)	July 19, 1997
Buh Buh Ray, D-Von Dudley (3)	August 17, 1997
John Kronus, New Jack	September 20, 1997
Little Guido, Tracey Smothers	October 18, 1997
Doug Furnas, Phil Lafon	December 5, 1997
Chris Candido, Lance Storm	December 6, 1997
Sabu, Rob Van Dam	June 27, 1998
The Dudleys	October 24, 1998
Masato Tanaka, Balls Mahoney	November 1, 1998
The Dudleys (2)	November 6, 1998
Sabu, Rob Van Dam (2)	December 13, 1998
The Dudleys (3)	April 17, 1999

ECW Television title

Champion	Won
Johnny Hot Body	August 12, 1992
Jimmy Snuka	March 12, 1993
Terry Funk	October 1, 1993
Sabu	November 13, 1993
Tasmaniac	March 6, 1994
J.T. Smith	March 6, 1994
Pit Bull	April 16, 1994
Mikey Whipwreck	May 13, 1994
Jason	August 13, 1994
2 Cold Scorpio	November 4, 1994
Dean Malenko	November 4, 1994
2 Cold Scorpio (2)	March 18, 1995

Champion	Won
Eddy Guerrero	April 8, 1995
Dean Malenko (2)	July 21, 1995
Eddy Guerrero (2)	July 28, 1995
2 Cold Scorpio (3)	August 25, 1995
Mikey Whipwreck (2)	December 7, 1995
2 Cold Scorpio (4)	January 5, 1996
Shane Douglas	May 11, 1996
Pit Bull II	June 1, 1996
Chris Jericho	June 22, 1996
Shane Douglas (2)	July 13, 1996
Tasmaniac (2)	June 7, 1997
Bam Bam Bigelow	March 1, 1998
Rob Van Dam	April 4, 1998

National Wrestling Alliance (NWA)/World Championship Wrestling (WCW) Heavyweight title

Champion	Won
George Hackenschmidt	May 5, 1904
Frank Gotch	April 3, 1908
Joe Stecher	July 4, 1915
Earl Caddock	April 9, 1917
Joe Stecher (2)	January 30, 1920
Ed "Strangler" Lewis	February 13, 1920
Stanislaus Zbyszko	May 6, 1921
Ed "Strangler" Lewis (2)	March 3, 1922
Wayne Munn	January 8, 1925
Stanislaus Zbyszko (2)	April 15, 1925
Joe Stecher (3)	May 30, 1925
Ed "Strangler" Lewis (3)	February 20, 1928
Gus Sonnenberg	January 4, 1929
Dick Shikat	August 23, 1929
Jim Londos	June 6, 1930
Ed Don George	December 10, 1930
Ed "Strangler" Lewis (4)	April 13, 1931
Henry DeGlane	May 4, 1931
Ed "Strangler" Lewis (5)	June 9, 1932
Ed Don George (2)	February 9, 1933
Jim Browning	February 20, 1933
Jim Londos (2)	June 25, 1934

Champion	Won
Danno O'Mahony	June 27, 1935
Dick Shikat (2)	March 2, 1936
Ali Baba	April 24, 1936
Everett Marshall	June 26, 1936
Lou Thesz	December 29, 1937
Steve Crusher Casey	February 11, 1938
Everett Marshall (2)	September, 1938
Lou Thesz (2)	February 23, 1939
Bronko Nagurski	June 23, 1939
Ray Steele	March 7, 1940
Bronko Nagurski (2)	March 11, 1941
Sandor Szabo	June 5, 1941
Bill Longson	February 19, 1942
Yvon Robert	October 7, 1942
Bobby Managoff	November 27, 1942
Bill Longson (2)	February 19, 1943
Whipper Billy Watson	February 21, 1947
Lou Thesz (3)	April 25, 1947
Bill Longson (3)	November 21, 1947
Lou Thesz (4)	July 20, 1948
Dick Hutton	March 15, 1956
Pat O'Connor	November 9, 1956
Buddy Rogers	November 14, 1957
Lou Thesz (5)	January 9, 1959
Gene Kiniski	June 30, 1961
Dory Funk Jr.	January 24, 1963
Harley Race	January 7, 1966
Dory Funk Jr. (2)	February 11, 1969
Harley Race (2)	May 24, 1973
Jack Brisco	July 20, 1973
Shohei Baba	December 2, 1974
Jack Brisco (2)	December 9, 1974
Terry Funk	December 10, 1974
Harley Race (3)	February 6, 1977
Dusty Rhodes	August 21, 1979
Harley Race (4)	August 26, 1979
Shohei Baba (2)	October 31, 1979
Harley Race (5)	November 7, 1979
Shohei Baba (3)	September 4, 1980
Harley Race (6)	September 10, 1980
Tommy Rich	April 27, 1981

Champion	Won
Harley Race (7)	May 1, 1981
Dusty Rhodes (2)	June 21, 1981
Ric Flair	September 17, 1981
Harley Race (8)	June 10, 1983
Ric Flair (2)	November 23, 1983
Kerry Von Erich	May 6, 1984
Ric Flair (3)	May 24, 1984
Dusty Rhodes (3)	July 26, 1986
Ric Flair (4)	August 9, 1986
Ronnie Garvin	September 25, 1987
Ric Flair (5)	November 26, 1987
Ricky Steamboat	February 20, 1989
Ric Flair (6)	May 7, 1989
Sting	July 7, 1990
Ric Flair (7)	January 11, 1991
Lex Luger	July 14, 1991
Sting (2)	February 29, 1992
Vader	July 12, 1992
Ron Simmons	August 2, 1992
Vader (2)	December 30, 1992
Sting (3)	March 11, 1993
Vader (3)	March 17, 1993
Ric Flair (8)	December 27, 1993
Hulk Hogan	July 17, 1994
Randy Savage	November 26, 1995
Ric Flair (9)	December 27, 1995
Randy Savage (2)	January 22, 1996
Ric Flair (10)	February 11, 1996
The Giant	April 22, 1996
Hulk Hogan (2)	August 10, 1996
Lex Luger (2)	August 4, 1997
Hulk Hogan (3)	August 9, 1997
Sting (4)	December 28, 1997
Sting (5)	February 22, 1998
Randy Savage (3)	April 19, 1998
Hulk Hogan (4)	April 20, 1998
Goldberg	July 6, 1998
Kevin Nash	December 27, 1998
Hulk Hogan (5)	January 4, 1999
Ric Flair (11)	March 14, 1999
Diamond Dallas Page	April 11, 1999

Champion	Won
Sting (6)	April 26, 1999
Diamond Dallas Page (2)	April 26, 1999
Kevin Nash (2)	May 9, 1999

NWA/WCW World Tag-Team title

Champion	Won
Ricky Steamboat, Jay Youngblood	May 10, 1980
Ray Stevens, Jimmy Snuka	June 22, 1980
Paul Jones, The Masked Superstar	November 27, 1980
Ray Stevens, Ivan Koloff	February 2, 1981
Paul Jones, The Masked Superstar (2)	March 22, 1981
Gene and Ole Anderson	May 1, 1981
Sgt. Slaughter, Don Kernodle	September 12, 1982
Ricky Steamboat, Jay Youngblood (2)	March 12, 1983
Jack and Jerry Brisco	June 18, 1983
Ricky Steamboat, Jay Youngblood (3)	October 3, 1983
Jack and Jerry Brisco (2)	October 21, 1983
Ricky Steamboat, Jay Youngblood (4)	November 24, 1983
Don Kernodle, Bob Orton Jr.	January 8, 1984
Wahoo McDaniel, Mark Youngblood	March 4, 1984
Jack and Jerry Brisco (3)	April 4, 1984
Wahoo McDaniel, Mark Youngblood (2)	April 27, 1984
Ivan Koloff, Don Kernodle	May 1984
Dusty Rhodes, Manny Fernandez	October 20, 1984
Ivan and Nikita Koloff	March 18, 1985
Rick Morton, Robert Gibson	July 9, 1985
Ivan and Nikita Koloff (2)	October 13, 1985
Rick Morton, Robert Gibson (2)	November 28, 1985
Dennis Condrey, Bobby Eaton	February 2, 1986
Rick Morton, Robert Gibson (3)	August 16, 1986
Manny Fernandez, Rick Rude	December 6, 1986
Rick Morton, Robert Gibson (4)	May 28, 1987
Arn Anderson, Tully Blanchard	September 29, 1987
Lex Luger, Barry Windham	March 27, 1988
Arn Anderson, Tully Blanchard (2)	April 20, 1988
Bobby Eaton, Stan Lane	September 10, 1988
The Road Warriors	October 29, 1988
Mike Rotundo, Steve Williams	April 2, 1989
The Freebirds	June 14, 1989

Champion	Won
The Steiner Brothers	November 1, 1989
Butch Reed, Ron Simmons	May 19, 1990
The Freebirds (2)	February 24, 1991
The Steiner Brothers (2)	March 9, 1991
The Enforcers	September 5, 1991
Dustin Rhodes, Ricky Steamboat	November 19, 1991
Arn Anderson, Bobby Eaton	January 16, 1992
The Steiner Brothers (3)	May 3, 1992
Steve Williams, Terry Gordy	July 5, 1992
Dustin Rhodes, Barry Windham	September 21, 1992
Shane Douglas, Ricky Steamboat	November 18, 1992
The Hollywood Blondes	March 2, 1993
Arn Anderson, Paul Roma	August 18, 1993
The Nasty Boys	September 19, 1993
2 Cold Scorpio, Mark Bagwell	October 4, 1993
The Nasty Boys (2)	October 24, 1993
Cactus Jack, Kevin Sullivan	May 22, 1994
Pretty Wonderful	July 17, 1994
Stars & Stripes	September 25, 1994
Pretty Wonderful (2)	October 23, 1994
Stars & Stripes (2)	November 16, 1994
Harlem Heat	December 8, 1994
The Nasty Boys (3)	May 21, 1995
Harlem Heat (2)	June 24, 1995
Bunkhouse Buck, Dick Slater	July 22, 1995
Harlem Heat (3)	September 17, 1995
The American Males	September 18, 1995
Harlem Heat (4)	September 27, 1995
Sting, Lex Luger	January 22, 1996
Harlem Heat (5)	June 24, 1996
The Steiner Brothers (4)	July 24, 1996
Harlem Heat (6)	July 27, 1996
Public Enemy	September 23, 1996
Harlem Heat (7)	October 1, 1996
Scott Hall, Kevin Nash	October 27, 1996
The Steiner Brothers (5)	October 13, 1997
Scott Hall, Kevin Nash (2)	January 12, 1998
The Steiner Brothers (6)	February 9, 1998
Scott Hall, Kevin Nash (3)	February 22, 1998
Sting, Kevin Nash	June 15, 1998
Scott Hall, The Giant	July 20, 1998

Champion	Won
Scott Steiner, Kenny Kaos	October 26, 1998
Curt Hennig, Barry Windham	February 21, 1999
Chris Benoit, Dean Malenko	March 14, 1999
Kidman, Rey Misterio, Jr.	March 29, 1999
Raven, Saturn	May 9, 1999

NWA/WCW United States Heavyweight title

Champion	Won
Ric Flair	April 19, 1980
Roddy Piper	January 27, 1981
Wahoo McDaniel	August 8, 1981
Sgt. Slaughter	October 4, 1981
Wahoo McDaniel (2)	May 21, 1982
Sgt. Slaughter (2)	June 7, 1982
Wahoo McDaniel (3)	August 22, 1982
Greg Valentine	November 4, 1982
Roddy Piper (2)	April 16, 1983
Greg Valentine (2)	April 30, 1983
Dick Slater	December 14, 1983
Ricky Steamboat	April 21, 1984
Wahoo McDaniel (4)	June 24, 1984
Magnum T.A.	March 23, 1985
Tully Blanchard	July 21, 1985
Magnum T.A. (2)	November 28, 1985
Nikita Koloff	August 17, 1986
Lex Luger	July 11, 1987
Dusty Rhodes	November 26, 1987
Barry Windham	May 13, 1988
Lex Luger (2)	February 20, 1989
Michael Hayes	May 7, 1989
Lex Luger (3)	May 22, 1989
Stan Hansen	October 27, 1990
Lex Luger (4)	December 16, 1990
Sting	August 25, 1991
Rick Rude	November 19, 1991
Dustin Rhodes (2)	January 11, 1993
Steve Austin	December 27, 1993
Ricky Steamboat	August 24, 1994
Steve Austin (2)	September 19, 1994

Champion	Won
Hacksaw Jim Duggan	September 19, 1994
Vader	December 27, 1994
Sting (2)	June 18, 1995
Kensuke Sasaki	November 13, 1995
The One Man Gang	December 27, 1995
Konnan	January 29, 1996
Ric Flair (2)	July 7, 1996
Eddy Guerrero	December 29, 1996
Dean Malenko	March 16, 1997
Jeff Jarrett	June 9, 1997
Steve McMichael	August 21, 1997
Curt Hennig	September 15, 1997
Diamond Dallas Page	December 28, 1997
Bret Hart	July 20, 1998
Lex Luger	August 10, 1998
Bret Hart (2)	August 13, 1998
Diamond Dallas Page (2)	October 26, 1998
Bret Hart (3)	November 30, 1998
Rowdy Roddy Piper	February 8, 1999
Scott Hall	February 21, 1999
Scott Steiner	April 11, 1999

NWA/WCW Television title

Champion	Won
Mark Youngblood	March 7, 1984
Tully Blanchard	May 1984
Dusty Rhodes	March 16, 1985
Arn Anderson	January 4, 1988
Dusty Rhodes (2)	September 9, 1986
Tully Blanchard (2)	November 27, 1986
Nikita Koloff	August 17, 1987
Mike Rotundo	January 26, 1988
Rick Steiner	December 26, 1988
Mike Rotundo (2)	February 20, 1989
Sting	March 31, 1989
The Great Muta	September 3, 1989
Arn Anderson (2)	January 1, 1990
Tom Zenk	December 4, 1990
Arn Anderson (3)	January 7, 1991

Champion	Won
Bobby Eaton	May 19, 1991
Steve Austin	June 3, 1991
Barry Windham	April 27, 1992
Steve Austin (2)	May 23, 1992
Ricky Steamboat	September 2, 1992
Scott Steiner	September 29, 1992
Paul Orndorff	March 2, 1993
Ricky Steamboat (2)	August 18, 1993
Lord Steven Regal	September 19, 1993
Larry Zbyszko	May 2, 1994
Lord Steven Regal (2)	June 23, 1994
Johnny B. Badd	September 18, 1994
Arn Anderson (4)	January 8, 1995
The Renegade	June 18, 1995
Diamond Dallas Page	September 17, 1995
Johnny B. Badd (2)	October 29, 1995
Lex Luger	February 17, 1996
Johnny B. Badd (3)	February 18, 1996
Lex Luger (2)	March 6, 1996
Lord Steven Regal (3)	August 20, 1996
Prince Iaukea	February 17, 1997
Ultimo Dragon	April 7, 1997
Lord Steven Regal (4)	May 18, 1997
Ultimo Dragon (2)	July 22, 1997
Alex Wright	August 21, 1997
The Disco Inferno	September 22, 1997
Saturn	November 3, 1997
The Disco Inferno (2)	December 8, 1997
Booker T	December 29, 1997
Rick Martel	February 16, 1998
Booker T (2)	February 22, 1998
Chris Benoit	April 30, 1998
Booker T (3)	May 1, 1998
Chris Benoit (2)	May 2, 1998
Booker T (4)	May 3, 1998
Fit Finlay	May 4, 1998
Booker T (5)	June 14, 1998
Chris Jericho	August 10, 1998
Konnan	November 30, 1998
Scott Steiner	December 28, 1998
Booker T (6)	March 14, 1999

Champion	Won
Scott Steiner (2)	May 9, 1999

WCW Cruiserweight title

Champion	Won
Shinjira Otani	March 20, 1996
Dean Malenko	May 2, 1996
Rey Misterio Jr.	July 8, 1996
Dean Malenko (2)	October 27, 1996
Ultimo Dragon	December 29, 1996
Dean Malenko (3)	January 21, 1997
Syxx	February 23, 1997
Chris Jericho	June 28, 1997
Alex Wright	July 28, 1997
Chris Jericho (2)	August 12, 1997
Eddy Guerrero	September 14, 1997
Rey Misterio Jr. (2)	October 26, 1997
Eddy Guerrero (2)	November 10, 1997
Ultimo Dragon (2)	December 29, 1997
Juventud Guerrera	January 8, 1998
Rey Misterio Jr. (3)	January 15, 1998
Chris Jericho (3)	January 24, 1998
Dean Malenko	May 17, 1998
Chris Jericho (4)	June 15, 1998
Rey Misterio Jr. (4)	July 12, 1998
Juventud Guerrera (2)	August 8, 1998
Kidman	September 14, 1998
Juventud Guerrera (3)	November 16, 1998
Kidman (2)	November 22, 1998
Rey Misterio Jr. (5)	March 15, 1999
Psichosis	April 19, 1999
Rey Misterio Jr. (6)	April 26, 1999

United States Wrestling Association (USWA) Heavyweight title

Champion	Won
Jerry Lawler	December 13, 1988
Master of Pain	April 1, 1989

Champion	Won
Jerry Lawler (2)	April 25, 1989
The Soultaker	October 23, 1989
Jerry Lawler (3)	November 6, 1989
King Cobra	December 30, 1989
Jerry Lawler (4)	January 8, 1990
Jimmy Valiant	February 26, 1990
Jerry Lawler (5)	March 12, 1990
Jimmy Valiant	April 28, 1990
Jerry Lawler (6)	May 5, 1990
The Snowman	June 18, 1990
Jerry Lawler (7)	October 8, 1990
Terry Funk	November 5, 1990
Jerry Lawler (8)	March 11, 1991
Awesome Kong	July 29, 1991
Jerry Lawler (9)	August 12, 1991
Dragon Master	August 26, 1991
Jerry Lawler (10)	September 2, 1991
Kamala	November 25, 1991
Jerry Lawler (11)	December 2, 1991
Kamala (2)	December 9, 1991
Koko B. Ware	February 24, 1992
Kamala (3)	March 16, 1992
Jerry Lawler (12)	May 4, 1992
Eddie Gilbert	June 15, 1992
Rick Morton	July 13, 1992
Eddie Gilbert (2)	July 20, 1992
Junkyard Dog	September 21, 1992
Butch Reed	October 12, 1992
Todd Champion	October 17, 1992
Jerry Lawler (13)	November 2, 1992
Koko B. Ware (2)	December 7, 1992
Jerry Lawler (14)	December 14, 1992
Papa Shango	May 3, 1993
Owen Hart	June 21, 1993
Jerry Lawler (15)	July 5, 1993
Tatanka	September 13, 1993
Jerry Lawler (16)	September 20, 1993
Randy Savage	October 11, 1993
Jeff Jarrett	November 22, 1993
Jerry Lawler (17)	December 20, 1993
Eddie Gilbert (3)	January 31, 1994

Champion	Won
Jerry Lawler (18)	February 7, 1994
Eddie Gilbert (4)	February 14, 1994
Jerry Lawler (19)	March 24, 1994
Sid Vicious	July 16, 1994
Jerry Lawler (20)	February 6, 1995
Bill Dundee	February 25, 1995
Razor Ramon	April 3, 1995
Jerry Lawler (21)	May 1, 1995
Ahmed Johnson	November 6, 1995
Jeff Jarrett (2)	December 13, 1995
Jerry Lawler (22)	March 4, 1996
Jeff Jarrett (3)	April 20, 1996
Jerry Lawler (23)	June 24, 1996
Sid Vicious (2)	August 30, 1996
Jerry Lawler (24)	September 2, 1996
The Colorado Kid	October 4, 1996
Jerry Lawler (25)	November 16, 1996
King Reginald	April 12, 1997
Jerry Lawler (26)	April 27, 1997
Dutch Mantel	August 8, 1997

USWA Tag-Team title

Champion	Won
Jeff Jarrett, Matt Borne	August 11, 1989
Sheik Braddock, Ron Starr	September 15, 1989
Jeff Jarrett, Matt Borne (2)	September 29, 1989
Robert Fuller, Brian Lee	December 1, 1989
Rex King, Steve Doll	February 3, 1990
Robert Fuller, Brian Lee (2)	February 6, 1990
Rex King, Steve Doll (2)	February 12, 1990
Brickhouse Brown, Sweet Daddy Falcone	April 28, 1990
Rex King, Steve Doll (3)	May 21, 1990
Tony Anthony, Tom Burton	June 2, 1990
Rex King, Joey Maggs	June 23, 1990
Brian Lee, Don Harris	August 11, 1990
Jeff Jarrett, Jeff Gaylord	September 3, 1990
Brian Lee, Don Harris (2)	September 10, 1990
Jeff Jarrett, Jeff Gaylord (2)	September 17, 1990

Champion	Won
Doug Gilbert, Tony Anthony	October 6, 1990
Jeff Jarrett, Cody Michaels	November 24, 1990
Doug Gilbert, Tony Anthony (2)	December 8, 1990
Stan Lane, Steve Keirn	January 7, 1991
Jerry Lawler, Jeff Jarrett	February 4, 1991
The Texas Hangmen	March 26, 1991
Jeff Jarrett, Robert Fuller	May 13, 1991
The Barroom Brawlers	July 8, 1991
Jeff Jarrett, Robert Fuller (2)	July 15, 1991
The Texas Outlaws	September 26, 1991
Jeff Jarrett, Robert Fuller (3)	October 7, 1991
Doug Masters, Bart Sawyer	November 4, 1991
Robert Fuller, The Young Gun	November 25, 1991
The Moondogs	November 30, 1991
Jerry Lawler, Jeff Jarrett (2)	June 29, 1992
The Moondogs (2)	July 6, 1992
Jerry Lawler, Jeff Jarrett (3)	July 20, 1992
The Moondogs (3)	August 10, 1992
Jerry Lawler, Jeff Jarrett (4)	August 17, 1992
The Moondogs (4)	October 3, 1992
Ron and Don Harris	December 28, 1992
The Moondogs (5)	January 11, 1993
Ron and Don Harris (2)	January 25, 1993
The Moondogs (6)	February 1, 1993
Ron and Don Harris (3)	February 15, 1993
The Moondogs (7)	February 22, 1993
Brian Christopher, Big Black Dog	March 8, 1993
The Moondogs (8)	March 15, 1993
Brian Christopher, Scotty Flamingo	March 22, 1993
The Moondogs (9)	March 29, 1993
Rex King, Steve Doll (4)	April 12, 1993
New Jack, Homeboy	June 21, 1993
C.W. Bergstrom, Melvin Penrod Jr.	July 5, 1993
The Moondogs (10)	August 2, 1993
The Dogcatchers	August 16, 1993
The Moondogs (11)	September 6, 1993
The Dogcatchers (2)	September 13, 1993
Moondog Spike, Mike Anthony	October 4, 1993
Rex Hargrove, Koko B. Ware	November 1, 1993
Brian Christopher, Jeff Jarrett	November 8, 1993
PG-13	November 27, 1993

Champion	Won
Mike Anthony, Jeff Gaylord	November 29, 1993
The War Machines	December 6, 1993
Far Two Wild	December 8, 1993
The Bruise Brothers	January 10, 1994
The Rock-n-Roll Express	January 23, 1994
The Moondogs (12)	January 31, 1994
Brian Christopher, Eddie Gilbert	April 23, 1994
The Eliminators	May 2, 1994
PG-13 (2)	June 13, 1994
Dante, The Great Mephisto	August 15, 1994
PG-13 (3)	August 29, 1994
The Phantoms	October 18, 1994
The Moondogs (13)	October 24, 1994
Jimmy and Ron Harris	December 26, 1994
PG-13 (4)	December 26, 1994
Doug Gilbert, Tommy Rich	January 9, 1995
PG-13 (5)	January 9, 1995
Doug Gilbert, Tommy Rich (2)	January 14, 1995
PG-13 (6)	March 13, 1995
Brickhouse Brown, The Gambler	April 15, 1995
PG-13 (7)	May 1, 1995
The Rock-n-Roll Express (2)	July 3, 1995
PG-13 (8)	July 10, 1995
The Heavenly Bodies	August 7, 1995
PG-13 (9)	August 28, 1995
Jesse James Armstrong, Tracey Smothers	October 28, 1995
PG-13 (10)	January 13, 1996
Jesse James Armstrong, Tracey Smothers	February 14, 1996
PG-13 (11)	February 17, 1996
Doug Gilbert, Tommy Rich (3)	March 4, 1996
The Cyberpunks	March 25, 1996
Bill Dundee, Jerry Lawler	May 18, 1996
Flex Kavana, Bart Sawyer	June 17, 1996
Brickhouse Brown, Reggie B. Fine	July 15, 1996
The Moondogs (14)	August 5, 1996
Bill and Jamie Dundee	August 20, 1996
Brian Christopher, Wolfie D	October 21, 1996
The Grimm Twins	November 9, 1996
Steven Dunn, Flash Flanagan	November 23, 1996

Champion	Won
PG-13 (12)	January 18, 1997
Flash Flanagan, Billy Travis	March 3, 1997
The Truth Commission	March 22, 1997
The Shooting Stars	April 12, 1997
The Truth Commission (2)	April 19, 1997
Paul Diamond, Steven Dunn	May 14, 1997
The Truth Commission (3)	May 28, 1997
PG-13 (13)	July 13, 1997
Steven Dunn, Flash Flanagan	August 8, 1997
PG-13 (14)	August 31, 1997

World Wrestling Federation (WWF)
World Heavyweight title

Champion	Won
Bruno Sammartino	May 17, 1963
Ivan Koloff	January 18, 1971
Pedro Morales	February 8, 1971
Stan Stasiak	December 1, 1973
Bruno Sammartino (2)	December 10, 1973
Superstar Billy Graham	April 30, 1977
Bob Backlund	February 20, 1978
Antonio Inoki	November 30, 1979
Bob Backlund (2)	December 6, 1979
The Iron Sheik	December 26, 1983
Hulk Hogan	January 23, 1984
Andre the Giant	February 5, 1988
Randy Savage	March 27, 1988
Hulk Hogan (2)	April 2, 1989
The Ultimate Warrior	April 1, 1990
Sgt. Slaughter	January 19, 1991
Hulk Hogan (3)	March 24, 1991
The Undertaker	November 27, 1991
Hulk Hogan (4)	December 3, 1991
Ric Flair	January 19, 1992
Randy Savage	April 5, 1992
Ric Flair (2)	September 1, 1992
Bret Hart	October 12, 1992
Yokozuna	April 4, 1993
Hulk Hogan (5)	April 4, 1993

Champion	Won
Yokozuna (2)	June 13, 1993
Bret Hart (2)	March 20, 1994
Bob Backlund (3)	November 23, 1994
Diesel	November 26, 1994
Bret Hart (3)	November 19, 1995
Shawn Michaels	March 31, 1996
Sycho Sid	November 17, 1996
Shawn Michaels (2)	January 19, 1997
Bret Hart (4)	February 16, 1997
Sycho Sid (2)	February 17, 1997
The Undertaker (2)	March 23, 1997
Bret Hart (5)	August 3, 1997
Shawn Michaels (3)	November 9, 1997
Stone Cold Steve Austin	March 29, 1998
Kane	June 28, 1998
Stone Cold Steve Austin (2)	June 29, 1998
The Rock	November 15, 1998
Mankind	January 4, 1999
The Rock (2)	January 24, 1999
Mankind (2)	January 31, 1999
The Rock (3)	February 15, 1999
Stone Cold Steve Austin (3)	March 28, 1999

WWF Intercontinental title

Champion	Won
Pat Patterson	September 1979
Ken Patera	April 21, 1980
Pedro Morales	December 8, 1980
Magnificent Muraco	June 20, 1981
Pedro Morales (2)	November 23, 1981
Magnificent Muraco (2)	January 22, 1983
Tito Santana	February 11, 1984
Greg Valentine	September 24, 1984
Tito Santana (2)	July 6, 1985
Randy Savage	February 8, 1986
Ricky Steamboat	March 29, 1987
The Honky Tonk Man	June 2, 1987
The Ultimate Warrior	August 29, 1988
Rick Rude	April 2, 1989

Champion	Won
The Ultimate Warrior (2)	August 28, 1989
Curt Hennig	April 23, 1990
Kerry Von Erich	August 27, 1990
Curt Hennig (2)	November 19, 1990
Bret Hart	August 26, 1991
The Mountie	January 17, 1992
Roddy Piper	January 19, 1992
Bret Hart (2)	April 5, 1992
Davey Boy Smith	August 29, 1992
Shawn Michaels	October 27, 1992
Marty Jannetty	May 17, 1993
Shawn Michaels (2)	June 6, 1993
Razor Ramon	September 27, 1993
Diesel	April 13, 1994
Razor Ramon (2)	August 29, 1994
Jeff Jarrett	January 22, 1995
Razor Ramon (3)	May 19, 1995
Jeff Jarrett (2)	May 22, 1995
Shawn Michaels (3)	July 23, 1995
Razor Ramon (4)	October 22, 1995
Goldust	January 22, 1996
Ahmed Johnson	June 23, 1996
Marc Mero	September 23, 1996
Hunter Hearst Helmsley	October 21, 1996
Rocky Maivia	February 13, 1997
Owen Hart	April 28, 1997
Stone Cold Steve Austin	August 3, 1997
Owen Hart (2)	October 5, 1997
Stone Cold Steve Austin (2)	November 9, 1997
Rocky Maivia (2)	December 8, 1997
Hunter Hearst Helmsley	August 30, 1998
Ken Shamrock	October 12, 1998
Val Venis	February 14, 1999
Road Dog Jesse James	March 15, 1999
Goldust (2)	March 29, 1999
The Godfather	April 12, 1999

WWF World Tag-Team title

Champion	Won
Eddie and Dr. Jerry Graham	1957
Mark Lewin, Don Curtis	December 12, 1958
Eddie and Dr. Jerry Graham (2)	May 27, 1959
Red and Lou Bastien	April 2, 1960
Eddie and Dr. Jerry Graham (3)	April 16, 1960
Red and Lou Bastien (2)	April 23, 1960
Al Costello, Roy Heffernan	July 21, 1960
Red and Lou Bastien (3)	August 8, 1960
Al Costello, Roy Heffernan (2)	August 24, 1960
Johnny Valentine, Buddy Rogers	November 19, 1960
Al Costello, Roy Heffernan (3)	November 26, 1960
Johnny Valentine, Cowboy Bob Ellis	January 11, 1962
Buddy Rogers, Handsome John Barend	July 5, 1962
Buddy Austin, The Great Scott	March 7, 1963
Skull Murphy, Brute Bernard	May 16, 1963
Killer Kowalski, Gorilla Monsoon	November 14, 1963
Chris and John Tolos	December 28, 1963
Vittorio Apollo, Don McClarty	February 1964
Dr. Jerry and Crazy Luke Graham	June 1964
Gene Kiniski, Waldo Von Erich	October 1964
Gorilla Monsoon, Cowboy Bill Watts	April 1965
Dan and Dr. Bill Miller	July 1965
Johnny Valentine, Antonio Pugliese	February 21, 1966
Baron Mikel Scicluna, Smasher Sloan	September 22, 1966
Spiros Arion, Antonio Pugliese	December 8, 1966
Captain Lou Albano, Tony Altimore	July 10, 1967
Spiros Arion, Bruno Sammartino	July 24, 1967
Victor Rivera, Tony Marino	December 8, 1969
Bepo and Gito Mongol	June 15, 1970
Crazy Luke Graham, Tarzan Tyler	June 1971
Karl Gotch, Rene Goulet	December 6, 1971
Baron Mikel Scicluna, King Curtis	February 1, 1972
Chief Jay Strongbow, Sonny King	May 22, 1972
Professor Tanaka, Mr. Fuji	June 27, 1972
Tony Garea, Haystacks Calhoun	May 30, 1973
Professor Tanaka, Mr. Fuji (2)	September 11, 1973
Tony Garea, Dean Ho	November 14, 1973
Jimmy and Johnny Valiant	May 8, 1974

Champion	Won
Victor Rivera, Dominic DeNucci	May 13, 1975
Blackjack Mulligan, Blackjack Lanza	August 26, 1975
Tony Parisi, Louis Cerdan	November 8, 1975
The Executioners	May 11, 1976
Chief Jay Strongbow, Billy White Wolf	December 7, 1976
Professor Tanaka, Mr. Fuji (3)	September 27, 1977
Dominic DeNucci, Dino Bravo	March 14, 1978
The Yukon Lumberjacks	June 26, 1978
Tony Garea, Larry Zbyszko	November 21, 1978
Johnny and Jerry Valiant	March 6, 1979
Ivan Putski, Tito Santana	October 22, 1979
The Samoans	April 12, 1980
Bob Backlund, Pedro Morales	August 9, 1980
The Samoans (2)	September 9, 1980
Tony Garea, Rick Martel	November 8, 1980
The Moondogs	March 17, 1981
Toney Garea, Rick Martel (2)	July 21, 1981
Mr. Fuji, Master Saito	October 13, 1981
Jules and Chief Jay Strongbow	June 28, 1982
Mr. Fuji, Master Saito (2)	July 13, 1982
Jules and Chief Jay Strongbow (2)	October 26, 1982
The Samoans (3)	March 8, 1983
Tony Atlas, Rocky Johnson	November 15, 1983
Adrian Adonis, Dick Murdoch	April 17, 1984
Mike Rotundo, Barry Windham	January 21, 1985
The Iron Sheik, Nikolai Volkoff	March 31, 1985
Mike Rotundo, Barry Windham (2)	June 17, 1985
Brutus Beefcake, Greg Valentine	August 24, 1985
The British Bulldogs	April 7, 1986
The Hart Foundation	January 26, 1987
Rick Martel, Tito Santana	October 27, 1987
Demolition	March 27, 1988
Arn Anderson, Tully Blanchard	July 18, 1989
Demolition (2)	October 2, 1989
Andre the Giant, Haku	December 13, 1989
Demolition (3)	April 1, 1990
The Hart Foundation (2)	August 27, 1990
The Nasty Boys	March 24, 1991

Champion	Won
The Legion of Doom	August 26, 1991
Ted DiBiase, Irwin R. Schyster	February 7, 1992
Earthquake, Typhoon	July 20, 1992
Ted DiBiase, Irwin R. Schyster (2)	October 13, 1992
The Steiner Brothers	June 14, 1993
Ted DiBiase, Irwin R. Schyster (3)	June 16, 1993
The Steiner Brothers (2)	June 19, 1993
The Quebecers	January 17, 1994
Men on a Mission	March 29, 1994
The Quebecers (2)	March 31, 1994
The Headshrinkers	April 26, 1994
Diesel, Shawn Michaels	August 28, 1994
Bob Holly, The 1–2–3 Kid	January 22, 1995
The Smoking Gunns	January 23, 1995
Owen Hart, Yokozuna	April 2, 1995
Diesel, Shawn Michaels (2)	September 24, 1995
The Smoking Gunns (2)	September 25, 1995
The Bodydonnas	March 31, 1996
Henry and Phineas Godwinn	May 19, 1996
The Smoking Gunns (3)	May 26, 1996
Owen Hart, Davey Boy Smith	September 22, 1996
Stone Cold Steve Austin, Shawn Michaels	May 25, 1997
The Headbangers (2)	September 7, 1997
Henry and Phineas Godwinn (2)	October 5, 1997
The Road Warriors	October 7, 1997
The New Age Outlaws	November 24, 1997
Terry Funk, Cactus Jack	March 29, 1998
The New Age Outlaws (2)	March 30, 1998
Kane, Mankind	July 13, 1998
Stone Cold Steve Austin, The Undertaker	July 26, 1998
Kane, Mankind	August 10, 1998
The New Age Outlaws (3)	August 30, 1998
The Big Boss Man, Ken Shamrock	December 13, 1998
Owen Hart, Jeff Jarrett	January 25, 1999
Kane, X-Pac	March 30, 1999

wwf European title

Champion	Won
The British Bulldog	February 26, 1997
Shawn Michaels	September 20, 1997
Hunter Hearst Helmsley	December 11, 1997
Owen Hart	January 20, 1998
Hunter Hearst Helmsley (2)	March 16, 1998
D-Lo Brown	July 20, 1998
X-Pac	September 21, 1998
D-Lo Brown	October 5, 1998
X-Pac	October 18, 1998
Shane McMahon	February 15, 1999

wwf Light Heavyweight title

Champion	Won
Taka Michinoku	December 7, 1997
Christian	October 18, 1998
Duane Gill	November 22, 1998

wwf Hardcore title

Champion	Won
Mankind	November 2, 1998
Big Boss Man	November 30, 1998
Road Dog Jesse James	December 15, 1998
Bob Holly	February 14, 1999
Billy Gunn	March 15, 1999
Bob Holly (2)	March 28, 1999
Al Snow	April 25, 1999

TWO-SPORT STARS

MUHAMMAD ALI

On June 25, 1976, Muhammad Ali fought wrestler Antonio Inoki to a 15-round draw in Tokyo. Ali later served as guest referee at WrestleMania I (March 31, 1985), for the main event of Hulk Hogan and Mr. T vs. Roddy Piper and Paul Orndorff.

PRIMO CARNERA

In 1941, at the age of 34, former Heavyweight boxing champion Primo Carnera embarked upon a career in wrestling. He won 321 matches in a row before being defeated by Antonino Rocca on April 20, 1949.

JIM COVERT

Chicago Bears lineman Jim Covert participated in a 20-man invitational battle royal at WrestleMania II, which was won by Andre the Giant.

JACK DEMPSEY

Former Heavyweight boxing champion Jack Dempsey served as special referee in a title match between Jim Londos and Ed "Strangler" Lewis on September 20, 1934. One month later, he refereed a boxer-vs.-wrestler match pitting Abe Kashey against Charlie Retzlaff. The wrestler, Retzlaff, scored a pin in the fourth round. On July 15, 1940, Dempsey became a competitor himself and beat wrestler Bill Curry in the second round.

BUSTER DOUGLAS

Buster Douglas shocked the world by beating Mike Tyson for the Heavyweight boxing title on February 11, 1990. Just 12 days later, Douglas appeared as special referee (replacing scheduled guest Mike Tyson) for a match between Hulk Hogan and Randy Savage.

BILL FRALIC

Veteran football player Bill Fralic participated in a 20-man invitational battle royal at WrestleMania II, which was won by Andre the Giant.

RUSS FRANCIS

Veteran football player Russ Francis participated in a 20-man invitational battle royal at WrestleMania II, which was won by Andre the Giant.

MARK GASTINEAU

New York Jets defensive end and sack specialist Mark Gastineau defeated AWA wrestler Derrick Dukes on June 8, 1991. Gastineau went on to a brief and unspectacular career as a boxer.

KEVIN GREENE

In 1996, Carolina Panthers defensive standout Kevin Greene, a lifelong wrestling fan, began making appearances at WCW events. He first feuded with Steve "Mongo" McMichael, but his most memorable match was the main event of Slamboree 1997; Greene, Roddy Piper, and Ric Flair defeated Scott Hall, Kevin Nash, and Syxx in a WCW-vs.-NWO showdown.

MARK HENRY

Four-hundred-pound Mark Henry, "the world's strongest man," was the captain of the weightlifting team at the 1996 Olympic Games. After signing with the WWF, he joined the Nation of Domination and acquired the nickname "Sexual Chocolate" after romancing Triple H's former bodyguard, Chyna.

ERNIE HOLMES

Veteran football player Ernie Holmes participated in a 20-man invitational battle royal at WrestleMania II, which was won by Andre the Giant.

WALTER JOHNSON

In a one-time-only event held on February 16, 1974, Cincinnati Bengals linebacker Ron Pritchard wrestled Cleveland Browns tackle Walter Johnson. Johnson won by disqualification.

ALEX KARRAS

On April 27, 1963, Detroit Lions star Alex Karras squared off against Dick the Bruiser before 10,000 fans at the Olympia in Detroit. Though Karras was pinned in front of his hometown fans, he sent The Bruiser to the hospital to get five stitches over his right eye.

JOE LOUIS

Legendary boxer Joe Louis wrestled throughout the 1950s, primarily to earn the money he needed to pay off his debts to the government.

KARL MALONE

Utah Jazz basketball great Karl Malone was voted one of The 50 Greatest Players of All Time by the NBA. At WCW's Bash at the Beach 1998, Malone and Diamond Dallas Page lost a tag-team grudge match by DQ to Hulk Hogan and Dennis Rodman. Malone executed a diamond cutter on the referee to protest the decision.

HARVEY MARTIN

Dallas Cowboys standout Harvey Martin participated in a 20-man invitational battle royal at WrestleMania II, which was won by Andre the Giant.

STEVE MCMICHAEL

After 10 years with the Chicago Bears, capped by a Super Bowl victory in 1990, McMichael embarked upon a second career in wrestling. He joined the WCW's Four Horsemen and reigned briefly as the US Heavyweight champion in 1997.

BRONKO NAGURSKI

A football Hall of Famer, Bronko Nagurski began wrestling in 1937. He became a two-time NWA Heavyweight champion, defeating Lou Thesz in 1939 and Ray Steele in 1941.

PATRICK O'CALLAGHAN

A physician who held the world record for the hammer throw in 1938, O'Callaghan wrestled during the 1940s.

KEN PATERA

In 1972, Patera represented the United States at the Olympic Games in super-heavyweight weightlifting. His first attempt at a wrestling career was cut short when he was arrested for assaulting a police officer and sentenced to two years in prison. After his release, he reigned as WWF Intercontinental champion and Missouri State Heavyweight champion.

WILLIAM "THE REFRIGERATOR" PERRY

The elephantine Chicago Bears star participated in a 20-man invitational battle royal at WrestleMania II, which was won by Andre the Giant.

RON PRITCHARD

In a one-time-only event held on February 16, 1974, Cincinnati Bengals linebacker Ron Pritchard wrestled Cleveland Browns tackle Walter Johnson. Johnson won by disqualification.

DENNIS RODMAN

Flamboyant Chicago Bulls star Dennis Rodman joined Hulk Hogan at Bash at the Beach on July 13, 1997, to battle the team of The Giant and Lex Luger. He returned to the ring one year later, again alongside Hogan, to defeat Diamond Dallas Page and Karl Malone.

BABE RUTH

Legendary home-run hitter Babe Ruth refereed two wrestling matches in April of 1945.

LEON SPINKS

Boxer Leon Spinks lost a boxer-wrestler match to the great Japanese champion Antonio Inoki on October 9, 1986. Three years later, on June 25, 1989, he lost a similar competition to the unheralded Greg Wojokowski.

JOHN L. SULLIVAN

In 1887, boxer John L. Sullivan wrestled Greco-Roman champion William Muldoon before a crowd of 2,000 in Gloucester, Massachusetts. The match was stopped after Sullivan was body-slammed and the fans rushed the ring.

LAWRENCE TAYLOR

At WrestleMania XI in 1995, New York Giants all-pro linebacker Lawrence Taylor pinned Bam Bam Bigelow. Taylor had trained for the match, and he surprised the fans with his mat-wrestling skills and a few moves from the top rope.

MIKE TYSON

Shortly after Tyson's infamous Heavyweight title fight against Evander Holyfield in which he bit off a portion of Holyfield's ear, he announced his participation in WrestleMania XIV. He was appointed "special enforcer" for the title match between Steve Austin and Shawn Michaels. At WWF events leading up to the pay-per-view, Tyson sported a Degeneration X T-shirt, but he revealed his allegiance to Austin during the match.

JERSEY JOE WALCOTT

Walcott battled Buddy Rogers, the first "Nature Boy," in a boxer-wrestler match held in Montreal on October 7, 1959. On April 15, 1963, Walcott was pinned by Lou Thesz in the fourth round of a match held in Memphis.

CHUCK WEPNER

Boxer Chuck Wepner, the man who inspired Sylvester Stallone to write *Rocky* through his strong showing against Muhammad Ali, joined forces with Andre the Giant in a tag-team match against Bruno Sammartino and Stan Hansen. The match, held at New York's Shea Stadium, drew 32,000 fans.

REGGIE WHITE

Green Bay Packers star Reggie White lost to former Chicago Bear Steve McMichael at wcw Slamboree on May 18, 1997. The match was intended to renew one of football's most enduring rivalries.

Bibliography

Bauer, Bud. "Goldberg's Deep Impact." *Wrestling World Presents Stone Cold Steve Austin and Other Hell Raisers* Nov. 1998: 44–46, 48–49.

Chapman, Mike. *From Gotch to Gable.* University of Iowa Press, 1981.

Ciacciarelli, Stephen, ed. Wrestling World *Presents Who's Who in Wrestling.* Sterling/MacFadden Partnership, 1998.

Collins, James. "Lords of the Ring." *Time* 29 June 1998: 67–68.

Epstein, Dorran Jack. "Mick Foley FAQs."

Fine. Marshall. "Say What You Will, He Fills Out a Tutu." *Los Angeles Times* 7 Oct. 1993: F4.

"Flair Hopes to Avoid Final Whooo!" *Charlotte Observer* 27 Dec. 1993.

Frankel, Bruce. "Ring Master." *People* 14 Dec. 1998: 121–22.

"The Future is Golden." WCW/NWO *Magazine* July 1998: 22–23.

Gardner, Ralph, Jr. "The Nitro Girls." *Penthouse* Aug. 1998: 90–92, 200.

Gipe, George. *The Great American Sports Book.* Hall of Fame Press, 1987.

Green, Michelle. "Musclebound for Glory." *People* 14 Oct. 1991: 61–63.

Greenberg, Keith Elliot. "Love and Stitches." *Raw Magazine* July 1998: 30–34.

Griffin, Ervin, Jr. "Diary of a Hitman: The Story of Bret Hart." http://users.aol.com/Solie/index.html.

—."Ironman: The Legend of The Road Warriors." http://users.aol.com/Solie/index.html.

—."Run, Blade Runner, Run." http://users.aol.com/Solie/index.html.

Heath, Chris. "Stone Cold Steve Austin." *Rolling Stone* 24 Dec. 1998: 123–130, 178.

Interview with Brian Bukantis conducted by the author, 20 Nov. 1998.

Interview with Mike Chapman conducted by the author, 5 Oct. 1998.

"Interview with The Giant." Union of Diamond Cutters Web site.
    http://wcwwrestling.com/indiv/ddp/.

"Interview with Bill Goldberg." Union of Diamond Cutters Web site.
    http://wcwwrestling.com/indiv/ddp/.

"Interview with Bret Hart." http: www.scoopscentral.com.

"Interview with Rey Misterio Jr." Prodigy chat, 6 Nov. 1997.

"Interview with The Ultimate Warrior." *The Wrestling Insiders Radio Show*,
    20 Mar. 1994.

Johnson, Kirk. "Professional Wrestling Cuts Good Guys from the Script." *New York
    Times* 30 Mar. 1998.

Leland, John. "Stone Cold Crazy." *Newsweek* 23 Nov. 1998: 60–64.

Lenker, David, ed. *Wrestling True-Life Stories*. London Publishing, 1998.

Lieberman, Paul. "The Ultimate Grudge Match." *Los Angeles Times* 15 Nov. 1998:
    8–9, 96, 98, 100.

Lipton, Michael A. "Incredible Hulk?" 23 Mar. 1992: 91–95.

Mooneyham, Mike. "Valentine Recalls Crash That Ended His Career."
    Charleston Post and Courier 3 May 1998.

The 1998 Wrestling Almanac. London Publishing, 1998.

O'Hara, Michael. "Goldberg versus the World." *New Wave Wrestling* Sept. 1998: 42–43.

Sandburg, Carl. *Abraham Lincoln: The Prairie Years and the War Years*. Vol. 1. Harcourt
    Brace, 1989.

"Sean Waltman." *Raw Magazine* July 1998: 36–39.

Shamrock, Ken, with Richard Hanner. *Inside the Lion's Den*. Charles E. Tuttle, 1998.

White, Ken. "Rising Star: Rocky Maivia leads WWF to Thomas and Mack Center."
    Las Vegas Review Journal 16 Jan. 1998: D1.

Wilson, Charles Morrow. *The Magnificent Scufflers*.